TOWN, GOV....

A CENTENNIAL HISTORY
OF THE
ABERDEEN UNIVERSITIES
OFFICERS TRAINING CORPS
1912-2012

JB DUFFUS

Published by James B Duffus
Printed and Bound by The Gatehouse, Robert Gordon University

Town, Gown and Gun

First published in 2012 by
James B Duffus
Lyndene
Deveron Road
Huntly
AB54 8DU

ISBN: 978-0-9571900-0-9

British Library Cataloguing-in-Publication Data
A catalogue record for this book is available from the British
Library

Printed and Bound in Great Britain
by
The Gatehouse - Design and Print Consultancy
Robert Gordon University
Aberdeen
www.rgu.ac.uk/gandp

CONTENTS

<u>Appendices</u>

PREFACE

For a century Aberdeen's Officers Training Corps, with a few slight changes of name along the way, has offered thousands of students basic military training, fun, adventure and comradeship.   Apart from during the World Wars, membership of the Contingent has been voluntary and with no commitment to further military service.   Indeed most members over the decades never donned uniform again. However even a limited and short experience of soldiering is surely of some value among the citizens of a democracy that still finds the need to put Service men and women in harm's way.   Some men and, for more than half of its existence, women, did go on to full or part time military careers.

That this unit has lasted for a century demonstrates that the University, the Army and generations of Aberdeen's students have thought its existence worth supporting.   It is sadly impossible to mention all the characters, events and places associated with it.   It is hoped however that what is included stirs happy memories for recent members while still providing the general reader or future historian with a reasonably robust record of what it was all about.

The problem of selecting photographs has been eased by the existence of a large photo archive on the internet. **Indeed this book should be viewed as a companion to the archive theoldboars.smugmug.com. Readers are urged to visit this site and indeed add to it.** If you are reading this many years after 2012, it may help to know that a copy of the archive should still be available in the University of Aberdeen Library in a format accessible with your technology.

AUOTC's story is told with reference to contemporary events in the University, Aberdeen, and British defence. Chapters are based on significant periods in Army history. This may seem grandiose. However it is this 'big picture' which ultimately shapes the civil and military societies within which the OTC operates and the level of resources made available to it. If nothing else it determines the course of the lives of the unit's military alumni and the people who come to train them.

Before following AUOTC's own story an initial chapter is dedicated to the long chain of events in the University, the Army, and the Country which led to the Contingent's formation only a couple of years before the start of World War I.

Chapter 1

THE UNIVERSITY AND SOLDIERING
1495-1912

Every November, sometimes in sunshine, occasionally in snow, AUOTC follows its Drums and Pipes through the gate near Bishop Elphinstone's empty tomb outside King's Chapel. Elphinstone, who actually rests inside the Chapel, established the University and King's College in 1495. The University was the third established in Scotland and the fifth in the whole of Britain. The following centuries saw clan wars, the Civil Wars of the Three Kingdoms, Jacobite Risings, counters to Napoleon's ambitions and miscellaneous imperial adventures. University students, staff and graduates therefore had ample opportunity by choice or by fate to go soldiering. Military life could be part-time or full-time, on active service or in peacetime training. Staff and graduates in their chosen professions would, because of their place in society, participate in, and in many cases lead, volunteer activity. When pay was offered, students would take even more interest in part-time soldiering. By the late 19th century and the first decade of the 20th Century the scope for volunteering and the keenness of University men to do so, brought about the formation of sub-units with direct links to the University, and before long the word 'University' appeared in their formal titles.

Long before the establishment of the University citizens initially from as young as 12 years old, were bound by law to 'prepare to watch and ward' their city. The year before the University formed, all Aberdonians between the ages of 16 and 60 were told to be ready for war with personal

3

equipment, artillery and carts. The principal threat was an English landing on the north side of the River Dee's harbour basin. The defence of the port and neighbouring coastline, against a succession of potential enemies, was the prime mission for Aberdeen's Volunteers until 1908 when an option for overseas deployment with the Regulars was built into their organisation, training and terms of service.

Throughout the 1500s regular 'Wapinschaws' were held where, in the face of penalties if they didn't, men mustered to have their weapons and equipment checked and recorded against lists of what was expected. Up the chain of command from the burghs, to counties and eventually to the Crown, an accurate assessment of military capability was maintained. In 1530 the threat loomed in the west rather than from the sea. An alarm system centred on St Nicholas' steeple would indicate by bell rings the number of 'gentlemen of the country' approaching. The town's quick reaction force would rush to the defence of the gates. Not all defensive arrangements were perfect. In 1532 a committee was formed to investigate mysterious discrepancies in the quantities of artillery and ammunition held at readiness.

The North East underwent Reformation with less violence than some areas but in 1559 the inhabitants of King's College actually found cause to organise a defence against a Protestant mob from the south. With time and a purge of staff, King's became Protestant in outlook.

The 4th Earl Marischal's new college in New Aberdeen was designed as a Protestant institution from the outset in 1593. The two colleges would argue over status, student recruitment and resources for centuries. The occasional raids and brawls conducted by one group of students against the other never really amounted to

4

'soldiering' but did sometimes call for a knowledge of 'hand to hand' combat. By the early 1600s King's and Marischal had around 70 undergraduates each, both colleges recruiting around 20 new students annually.

After a period of waning interest in part-time soldiering, regular Monday drill nights were resumed in 1638 but only on the understanding that everyone would go home afterwards without shooting and 'spending powder' to the alarm of fellow citizens. Officers for this newly energised force were appointed by the Town Councils. These appointees however promptly resigned the following year on the approach of Montrose's army.

17th Century Old Aberdeen was protected against trouble by a dozen or so volunteers armed with muskets and bolstered by four better trained militia men. In 1686, once more responding to a threat of invasion from the west by 'Hielan' Men', it was thought necessary to arm all capable inhabitants and, by 1689, 24 armed men would parade at a daily rendezvous on the King's College Bowling Green.

Holland became a threat in 1665 and the defences damaged during the Civil Wars were repaired and cannon repositioned. By 1696 the French had replaced the Dutch as the principal potential enemy. In 1708 the whole town 'stood to' with its professional class, many products of the Universities, in command. Apothecaries, advocates and merchants led companies, each with areas of responsibility throughout the town. This scare, like many, came to nothing. There was however nothing imagined about the Jacobite capture of the town seven years later in 1715. The Jacobites' quick and easy success was helped by two factors. Firstly, the town's gunpowder stocks had been removed with the departure of King George's troops. Secondly, the command

and control arrangements evaporated with the precipitate departure of the Town Council. At this time King's and Marischal were united in their generally pro-Jacobite feelings. As after the Reformation, post-1715 staff purges ensured that New and Old Aberdeen's colleges adopted a pro-Government outlook. Continued and much needed access to Government funding was thus assured. However, when Bonnie Prince Charlie came across the water thirty years later in his attempt to take the throne for his father, the shires of North East Scotland would prove to contain his strongest and most consistent supporters.

Dr Samuel Johnson, England's great man of letters and commentator on 18th Century life, observed that the Scottish Universities took in boys and finished with them before they were adults. These boys could not expect *'to be often decorated with the splendour of ornamental knowledge, but they obtain a mediocrity of knowledge , between learning and ignorance, not inadequate for the purposes of common life'.* This opinion was formed when England had two universities against Scotland's five. Two of the latter were in Aberdeen. Scotland's gentry and professionals were as well educated as their English equivalents. Most burghs had grammar schools, and the sons of the better off could travel further afield for their schooling before, if they chose, university. The officers of the Lowland and Highland regiments which would participate in the '45 were at least as educated and informed as the leaders of continental armies.

In 1739 the town authorities did not share the rural enthusiasm for the Pretender. Anxious to boost local defence Aberdeen bought 300, probably obsolescent, muskets from the wily old Quartermaster of the regular regiment quartered in the town. These arms were thus available for forces raised in defence against the Jacobite Rising of 1745. This time magistrates appointed officers to lead 12 citizen companies. Their endeavours were somewhat undermined by the removal of the coast defence cannon from the harbour mouth to Edinburgh Castle. Sir John Cope took them with him as he sailed for the Forth and lasting fame in the song 'Hey Johnny Cope are ye wakened yet ?'. Cope's decision to take the cannon despite the remonstrations of the town elders, was perhaps based on doubts about the town's future loyalty and affiliations.

On 25 Sep 1745 an armed band from Strathbogie rode in, abused and kicked out the councillors, opened the jails and made everyone drink toasts to Prince Charlie. Foreseeing the Jacobite occupation of the town , councillors and magistrates had in good time appointed stay-behind 'spys' for intelligence purposes.

In December 1745 a former Principal and Professor and a group of students were included in a small band of Aberdeen volunteers which joined a Hanoverian force holding Inverurie. They were all captured by Lord Lewis Gordon's Jacobites in a running street battle through the moonlit and frosty streets. Not a great success for this first recorded formed, but untrained and ill equipped, body of Aberdeen student soldiers.

The Jacobites held Aberdeen in a state of extortion for five months before departing in February 1746 on the approach of Cumberland's Army. A Provost was reappointed, a regular army garrison of 200 established in Robert Gordon's Hospital dubbed 'Fort Cumberland', and 400 citizens enrolled in the Volunteers. Among their officers were Professor David Verner of Marischal College as Captain, with Francis Skeen, Professor of Philosophy, as his

7

Lieutenant. The Volunteers policed the town and searched for lingering 'rebels'. With great enthusiasm Aberdeen's new Volunteers paraded, despite a 30% shortage of small arms, to fire volleys to mark Cumberland's birthday. A few days later, the Volunteers were on parade again to mark his decisive victory on Culloden Moor. The Volunteer officers were invited to the Town's House for, given the many toasts proposed, lots of drink.

1756-59 saw the first conflict on a global scale when campaigns were fought against the French in North America and elsewhere. The threat of invasion and the raising of local volunteers was marked by a piece of verse in Aberdeen's *'Gentleman's Magazine'*, no doubt enjoyed by University staff and students.

> *'Tis hoped they'll make a bold resistance*
> *And cause Monsieur to keep his distance*
> *Should he attempt to land his host*
> *Upon the Aberdonian Coast.*

With the American War of Independence underway in 1778 the Town Council offered to fund and raise the Aberdeen Volunteers for the 'duration'. This offer was declined. At first William Pitt's military priorities for Scotland were the raising of clan-based regular regiments. The new regiments would provide sorely needed deployable force, and effectively disarm the Highlands, thereby removing any risk of a repeat of the '45 Rising. Pitt did recognise a real invasion threat and moved his Volunteer Bill for companies to be raised for local defence only, particularly in maritime areas. Men would come from the county gentry and yeomanry classes. Unemployed lieutenants on half pay were invited to raise Independent Companies of Fencibles. If they succeeded they would receive full pay and be allowed to sell on their post to a successor. Landowners tried to outdo each other's shows of loyalty by raising the most Fencibles. They were assisted by the promise of large bounties for recruits. The scheme soon showed signs of being too successful, robbing the Army and Royal Navy of recruits, and Fencibles became limited. Fencibles could be deployed elsewhere in Britain and Ireland to protect coasts vacated by regulars sent overseas. In addition to any Fencibles, Aberdeen and the Shire were authorised to raise an infantry company. To man the 'great guns' defending the harbour, an artillery company of 40 men with 20 firelocks was formed.

In 1782 Old Aberdeen's Professors and Baillies, sitting on the regulating committee of the town's Military Association, resolved to raise a force of 70 volunteers. Higher authorities were requested to provide arms and properly qualified instructors. Old Aberdeen had a total population of 1,700 while New Aberdeen was home to over 20,000 and could thus sustain many more volunteers.

By 1794 the Aberdeen Corps of Volunteers was raised as a territorial based defence against French Invasion. The unit consisted of five companies, each of 60 men. Artillery officers and then infantry officers were, for the first time, properly and formally 'gazetted' in the London Gazette. Seniority among the lieutenants was resolved by ballot. The first commander of these 'gentlemen volunteers' from the professional and commercial classes, was Marischal College educated advocate and landowner Alexander Moir of Scotstown. He supervised the training regime of one drill night per week and a general field day once per month somewhere in the town or out on the Links. In Oct 1795 each

9

man was issued with 12 rounds of ball ammunition in preparation for what would now be termed a Military Aid to the Civil Power (MACP) task to quell riots. In recognition of the legal aspects of such operations a magistrate would accompany the troops. Riots did occur the following year and the prompt action by the Volunteers to keep the peace and protect property and persons was praised.

The maintenance of proper discipline and standards was as ever a constant issue and Serjeants were asked especially to watch over the morals of the drummers. These gentlemen volunteers although armed by the Government received no pay and met their own expenses. They were therefore rather exclusive in membership and as, after naval victories, the perceived threat abated, they were increasingly the butt of jokes, ridicule and press satire. Attendance at drills fell to the point that many were being admonished as being, in the event of a real emergency, more of a threat to their friends than their enemies.

In 1797 for the first time in generations a militia system was applied to Scotland. Those citizens in Volunteer units would be exempt from the regular ballots for Militia service which could involve service away from home. Needless to say the Militia ballot renewed enthusiasm for Volunteer service.

The following year, 1798, saw the zeal for the defence of the nation and the raising of volunteers matched by personal cash contributions. The King gave £20,000 and Cabinet ministers £2,000 each. Personal cash being 'put where mouths were' in defence matters is interesting to note in our more sophisticated times.

French landings could be expected almost anywhere on the coast and had already happened in Pembrokeshire.

Landowners in addition to raising volunteer units offered their carts, horses and servants for logistical purposes within 18 miles of their homes. Shire and City were now in these times very much on the same side.

Old Aberdeen's Volunteer Association resolved to raise and equip the Old Aberdeen Voluntary Light Infantry, the London Gazette indicating its first commander to be Dr Gilbert Gerard, Minister of Old Machar and Professor of Divinity at King's College. The unit would exist during the first Napoleonic scare from 1798 to 1802 when the Treaty of Amiens brought, it was thought, lasting peace.

In 1799 in a bid to open up volunteering beyond the professional classes and into the ranks of tradesmen, the Royal Aberdeen Light Infantry Volunteers formed under the command of Alexander Dauney, an advocate and Professor of Civil Law at King's College. Dauney was an active and much respected Volunteer. His performance as a Professor however left much to be desired. To a panel of Commissioners investigating the inefficient, and in places corrupt, state of Scotland's universities in 1826 Dauney stated that since becoming Professor in 1793 he had never been called upon to give any lectures. In 1824 at the age of 79, in response to a reforming Chancellor's prompts, he gave his first performances in a lecture room. After the novelty of his appearance in front of undergraduates had worn off, attendance declined and the Professor reverted to his old ways. He attributed his lack of presentational skill to his late start.

Dauney's unit disbanded with the Treaty of Amiens. Indeed all Government enthusiasm for expensive defence arrangements disappeared rapidly. Regular units, Militia, Fencibles and Yeomanry returned to their home areas.

11

Volunteers were relieved from further service and handed in their arms and equipment.

The startling outbreak of peace was short-lived. In March 1803 strong enemy amphibious force preparations were detected in Dutch and French ports. The Militia were again activated to free up the Regulars and Lord Lieutenants were deluged with offers from Volunteers to reform. War broke out again in May 1803 and within a few months Volunteer Forces were back in greater strength than before. Dauney's light infantry offered to reform but due to political manoeuvrings, the existence of other units, and a woeful shortage of arms, the offer was refused.

In July a Bill for a *levy en masse* called for the arming of all men between the ages of 17 and 55. Offers exceeded quotas by several times and many were snubbed. Measures to repel invaders and maintain civil order were drawn up. Signal light chains stretched inland from ports to facilitate calls for assistance. Coastal merchantmen were armed. Plans were made to move livestock and corn inland in the event of an enemy landing.

Any student Volunteer infantryman of 1804 would need arms, ammunition, one shirt , one pair of shoes, one pair of stockings, combs and brushes, 3 days worth of bread , a blanket or greatcoat and a water bottle. In addition to individual kit, unit stores, the equivalent of the modern G1098, were listed and checked. The New Town of Aberdeen could boast four volunteer corps.

The Loyal Aberdeen Volunteers or Capt Finlason's Fencibles, were well officered by Finlason of the 89th Foot himself, and other half-pay officers. This unit soon had a strength of over 800 and the Duchess of Gordon presented their Colours in February 1804. The 'wet weather' option was conducted in the barracks courtyard, the Links that day, being too inhospitable for ceremony. The consumption of several hogsheads of porter marked the occasion. The following year the unit's members would all donate a day's pay towards the care of the wounded sailors returned from their triumph at Trafalgar.

The Royal Aberdeen Volunteers were, as already described, a corps of gentlemen receiving no pay, and somewhat exclusively 'upper middle class'. On paper they were 480 strong but the new call to arms was met with a lukewarm response.

In other Aberdeen communities even a shortage of firearms did not stop enthusiasm and progress. Two units formed with pikes as their principle weapons.

The Gilcomston Pikemen formed part of Old Machar's parish efforts and 180 men joined. In direct support were horses, carriages and the servants to operate them, donated by the local Gentry. Their leader was Lt Col James Chalmers, a Marischal College educated, printer and publisher.

To the south, The Aberdeen Pikemen formed from the shipyard workers around Footdee ('Fittie'). They drilled with Finlason's 'Fencibles' and included in their ranks, additional gunners for the big artillery at the harbour.

Pikes were replaced by muskets in 1807 and the two units renamed as the Gilcomston Light Infantry and the Aberdeen Light Infantry.

In the early 1800s Aberdeen's two universities were under-funded, housed in old and deteriorating buildings, and generally hostile to each other. This did not stop them attracting and educating talented individuals.

A King's College graduate could occasionally be

found wildfowling in Belhelvie Parish, north of Aberdeen, inland from the Balmedie dunes. The Reverend Alexander John Forsyth LLD pondered the annoying passage of time between the warning puff of smoke from his flintlock's priming pan and the arrival of shot anywhere near the birds in his sights. His solution was the use, in place of flint, steel and powder, of recently discovered fulminate chemicals. These compounds exploded in response to friction or shock. His work at King's College and at the Tower of London would eventually result in the percussion cap. In addition to reducing warning times for Belhelvie ducks, the cap gave muzzle-loaded muskets an almost all-weather capability. It is said Napoleon offered Forsyth £20,000 to go to France and develop his invention. Forsyth's loyalty to King and Country was rewarded by the British Government with rather more limited cash instalments forty years later, and long after his death. Forsyth and his invention are commemorated by a wall plaque in the blustery gap that leads from the King's College Quadrangle out towards Elphinstone Hall.

In addition to his significant military technical work Forsyth was the leading light in the, 90 strong, Belhelvie Company of The Aberdeenshire Volunteers. Forsyth's company was one of around fifty raised in the small towns, villages and agricultural districts of Aberdeenshire, Banffshire and Kincardine after the Truce of Amiens collapsed in 1803. Previously Volunteers had signed up to defend their own homes and localities. But this time 4000 volunteers undertook to deploy away from home to meet a hostile fleet, initially anywhere in the three counties, and subsequently anywhere in Great Britain. Volunteers were also required to leave home for Garrison duty and continuous training periods for anything between a week and a month.

Although mostly volunteer infantrymen, in the coastal towns some men manned the coastal artillery. Peterhead's Volunteer Battery 'saw off' a lurking French privateer.

The University provided officers and men for the Volunteers, but was also contributing to the developing Army Medical Staff caring for the Regular Army. The University had a claim to have established the first medical school in the English speaking world. The very strong link between the University and Army medicine is traceable through the Volunteer movement right up to and beyond the formation of the OTC in 1912.

In Duthie Park, on top of the bank above the River Dee, towers a 21 metre high obelisk. The monument, originally erected at Marischal College in 1860 was moved in 1906 to allow extensions to the College. The monument celebrates the life and achievements of James McGrigor. On the Iberian Peninsula at the start of the 19th century Arthur Wellesley, not yet the Duke of Wellington, was organising and deploying an increasingly professional field army to remove Napoleon's armies. He had organised his force for the first time into self contained divisions with their own artillery and supporting arms, a structure recognizable a century later in World War I. James McGrigor (1771-1858) was Wellesley's Chief of Medical Staff. He was born in Cromdale and attended the Aberdeen Grammar School and Marischal College. He and eleven other students founded the Aberdeen Medical Society in order to supplement the disappointing level of medical teaching offered at that time by both King's and Marischal Colleges.

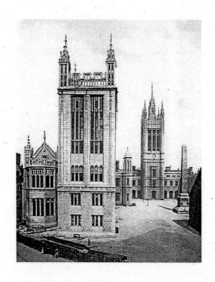

McGrigor's Monument inside the developing Marischal College. It was later moved to Duthie Park.

McGrigor became a surgeon in the 88th Regiment of Foot (Connaught Rangers), serving in Flanders, the West Indies and Egypt. He was appointed to the post of Deputy Inspector-General of Hospitals in 1805 and took part in the Walcheren expedition before his appointment as Inspector-General of Hospitals in August 1809. In 1811 he was appointed Chief of the Medical Staff of the Peninsular Army, serving in Spain, Portugal and France until the end of the war in 1814.

McGrigor introduced a system of staged evacuation of sick and wounded men. He also persuaded Wellesley to mention medical officers in official dispatches for the first time. He came out of retirement in June 1815 to accept the post of Director-General of the Army Medical Department, a position he held until 1851. McGrigor introduced several important changes including regular medical reporting from military stations across the Empire, and the provision of assistance to widows and dependents in the form of the Army Friendly Society (1816) and the Army Benevolent Society (1820). He initiated research into all aspects of army health and the development of chairs of military medicine in Dublin and Edinburgh. He improved the system for selecting men for commissions in the medical services and secured proper Royal status for those commissions. He served as Rector of the University of Aberdeen on three occasions.

Not all the University's military men were medics. In these times mere boys attended University, attempted to learn what was needed for their vocation, and left. Most did not properly graduate. Harry 'Joe' Lumsden left King's at 16 and returned to India to serve in the Indian Army as his father had done.

Harry 'Joe' Lumsden. Pioneer of 'khaki' uniform.

In 1847 Lt Lumsden was tasked to raise the elite Queen Victoria's Own Corps of Guides on the NW Frontier. Concluding that brightly coloured, tightly fitting uniforms were not the best apparel for the climate or the new unit's 'special forces' role, he clothed his men in loose fitting 'khaki'. Lumsden's example would eventually be followed some 60 years later by the whole British Army.

Forty years after Waterloo, Napoleon III's steam-age France caused several flurries of invasion fever and Volunteering. In the midst of this general suspicion, France was however the key ally of Britain in the Crimean War against Russia in the 1850s. Many of the hard learned lessons of the Napoleonic period had been forgotten. Appalling incompetence was brought to the notice of politicians and the British public by newspaper war correspondents such as WH Russell of the Times.

Logistics and administration were a debacle at the start due to insufficient resources, poor training and almost no planning. Everything was hampered by the separation of responsibilities in the field and at the highest levels. Supply and Transport belonged to the Treasury and arrangements to support the Army were improvised in the field only after deployment. Guns, ammunition, the Royal Artillery and the Royal Engineers belonged to the Master General of the Ordnance. The Army Medical Department was an independent organisation. Outfitting the men of infantry and cavalry regiments was the responsibility of each individual Colonel. In 1854/55 everything was brought under a single War Department and Secretary of State.

Matters improved steadily as the war progressed but the government and military establishment were shaken by the Army's performance against a European enemy.

Wellington's army in the Peninsula in 1808 had benefited from 15 years of bitter war experience. The Crimean emergency had seen a force plunged straight from peace to war.

The shock of the Indian Mutiny soon after the Crimea lent further impetus for a protracted series of committees, studies and reforms over the next quarter century. Many senior commentators at the time thought it fortunate that the Crimean and Indian emergencies had not occurred simultaneously. Britain had insufficient strength to handle both at the same time. The legendary Thin Red Line of Crimean battles and later oil paintings, was 'thin' largely due to a serious shortage of trained reinforcements after the initial deployment of 26,000 men. Britain, unlike its ally France, had no system for manning, sustaining and activating a large reserve of trained manpower. It also seemed that Britain must learn from continental armies and undertake systematic training during peacetime, especially for staff and technical officers.

The Prussian system of short term compulsory universal conscription to produce large numbers of trained reserves with strong local attachments seemed to offer the best model. In Britain, not historically or culturally compatible with modern Prussian ways, a voluntary system would need to meet the conflicting requirements of the Empire and Continental threats.

To improve staff officer education, the senior bit of the Royal Military College Sandhurst was expanded and transformed into the Staff College. Here students learned from historical studies and developed the knowledge and personal competence required to manage a large army in the field.

Edward Cardwell, Secretary of State for War (1868-74), in a bid to save money as much as to improve the Army, built on the considerable progress achieved since the Crimean War. Half way through Cardwell's period in office, it was still a weak Britain that watched Prussia mobilise at an astonishing rate and smash the former superpower, France. The Franco-Prussian War (1870-1871) demonstrated just how much had been changed by industrialisation, social progress and scientific invention. It also illustrated the 'force-multiplying' effect of a well trained and practiced staff system.

Cardwell's reforms put the finishing touches to the design of the late Victorian army. Recruits would now sign-up to a shorter period of regular service followed by a reserve liability. Better links between the country and its Army were forged by a comprehensive military system based on local depots with strong connections to the surrounding towns and counties.

To facilitate all these changes Cardwell had also ended the practice of purchased commissions. Attendance at the Royal Military College Sandhurst now became the usual route to a Regular Commission for those other than gentlemen cadets of the Royal Artillery and Royal Engineers who continued to go to the Royal Military Academy at Woolwich, as they had done since 1741.

A few years after the Crimean War, King's College and Marischal College were at last permanently united to form the University of Aberdeen in 1860. The local Volunteer movement waxed and waned but in July 1862, a crowd of 30,000 assembled on and around the Broad Hill to enjoy a colourful parade of 2,500 regulars, militia and volunteers in kilts, bearskins and feather bonnets. Officers in cockaded and plumed headgear galloped purposefully about in the background. This, the first 'modern' Wapinschaw, was repeated as an annual event in a steadily less flamboyant manner at Black Dog Ranges into the first decade of the 21st Century.

1862 also saw Aberdonian Alexander Ogston start his medical training at Marischal College. After qualification and further education in Europe, Ogston rose through the ranks of the medical teaching staff eventually being Professor of Surgery from 1882 to 1909. Professor Ogston, learning from and observing Lister's work, introduced the rather conservative Aberdeen medical establishment to the concept of antiseptic surgery. He interrupted his considerable duties in Aberdeen to work for the Army during the 1884 Egyptian War and the Second Boer War 1899-1902. Instrumental in the creation of the Royal Army Medical Corps, in his seventies he again deployed with the Army during World War I, to assist in the management of severe trauma. He died as Sir Alexander Ogston KCVO MB CM MD in 1929. A University surgery society and an award for best student bear his name to this day. With a long lifetime of achievements Ogston ranks with James McGrigor of Napoleonic times in the band of Aberdeen University medics who did so much to improve Army medicine.

In 1878, at the express wish of Aberdeen's Rifle Volunteers, a Volunteer Royal Engineer unit was established, initially sharing the accommodation and weapons of the artillery volunteers. A senior RE officer came south from Fort George to inspect the unit, and conduct formal exams to assess the competence of the officers. One essential skill of the volunteer RE officer was the ability to beg, borrow and steal instructors capable of teaching the wide range of Sapper skills. For the first 6 years of its existence the unit shared its Adjutant and Sergeant Major with its Lanark equivalent but came of age when it finally received its very own experienced Adjutant.

The new unit progressed, became popular and was increased in establishment. The multitude of skills involved must have attracted some University staff and students to its ranks. There they would learn the mysteries of knotting, splicing, lashing, siege works, water supply, and telegraph lines. Bridges nearly 300 ft long were thrown across the River Dee and eventually the unit had its own watermanship hut near the Wellington Suspension Bridge and a 5 acre training ground in Torry. All the Volunteer units followed a cycle of drill nights and annual camps with the opportunity for some to go to Regular corps depots for specialist courses. For Sappers such training took place in Chatham.

From time to time Government encouraged universities to form their own volunteer units. In 1860, Edinburgh University formed No. 4 Company of the Queen's Edinburgh Rifles. In 1882 St Andrew's formed No. 7 Company of the 1st Fife Royal Garrison Artillery Volunteers. Although the Volunteer Rifles, Artillery, and Engineer units in Aberdeen were open to recruits from the University, there was still no 'University unit'. This changed in 1885 when the University formed No 8 Battery as a new sub unit of the 1st Aberdeenshire Artillery Volunteers. The existing 8,9 and 10 batteries renumbered, much to the joy of sign writers. The Battery Commander was yet another medic, Captain William Stirling, Professor of Physiology. Professor Trail of the Botany Dept also became involved. The unit had been receiving depressingly unsatisfactory annual reports but by 1887 things had been sorted out.

Soon after the establishment of the University Artillery Battery, in February 1886, the Aberdeen Ambulance Association met for the first time and agreed that they wanted a Volunteer Bearer Company formed from the University. Eighteen months later 101 medical students and staff formed a new, War Office approved, local branch of the Medical Staff Corps. Funding followed a year later and training for the 7th Division Volunteer Medical Staff Corps began in earnest. Stretcher drills and first aid training got underway and everyone was issued with a smart dark blue uniform with red facings, white belts, swords and the Geneva Badge of a red cross on a white background. In 1889 the officers received their commissions and the new unit under Surgeon Captain Alexander Macgregor was soon ready to march out the North Deeside Road headed for Cults and its first regimental camp. Camp would regularly involve 4 mile speed marches accompanied by ambulance wagons and pack horses. Reaching a designated scene of 'battle', the student soldiers were required to find and evacuate simulated battle casualties scattered throughout the woods. With casualties safely delivered to deployed Dressing Stations the unit would then set off on a 4 day march around the parishes of Culter and Skene. Each year, fifty or so selected individuals would go to a Brigade Camp in Aldershot. On one occasion the Aberdeen men would be reviewed by no less than the German Kaiser. The 1895 Camp was held at Birkhall where the unit was inspected by Queen Victoria. In 1905 the unit expanded with a second company, transport sections for two field hospitals and a bearer company for the Gordon Highlanders Volunteer Infantry Brigade. Headquarters were at the Albert Hall in Union Wynd.

The 1890s saw the admission of women to the

University with the first four graduating in Arts in 1898. It would not be until 1903 that a woman joined the academic staff and it would be another half century beyond that before female participation in student soldiering.

Old Aberdeen was incorporated by Act of Parliament into Aberdeen in 1891. Four years later in March 1895, No 8, (the University) Battery was absorbed into 1st Heavy Battery. In early 1896 all Aberdeen's Volunteer units were tested together. Alarm rockets were fired and 1500 rifle, artillery, engineer and medical volunteers mustered . The artillery were soon in action against notional enemy landings on the beach, engineers prepared emergency defensive earthworks, and the rifles hurried to counter a flanking assault at the mouth of the River Don. Later in the year more carefully umpired all-arms battle exercises were fought around Tullos. But by 1897 enthusiasm for artillery life was waning among the student population.

An infantry volunteer unit was however increasing in popularity. G Company of the 1st Volunteer Battalion Gordon Highlanders was based in Woodside, then just outside Aberdeen's boundary, but only a half hour walk or so from Old Aberdeen and the surrounding student digs. A University detachment formed in late 1897 under Captain WO Duncan, a Cambridge graduate, accomplished oarsman, and partner in an Aberdeen legal firm. The legal profession had, and would continue to have, a strong role in the local volunteer units. The CO of the 1st Volunteer Battalion was a local advocate.

U Company is Born

By 1898 numbers, and the wishes of Duncan's student soldiers, justified the formation of a new Company. Additionally Duncan thought that a separate University Company would increase the rather poor attendance statistics for training sessions and Annual Camp. A case was made to the Battalion CO and University or 'U' Company, 1st Volunteer Battalion The Gordon Highlanders, was born on 10 November 1898 with William Duncan as its first OC. 'U' Company would quickly establish itself as the battalion's best sub-unit in drill, shooting and general efficiency. Within the University structure of student societies and clubs, 'U' Company's members established a Gordon Highlanders Club thus gaining access to grants for gymnastic training. Other Club activities were grouped under the headings of General, Amusements, Shooting and Ambulance.

Duncan analysed the problems the Gunners had experienced in student recruiting. By 1897 the University Battery had dwindled almost to insignificance. Duncan adjusted the mandatory drill night commitments to allow for students' studies. Also thinking that the Battery Sgt Major of the Gunner unit had been in post far too long, he instigated a system of promotion whereby Sgts held their rank for only one year before reverting to Private thus making way for others to practice leadership. Men would continue to serve with the Company after they graduated. Duncan was also suspicious of too great an involvement in student volunteer units by the professors.

In 1899, with the outbreak of the South African War or Second Boer War (1899-1902), the British Army was committed to its biggest large-scale overseas deployment since the Crimea. Some of the many reforms by Cardwell and others would be tested.

U Company

The Shooting Team - February 1899

William Duncan and his 1899 U Company Shooting Team

The manning demands of the Boer War soon exceeded what the regulars could provide and the call went out to the nation's Volunteer units. Each Volunteer Battalion was authorised to form a Volunteer Service Company for deployment overseas. Volunteers were to be 20-35 years old, fit, first class shots, and of good character. Preference would be given to the unmarried and widowers without children. They would sign-on for one year or the duration of the war, receive full pay and a Volunteer gratuity of £5 on return. They would have full entitlement to pensions for wounds.

All this represented a most significant change in the relationship between the Regular Army and the Volunteers. Until 1889 Volunteers existed solely to defend the homeland.

26

Now some of them would opt to accompany the Regular Army in expeditionary warfare. The 1st Volunteer Battalion Gordon Highlanders from a strength of 809, formed a Service Company of 129, led by 'U' Company Commander Lt (Volunteer Capt) WO Duncan. He and others would thus gain valuable operational experience. Aberdeen's medical volunteers sent 6 men to South Africa, one was killed and one received a commission in the field. The Engineer Volunteers sent 54 men.

Direct 'university' involvement in the Boer War was in the form of a detachment from The Cambridge University Rifle Volunteers (CURV) sent to augment the Suffolk Regiment. The only strictly university unit to see active service, the CURV earned the Battle Honour 'South Africa 1900-01'.

In 1903 The Report of His Majesty's Commissioners on the War in South Africa indicted almost every aspect of the army from the Commander in Chief down. Whilst strategic intelligence, though largely ignored, had been excellent in the run up to war, planning and operational staff work was dire, standardised division of responsibilities and procedures non-existent, equipment and supplies poor and manpower wanting in both quality and quantity. The physical and mental qualities of British officers and men were all heavily criticised. Although in theory commissions were available to anyone of the right quality it was concluded that regimental life still required an officer, whatever his competence, to have considerable personal income.

The worry caused by the bitter lessons of the Boer War was exacerbated by the rise of the Prussian threat. To win the war in South Africa Britain herself had been left virtually defenceless against any serious threat from Europe.

To cover the three conflicting demands of Empire, home defence and Continental force projection, further great reforms were needed.

After the Boer War, 'U' Company continued to thrive and maintain high standards. For example, in the summer of 1906, the Company having completed its annual camp at Barry Buddon, marched all the way back to Aberdeen.

U Troop, The Scottish Horse

For those students more inclined to cover distance on horseback a University Troop was formed during the early 1900s within Aberdeen's own Yeomanry cavalry, G Squadron of The Scottish Horse. Two early members of the Troop are recorded in the University Roll of Honour for World War One. Both men progressed into reserved occupations but loyalty to their old student units made them enlist.

Arts student, William Urquhart, valued his time with the Troop so much that on the outbreak of World War I, he felt he owed his country a debt. He left his post as Minister at Kinloch Rannoch and enlisted as a Private in the Royal Scots. Commissioned into the Black Watch he was killed leading his men at Mametz Wood in 1916.

Williejohn Gilmour, another Arts student, by the summer of 1914 was a schoolmaster in Leith. Despite being offered a commission in the Gordons, he joined the Scottish Horse as a Trooper. After valued service as Quartermaster Sergeant with his Regiment in Gallipoli, he was commissioned. In Salonika, while attached to the South Notts Hussars, he was killed during a patrol.

28

William Urquhart and Williejohn Gilmour.
Once members of U Troop, The Scottish Horse.

The Royal Army Medical Corps (RAMC) is Formed

In 1902, the year Aberdeen's tram system was electrified, the Medical Staff Corps was renamed to become the Royal Army Medical Corps (Volunteers). There continued to be more recruits than vacancies and the War Office took some time to sanction establishment increases. By 1905 the University's own medical unit could field all the men, transport and kit necessary to build and operate two field hospitals and be the Bearer Company for the Gordon Highlanders Volunteer Brigade. The unit was now 400 strong and had its own bugle and pipe bands.

The effectiveness of the unit was demonstrated to the public by the rapid deployment of one complete field hospital at Hazlehead. The unit was of practical assistance to the town when it provided all the medical cover for the crowds thronging a Royal Visit on 27th September 1906 when King Edward VII and Queen Alexandra visited Aberdeen to open a new extension to Marischal College. This is the work that required the rustication of McGrigor's Monument to Duthie Park. An especially smart detachment from the University Company RAMC formed a Royal Guard of Honour at Marischal College. All of this was captured on film and the student soldiers and other highlights of the visit can be viewed online at the National Library of Scotland, Scottish Screen Archive website.

With less pomp and ceremony winter drill nights were spent learning more about sanitation and first aid. An annual cycle was established of drill nights, lectures, field exercises, annual camps and occasional special tasks. This training routine would be familiar to the officer cadets of 2012.

The 1900s saw various Secretaries of War and progressive staff officers gradually improve the situation exposed by the Boer War. A proper General Staff and War Ministry were finally established. Clear responsibilities were allocated to cover personnel, operations and planning, staff duties, recruiting, doctrine and training. Without this basis Britain would never have been able to cope with the massive and complex undertakings involved in the 20th Century's two World Wars.

Building on his predecessors' work but achieving the biggest change was Richard Haldane, born in Edinburgh and a graduate of Edinburgh University. He served as Secretary of State for War between 1905 and 1912. Reconciling the needs of a far flung Empire and the challenge of a growing German threat on the continent had to be attempted within, as

30

ever, a constrained budget. Indeed it was Haldane's success in achieving considerable savings that gave him political leverage during his expert politicking for reform.

At the start of the Boer War Britain's reserves other than the pool of ex-Regulars, had fallen into three categories.

Firstly, the Militia, administered by the Regular Army, consisted primarily of agricultural and casual labourers who could attend the initial 6 week training period and the one month per year thereafter. For officers the militia provided a back door into the Army avoiding Sandhurst. Militia units were predominantly infantry, with some coastal artillery, fortress engineers, and a small medical staff. Units could, as during the Crimean War be sent overseas to relieve Regular Garrisons, but the Militia as a whole was not a coherent force.

Secondly, the Yeomanry provided 38 regiments of cavalry manned by generally wealthy members who funded their unit and provided their own horses, uniforms and equipment. Fit for local defence and quelling internal unrest on behalf of the civil authorities, they lacked the resources and expertise to mobilise for more distant deployment.

Finally, the Volunteers, more urban, from small businesses, the artisan trades and professional occupations, were responsible for local defence against invasion ever since Napoleon's time. Although some central funding was available the units often depended on local subscriptions and the generosity of their commanders.

Despite all-arms grouping and cooperation in some instances, the reserve units were not organised into the coherent field formations needed to expand the British Army in the face of a serious Continental threat. In 1906 a War

Office committee, which included representatives from schools and universities, concluded that all the categories of reserves were deficient in officers. There soon followed recommendations for the formation of an Officers' Training Corps, directly funded by the War Office.

In August 1907 Haldane's Territorial and Reserve Forces Act received Royal Assent and on 1 April 1908 the Territorial Force (TF) officially came into being. Militia, Yeomanry and Volunteer units were reorganised, renumbered and renamed. For example, the 1st Volunteer Battalion Gordon Highlanders became the 4th Battalion Gordon Highlanders under the command of former 'U' Company Commander and Boer War veteran, Lt Col William Duncan.

Units were grouped into field divisions with strong regional identities. One of the 14 TF infantry divisions was the Highland Division which included Aberdeen and its surrounding shires in its area. By 1910 the new 'Territorials' numbered some 276,618 officers and men, 88% of establishment. Haldane's plans worked.

The individual units that made up each division or brigade were administered by County Associations, with the local Lord Lieutenant presiding over military members chosen from the unit COs; representative members nominated by the county councils and boroughs; and co-opted members, often retired military officers.

As Territorials, members of the TF were not obliged to serve outside Britain. In 1910 a call for registration of volunteers for Imperial Service overseas would yield only 10% of the total strength. Those who did volunteer were entitled to wear an 'Imperial Service' badge.

Haldane's reforms included the formation, under Army Order 160 of June 1908, of the Officers' Training Corps (OTC) which would help satisfy the TF's requirement for young officers.

There would be 23 OTC contingents of the 'Senior Division' at Universities and 166 of the 'Junior Division' at schools. The Inns of Court would also have an OTC contingent. The school contingents would focus on basic infantry skills while all the arms and services would be represented among the Senior Division contingents. The War Office would determine what specialised training and qualifications each applicant university could offer. The overall selection included the infantry, cavalry, Royal Artillery, Royal Engineers, Army Service Corps, Royal Army Medical Corps and the Army Veterinary Corps. Obviously not every university could set up every speciality.

To administer and support the University contingents Haldane required a Military Education Committee (MEC) to be set up in each University. Through the MECs the OTCs and their parent universities would have a direct link to the War Office, setting them administratively apart from the TF Associations and units.

In the absence of an OTC at Aberdeen, for a few years after 1908, U Company of the now 4th Gordons continued to thrive as the most popular unit for students. One U Company private of this time is an example of those who chose Regular soldiering as a career. Robert Dunlop Smith was the second son of Principal, the Very Rev. Sir George Adam Smith. He was an Arts student at Aberdeen 1910-11 and entered the Royal Military College Sandhurst, in 1912. He received a commission in the Indian Army and eventually

33

joined the 33rd Punjabis. His example proves the point that university men, although nowhere near the majority achieved near the end of the 20th Century, were far from unknown in the Regular Army officer profession. Of course the Army's own specialist schools provided tertiary education in some subjects easily comparable with many civilian colleges.

Robert Dunlop Smith.
Graduate entrant to Sandhurst in 1912.
Later of the 33rd Punjabis, Indian Army

Many Universities established their OTCs at the earliest opportunity in 1908. For example Glasgow did so and soon consisted of three infantry companies and an engineer company. Aberdeen, a smaller establishment, would take until 1912, under a keen Principal, to form its own contingent.

Chapter 2

FORMATION AND WORLD WAR I
1912-1919

The winter of 1912/13 had brought the sadly routine string of tragedies at sea. The Great Gale of mid January had killed 70 people lost in wrecks at Port Erroll, the Bullers of Buchan and Spey Bay. The world would be shocked by the loss of the unsinkable liner *Titanic* in April.

Aberdeen shared in all the bustle, industry and rapid technological developments of the early 20th Century. The city had inaugurated its first telegraph letter service with London on 1 January 1912 and had enjoyed public electric lighting for 17 years. Students had been able to use the tram network operating as far out as the Bridge of Don for nearly two decades. The Gaiety had become Aberdeen's first permanent cinema in 1908. Contemporary political action included a five week coal strike. Suffragettes increasingly appeared in the Courts and in May 1913 they would successfully set fire to Ashley Road School.

The University was growing. In addition to the recent Marischal College extensions, at Old Aberdeen the New King's teaching building was nearing completion. It would open in 1913. The new building was overshadowed by a, soon to be demolished, large professorial manse sitting between it and the Chapel.

On 17 May 1912 several eminent men from the University and the local community met in Marischal College to plan the formation of an Officers' Training Corps Contingent at the University of Aberdeen. There was a certain urgency to get on with things. The real driving force who chaired this first meeting of the Military Education Committee (MEC) was Principal and Vice Chancellor, George Adam Smith. A volunteer rifleman in his own student days at Edinburgh he went on to be a great traveller and active Victorian alpinist with the Matterhorn and other peaks under his belt. He was a renowned Biblical Scholar, and historical geographer of the Holy Land. His maps would be of great use in the coming war. Smith served as Principal from 1909 to 1935.

Principal George Adam Smith - AUOTC's Founding Father

Several other professors were at the table including Professor Trail of the Botany department, a former officer of the University Battery in Aberdeen's Artillery Volunteers. Also present was former Lord Provost and future Liberal MP for Aberdeen South, Sir John Fleming.

There too was Colonel William Johnston. A product of Aberdeen Grammar School, Johnston had studied for his MA and part of his medical course at Aberdeen before completing his studies at Edinburgh. He had gone on to active service as an Army Medical Officer in the first South African War of 1878, the Zulu War of 1879 and the short First Boer War of 1880/1881. By the time of the Second Boer War (1899-1901) he was Assistant Director General of Army Medical Services at the War Office. He was now retired from the Army, settled in Newton Dee, and employed in administrative work for Aberdeen Royal Infirmary and other city hospitals. His hobbies included writing a history of the Royal Army Medical Corps. He with fellow Aberdonian Sir Alexander Ogston and others had played a significant role in the formation of the RAMC. His experience would be particularly valuable since the War Office had very recently approved the University's application for a Medical Unit of the Senior Division of the Officers' Training Corps.

Opposition from the local Territorial Force (TF) Association and local Volunteer units, especially 4th Gordons with it's strong 'U' Company, had stymied a simultaneous application to form an Infantry Unit. The local TF rightly surmised that a big OTC, open to all undergraduates, would seriously degrade the quantity and quality of recruitment and retention in the existing units. But at least a Medical Unit was a start, and most appropriate given the University's long and distinguished association with Army Medicine.

The meeting confirmed the membership and duties of the new committee before the Principal described how the OTC was already being operated at Glasgow and other Universities. He had drawn up a draft 'Contract of Service'

37

which would be signed by all students applying to join. As at other OTCs all students joining would pay a deposit of 10 Shillings. 79 students had already indicated their interest, 41 of whom were, or had been, in the TF. These latter students would hopefully make it easy to appoint Cadet NCOs quickly. Finding officers was a bigger problem. The local RAMC would be asked to temporarily loan a suitable officer to get things going. Leaflets calling for volunteers would be printed and distributed throughout the University and the Principal and Secretary would seek out suitable accommodation.

A second MEC meeting was held in July 1912, where it was agreed to nominate to the War Office, Dr George Alexander Williamson as Commanding Officer. Williamson was a graduate of Aberdeen who had enlisted in the Medical Staff Corps Volunteers in 1889. He was now a Lecturer in Hygiene at the Aberdeen Teacher Training Centre. The War Office would also be asked to provide an Adjutant and Sergeant Instructors. Students would be enrolled at the start of the Winter Term 1912. The Committee then discussed the *'Rules for the Aberdeen University Contingent (Medical Unit) of the Officers' Training Corps'.*

The MEC would administer finance, uniforms, equipment, HQ accommodation, a drill ground, and the granting of expenses for administration and training including Annual Camps.

The Contingent would have two classes of membership:

Class 1 - Matriculated students studying medicine or proceeding to study medicine. (It was common to do an MA course first). Graduates or non-members of the University who desired to gain the proficiency Certificates obtainable in the OTC.

Class 2 - Honorary members nominated by the MEC.

All members were to be British Subjects of pure European descent, and would sign a contract making themselves subject to rules and regulations. The latter required every man to make himself 'efficient' for a minimum period of two years which could be extended at the CO's discretion. 'Efficiency' was well defined and related to attendance, conduct and proficiency. The unit's 'Efficiency' ratings would dictate how much money the War Office would grant to the unit's annual budgets.

Proficiency Certificates or 'Certs' were set at two levels and were specific to arm, for example in Aberdeen's case, to the RAMC. Cert 'A' covered basic knowledge and competence and Cert 'B' the higher level of training expected of senior cadets. Certs would be granted to those who passed written and practical tests.

By the end of 1912, Williamson had been properly listed in the London Gazette as a Lieutenant in the TF RAMC, supernumerary for service with AUOTC. He was receiving valuable support from Major Farquhar McLennan MB RAMC, the Adjutant of Aberdeen's TF School of Instruction who acted as OTC Adjutant during the formation period. Rooms for an Orderly Room and store had been found in Marischal College and needed £20 - £30 for furniture and equipment. This would come from the initial grant available on application from the Army Audit Office, Edinburgh. Interestingly the MEC had asked for the stipulation regarding ethnic suitability to be deleted from the

Rules but the War Office had declined the request.

Finding suitable drill hall accommodation had been difficult. The first option, the Marischal College Gymnasium, was too small for the drilling of 50-60 men. The TF Woolmanhill Drill Hall was available one night per week but was too small for stretcher drills and would incur a lighting charge. Finally the free use of the Hardgate Drill Hall was agreed upon, for which the TF Association was duly thanked.

63 cadets had enrolled in the Winter term of 1912 and dressing them in suitable uniforms became the next challenge. The uniform was based on that of Edinburgh OTC and would consist of cap, jacket, breeches, long puttees, brown boots and an overcoat. Bright buttons would bear the University Crest less the motto, and shoulder badges would indicate membership of Aberdeen University Officers' Training Corps.

Training pamphlets and books would cost 5 Shillings per set and £6-00 was allocated. Standing Orders were to be printed. The entitlement of the Cadet Sergeant Major to allowances for clerical work was to be investigated. On the social front the unit had already applied for a contribution towards the costs of a Corps Smoking Concert. The Principal undertook to meet this request without drawing on OTC funds.

Clearly, setting up and running a new unit was going to be an expensive task and any War Office assistance was tightly controlled. Fortunately a former Rector and current Chancellor of the University had a better grasp of the costs involved than most. The Lord Strathcona and Mount Royal had left his hometown of Forres as Donald Alexander Smith, bound for the Labrador wilderness as a Hudson Bay

40

Company fur trapper and trader. He had risen through the ranks of the Company to become a leading entrepreneurial participant in the birth of modern Canada in the fields of business, railways and government. In 1912 he was one of the few men still living in the Empire who had raised, financed and deployed his own Regiment. The Strathcona Horse had served in the Second Boer War. Strathcona made a private, unpublicised contribution of £120 (£9000 at 2010 values) to the new Medical Unit.

Lord Strathcona

In the first months of 1913 just over 60 cadets were drilling regularly. Roughly half were new to soldiering, and half had come from 'U' Company, the RAMC(TF) and the Scottish Horse. One recruit had left and gone abroad, while 15 of them had already sat their Cert A exams. The contingent included some pipers and all were looking forward to a fortnight's Annual Camp under canvas at the RAMC depot in Aldershot in July.

AUOTC resting during their first Camp, Aldershot, 1913

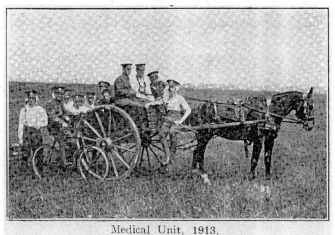

Medical Unit, 1913.

Bicycle, RAMC Cart and Horse in formation, Summer 1913

Among the former U Company members joining the OTC was Arthur Landsborough Thomson who had served with U Company from 1909 to 1912. While serving with the OTC he would become a University assistant in the Zoology Department in 1914. In 1915 he would be commissioned into the Argyll and Sutherland Highlanders and rise up the ranks to become a Lt Col (Assistant Quartermaster General) and be awarded an OBE.

The University still of course recognised U Company as its own and acknowledged the fact in various ceremonies. For example in 1913 U Company, led by the Pipes and Drums of the 4th Gordons, marched from Marischal College to King's College for a Church Service. Following an inspection in the King's quadrangle, they marched back to Marischal via King Street. In 1913 Duncan had handed over command of the Battalion to another former 'U' Coy Commander Capt Edward Watt: leader of the 1906 March from Barry to Aberdeen; former editor of the University's paper, *Alma Mater*; and a future Lord Provost. 'U' Company was now under the command of Captain Lachlan Mackinnon, another lawyer, and from a long family line of advocates. Mackinnon had come up through the ranks and affirmed that being a Private was much more fun than being the Captain. Thus William Duncan's long service with the Volunteers was over but a century later his claymore still has pride of place in the AUOTC and is carried as the Sword of Honour by the Senior Under Officer on formal parades such as that held on Remembrance Sunday outside King's Chapel.

Some other Marischal men, medics and some agriculture students, remained with the RAMC(TF) 'Terriers' particularly in the Transport Section. The latter offered 'real

43

live horses to ride' and a comfortable dry snooze on the baggage wagons.

The new OTC Medical unit was deemed 'Efficient' at Aldershot on its very first Camp, despite three cadets failing to attend and thus not earning that all important designation for themselves. The MEC considered each case of absence and allocated fines according to the quality of excuse. One cadet had been otherwise engaged professionally and one had never attended drills anyway. The third had experienced the unpleasant sensation of watching the unit's train from Aberdeen steam straight through Stirling Station where he had hoped to join it. Missed trains apart, the unit had got off to a good start. 10 cadets had passed their Cert A earning the unit £20 from the War Office in an admirable 'output based' reward system. These grants were payable when the cadets completed their 2 year commitment. One cadet had received a commission in the Royal Field Artillery (TF) with a view to joining the Regular Army. The unit had 38 candidates for Cert A and 10 candidates for the more advanced Cert B. In the interests of the progress of these individuals and with the attraction of further War Office grants, the question of running an additional Camp in the Spring was being actively discussed.

In mid November 1913 a special 'Military Number' of *Alma Mater* was distributed. This, the University's own weekly magazine, was available to all at two pence per copy or through a half-crown annual subscription. In addition to providing entertainment and commentary on topical issues the *Alma Mater* was an important means of communicating with the student body on routine arrangements for all academic and extra mural activities. The Military Number included articles by the Principal who urged more to join for the obvious physical, mental and moral benefits. He was, he wrote, proud to have been a Volunteer during his student days. Things had improved since his day with an efficient and more liberal system now in place to offer students some military education. In Aberdeen's case the training focussed on practical Army medical knowledge and skills. Valuable certificates could be gained to supplement what students were doing in their courses. He felt it was *'the duty of every able bodied youth to take his share of national service which is still happily entrusted to the goodwill and sense of honour of the men of these islands'*. The magazine continued with a contribution from the War Office explaining the OTC system particularly for medics. One third of the current medical mobilisation system it explained relied on civilian doctors. Experience had shown that to function effectively military doctors needed military knowledge as well as their medical skills.

The special edition finished off with articles from the Aberdeen OTC CO, Williamson, and a cadet NCO. The latter commented that *'as a pastime and efficient relaxation from the untold drudgery of an academic year, a typical OTC lecture cannot be surpassed.'*

Setting the overall tone however was the preface by no less than Field Marshal Earl Roberts. He wrote: *'I am very glad that a special effort is being made at the University of Aberdeen to stimulate recruiting for the University Company of the Territorial Force and for the Officers Training Corps. The shortage of officers for our defensive forces is a most serious matter and one that must be faced and remedied. I commend the movement to the students, and trust they will avail themselves of the opportunity afforded them to do a real*

45

service to their country by fitting themselves to fulfil the sacred duty of defending her in her hour of need.'

'Bobs' Roberts of Kandahar, one of the ablest British commanders of the 19th Century, would die just one year later at the age of 82 while visiting Indian troops fighting in France.

In January 1914 Lord Strathcona, the University's Chancellor, died. He had gifted personal funds to many University projects including the establishment of the OTC. The OTC paraded at the funeral service but U Company did not. This was commented on rather bitterly in *Alma Mater* from someone pointing out that U Company was *'twice as strong and infinitely richer in years'*. It seems communications were not all that they might have been in preparations for the ceremony since even the Students Representative Council failed to attend despite, it was claimed by the authorities, being invited.

On a lighter note, students of both sexes could, from February 1914, enjoy mixed bathing at the Aberdeen Bathing Station, an indoor pool with heated sea water.

At Annual Camp on Salisbury Plain in July 1914 the unit could look back on another year of success. Exams held in November and March had yielded good pass rates in Certs A and B, earning another £224 in War Office grants. The size of the AUOTC enterprise was indicated by the annual accounts showing both expenditure and income at around the £500 level. Strength was at 1 Officer, 74 cadets and 1 Sergeant Instructor. Of these, 54 were at Camp. Williamson demonstrated good care for his men when he overruled the protestations of officious railway staff and allowed his cadets to make the long journey home in mufti (an old Army expression for comfortable civilian clothes) rather than uniform. In the year 1913/14 the unit had produced 11 commissioned officers for the RAMC Special Reserve of Officers (SRO). Social life went on apace if not always fully financed. A Dance, held the night prior to Hogmanay, had created a deficit which the MEC refused to correct from its funds. The Inspection report for the unit at camp showed good standards of squad, company and ambulance drill. Field ambulance manoeuvre and tactics were good, as was discipline. A *'spirit of willing obedience'* was noted by the Inspecting Officer who found this most impressive given the *'state of emancipation of the medical student in a non-resident University'*. All of this reflected great credit on the new CO and his inexperienced NCOs. Unit standards and the output of Cert passes and SRO commissions were remarkable. It was noted though that nearly all administration and instruction rested directly on the shoulders of Lt Williamson and that his loss or resignation would be a great calamity. Another officer should be sought as a matter or urgency.

A far greater calamity did occur later in the Summer with the outbreak of World War I. Some University men volunteered immediately for service. Those already serving in the Territorial Force were mobilised with their various units. Aberdeen's industries lost up to half their workforce to the TF and other volunteering. Companies geared up for the war eventually becoming key producers of heavy linen, preserved foods and boots. Fishermen and their boats were progressively commandeered for minesweeping and coastal defence. The shipyards did the necessary alterations.

U Company is Mobilised

Aberdeen University's own TF unit, 'U' Company, 4th Gordons, was at Tain, by the Dornoch Firth, with the rest of the Battalion on their fortnight long Annual Camp. Three in four of the young men were from the Arts Faculty with the remainder from the faculties of law, science, medicine and agriculture. Hard military training, live firing and route marches out in the fresh air had helped everyone recover from their end of year exams. Sea swimming and golf was enjoyed

U Company by the Dornoch Firth 1914

as was the odd rowing expedition across the Firth to Dornoch itself to 'give the girls a treat' and regale the locals with student songs. On 30 July news reached Tain of imminent war and everyone returned home to prepare for mobilisation.

They were all soon on their way, via a stopover in Perth, to Bedford to join the rest of the Highland Division in training for the Western Front. Although in theory still not obliged to serve overseas, most of the TF quickly volunteered for operations in France and Belgium. This uncertainty around TF divisions deploying overseas was one of the factors behind Kitchener's separate building of his 'New Army' formed initially by volunteers, such as those in the famous 'Pals' battalions. After them the attrition of war demanded conscripts.

The OTC

In late 1914 and early 1915, the OTC dispatched a number of cadets with recommendations for Commissions in the Regular Army for the duration of the war. One example of these cadets is probably William Davidson of Blythewood Inverurie. He was educated at the Grammar School and Gordon's College, Aberdeen, and later at Trinity College, Glenalmond. He began his medical studies at Aberdeen in 1912. In January 1915 he entered the R.M.C., Sandhurst, and after a few months of training was gazetted to the Gordon Highlanders, 2nd Battalion, with which he served in France till the following September, when, having been wounded in action near Hulluch, he was invalided home. On recovery, and after a short period of home service at Stoneywood Wireless Station, he rejoined his regiment in France; three months later he was mortally wounded in action near Mametz, and died on 2 July 1916. Officers and men alike testified to the bravery with which Davidson led his men in the face of terrible odds ; his gallantry and pluck were praised by all who knew him under the difficult active service.

*William Davidson, one of the first OTC members
to go off to War*

As an aside, the Stoneywood Naval Wireless Telegraphy Station is frequently mentioned in the comings and goings of those mobilised for the Gordons or as in this instance on spells of home service. The 3rd Gordons was the Regiment's reserve battalion responsible for the administration of men coming from or going to the other battalions. These men while attached to the 3rd Battalion were employed on garrison defence duties including spells of duty at Stoneywood. The wireless station had been built in 1909 as one of a network of Royal Navy shore stations responsible for 24 hour embryonic wireless communications between the Admiralty and Fleet commanders at sea on battleships. Stoneywood was one of three medium power stations having an operating range of 500 miles. Thus Stoneywood coverage included the entrances to the Baltic, Southern Norway, much of the North Sea and the strategic Home Fleet harbour at Scapa Flow in Orkney. The station was manned by an RN officer, a Chief Petty Officer, and a few telegraphers trained in this new cutting edge technology. The Stoneywood site was of key military significance and worthy of close defence against any threat conceived by the Hun.

In November 1914 a mass meeting of the University's lecturers, assistants and students petitioned for the establishment of another OTC unit for students other than those from the Medical school. They wanted an Infantry Unit or at least an Artillery Unit. The War Office refused the University's request, having enough to do, one imagines, without forming new OTC units. In December 1914 Principal Smith explained the War Office position in *Alma Mater*. The War Office was concentrating on establishing new schools of instruction for those seeking temporary commissions, including those with no previous military experience. As a result new OTC contingents would not be authorised. Principal Smith hoped that those who had campaigned for an infantry OTC would avail themselves of the opportunities offered by the local Military Training Association. Groups of the public, sufficient in number, could elect their own instructors and book one hour drill periods at the Gymnasium and Drill Hall on Crown Street. A modest subscription of one shilling would entitle students to 40 drill periods at a rate of up to three per week. All interested in this option were asked to contact Ian Innes of the Agricultural Chemistry Department at Marischal.

U Company in Bedford

Alma Mater at this time included frequent *'Notes from Bedford'* from the young men of U Company, currently stuck in training billets and becoming increasingly frustrated at not being in France doing what they were trained for. Many found it difficult to switch from the relaxed camaraderie of peacetime soldiering to the necessarily stricter discipline and more obvious hierarchy required of a fighting battalion. The special circumstances in U Company made things even harder to swallow. Everyone knew each other well, perhaps too well. The policy of rotating ranks meant that experienced men who had been sergeants were now again privates. The CSM, an assistant chemistry lecturer, had two first class degrees, and was more academically qualified than most of the officers. Those with rank found it as hard to adjust to a regime of instant obedience as those under them. Life was made a bit more bearable by the social life shared with the Bedford people after the latter got over initial worries about claymore wielding savages descending on them. This notion of the 'wild Highlanders' was positively encouraged with great glee by the comedians in the U Company ranks. But periods of boredom and frustration were increasingly experienced and in October there were garrison outbreaks of the then deadly scarlet fever, measles and diphtheria. These diseases mostly killed among other units of the Highland Division especially young Cameron Highlanders from the Western Isles who had no natural immunity. In the last three months of 1914 some U Company members were applying for commissions in other units, to escape Bedford and to ensure that they did not 'miss the war' which of course would probably 'be over by Christmas'. There was also a stampede of volunteers to replace casualties suffered by 6th Gordons and 4th Seaforths who were already in France. The CO 4th Gordons was worried that the very backbone of his battalion was being depleted, and he feared that his unit's deployment to the Continent would be further delayed.

German Students at Ypres

Having described U Company's student soldier experiences in the closing months of 1914 it is appropriate to salute the sacrifice of their German equivalents. November 1914 saw the closing stages of the 'Race to the Sea'. A series of outflanking manoeuvres had brought the Allied and German armies to the vicinity of Ypres. Beyond Ypres stood the Channel ports essential to the supply and expansion of the British Army in France and Belgium. The First Battle of Ypres marked the transition from mobile operations to static trench warfare. Employing tactics better suited to Napoleon's time, waves of fresh German Volunteer infantrymen were repeatedly thrown against heavy artillery and devastating machine gun and rifle fire from French and British defensive positions. Among these German formations were thousands of poorly trained but enthusiastic student volunteers not long released from their studies. Perhaps to camouflage the disastrous waste of life, the German authorities nurtured stories about lines of singing students marching arm in arm into the hail of Allied lead. Subsequent research into German and Allied records has indeed identified very brave actions by waves of young volunteers in different parts of the battlefield and at different times. Singing did happen too. Whilst the number of students involved is still disputed, many hundreds of German student soldiers were indeed killed around Ypres.

The legend of this *Kindermord bie Ypern* (massacre of the innocents of Ypres) grew during and after the Great War eventually becoming part of Nazi mythology. In November 1914, U Company's own part in vicious reality and the forging of legend around Ypres, still lay many months off.

The OTC

Back in Aberdeen, the OTC was about to lose grant income. Cert A and B training had been suspended for the War's duration and most of the current cadets were unlikely to complete the required 2 years OTC service. The War Office intimated that other grants would be made in lieu, especially in recognition of all those unit members who had enlisted in the Regulars, the Special Reserve, or the Territorial Force since mobilisation. As 1914 drew to a close John Kinloch, a Lecturer in Public Health, applied for a Lt's commission for service in the OTC. Kinloch had been a member of Glasgow High School's contingent of the OTC Junior Division before attending Glasgow University. The MEC meeting in March 1915, was pleased to note that Lt Kinloch was now in post and just in time to replace Capt Williamson as CO when the latter departed for service overseas. Williamson who had been mobilised in August 1914 stayed in the UK until March 1915 when he went off to serve with the Egyptian Expeditionary Force. He worked in the Officers' Hospital in Cairo and later as the Senior Medical Officer for Prisoner of War camps in Cyprus. He was mentioned in dispatches in 1918 and demobilised in February 1919. His experience in this theatre of war equipped him to become a lecturer in tropical medicine when he returned to work in Aberdeen University.

Cadet strength stood at 79 with only 3 deemed not 'Efficient'. One of these three appears nevertheless to have been an active soul who had taken himself off to the Western Front in France to act as a medical 'dresser'. The MEC took satisfaction from the glowing report the unit had earned from its 1914 camp and the 35 commissions granted to former members of the Contingent. In addition 10 men had gone to France as hospital dressers and a further 5 had gone to serve in the ranks of various service units.

U Company Goes to War, February to July 1915

In February 1915, to everyone's relief, the 4th Gordons at last marched through Bedford behind its Pipe Band to entrain for Southampton Docks. The battalion's highly respected RSM, who had done more than most to prepare his volunteers for war, did not go with them. After a sudden and short illness he had died only days earlier. At Southampton, U Company occupied a low deck in the fore-hold of the old Liverpool cattle boat , the *'Archimedes'*, a deck below the battalion's horses. Even in an infantry unit there were dozens of horses: riding horses for the officers; draught animals for the ammunition, stores and medical wagons; and pack horses. A 'lights out' crossing, escorted by torpedo boat destroyer, brought man and horse to Le Havre.

From Le Havre a series of transit billets, slow train rides and route marches brought the Student Soldiers through France and into what remained of unoccupied Belgium. They took over rear area huts at La Clytte, south west of Ypres and only 10 miles from the front line. A new 'double company', D Company, formed from U Company and the Grammar and Robert Gordon's Schools Company. The Battalion's war organisation was of four not eight rifle companies. The U Company designation was retained in informal conversation. Just over a fortnight after leaving Bedford, D Company , on 8 March 1915, was in the trenches learning how to live and fight from men of the Suffolk Regiment. Thus began a rotation between trench life in the 'Wipers' Salient, and rest and training at various sites to the west of Ypres.

During the last week in May 1915 the 4th Gordons took over trenches near what remained of the small village of Hooge on the Menin Road, only 3 miles from the centre of Ypres. U Company's place in history was made either side of the Menin Road, firstly to the north in Y Wood and Bellewaarde, and later to the south in Sanctuary Wood. In the last week of May, D Company alternated with the other companies between the front and reserve trenches. The month ended and June began with heavy German shelling. After a rest spell back in Vlamertinghe the 4th Gordons moved into the Bellewaarde area and dug in amidst severe artillery bombardment which included gas shells. 16 June brought temporary escape as the Gordons were relieved in place at midnight. The Battalion then formed the brigade reserve, still under shellfire, until 19 June when it marched back to Vlamertinghe and Brandhoek for three weeks rest and training 'out of the line'.

The British line around Hooge continued to be unstable with the Germans having gained positions on relatively high ground. They were strengthening their hold on Hooge with concrete fortifications. Back in the trenches, this time south of the Menin Road, in Sanctuary Wood, the Gordons witnessed the British attempt to improve the situation with the detonation of the largest underground mine to date. This first use of ammonal explosive left a huge crater, a new topographic feature in the desolate landscape. At the end of July 1915 the Gordons left the trenches for the rear area just before the Germans unleashed one of their own terror weapons, liquid fire from their flamethrowers, against the British defenders of Hooge.

The OTC, Summer 1915

Summer Camp 1915 was held at Rumbling Bridge in Perthshire, with the Medical Unit of Edinburgh University OTC. The joint corps of Medics supported an Infantry Brigade with a train of ambulance and store wagons. On schemes in the nearby Ochil Hills they erected and operated a fully equipped Advanced Field Hospital and practiced the collection, dressing and conveying of wounded. Two AUOTC Cadet Sgts were recommended for RAMC Commissions.

U Company's Last Battle, September 1915

The British and French intended to launch a massive Autumn offensive against the Germans. The main British effort would be through the spoil heaps and pitheads of the Loos coalfield, over twenty miles south of Ypres. The attack would involve the first large scale use of Kitchener's New Army. To add to the hoped for shock effect large mines would again be exploded under the German trenches and the British, if the winds were favourable, would employ poison gas for the first time. The role of the University's Gordon Highlanders and the other men in the Ypres Salient was to conduct containment attacks to prevent the Germans from moving troops south against the main British thrust at Loos.

In the first week of September, D Company was living in very wet conditions in a mix of huts and bivvies around Ouderdom. Battalion officers were going forward in small groups to recce around Hooge and Sanctuary Wood. Formal warning for an attack came on 8 September. Four days later the Battalion moved up to the trenches and former divinity student Sgt Forbes and his snipers conducted close recce patrols on the German positions even in daylight getting to within 10 metres of 'Fritz'.

JK Forbes.
Divinity Student, Musician, Linguist, Sniper Sergeant

Epitomising more than most the unusual nature of an infantry company formed entirely from University men, Forbes deserves further mention here. In later tributes friends recalled his marvellous feats of endurance as a climber and hill walker involving 'prodigious tramps' by day and night often in foul weather. Graduating in 1905 Forbes initially followed the profession of teaching near Buckie before enrolling in Aberdeen's United Free Church College in 1912 to train as a minister. A talented and natural musician and linguist (Greek, Hebrew, German, English and The Doric) he was acknowledged as an outstanding student even against the very high standards of the Free Church Colleges. A former member of U Company he enlisted as a Private in the 4th Gordons in October 1914. A highly intelligent and mature man in his thirties he hated the petty discipline of barracks in Bedford but once in the field he thrived as leader of the Battalion's snipers. His prowess in sniping and the reconnaissance of enemy positions soon gained the attention of his Divisional Commander and the Germans. The latter placed a price on the head of this no-man's land 'personality' who passed his spare time translating ancient Hebrew texts using German commentaries.

By 17 September, the Gordons were pleased to be again holding ground lost to the Germans five weeks previously. On 18 Sep the Battalion moved back behind Ypres for final rehearsals and rest before the big attack. Sgt Forbes and six of his snipers remained in the forward trenches to report any last minute changes to German trenches and wire entanglements.

Ominously, on the 22 Sep, no less than Field Marshal Lord Kitchener came to inspect the Brigade and commend them for the excellent work done so far. He was sure they would do the same in the events which were to take place in the next few days.

On 23 Sep the 4th Gordons set off for Sanctuary Wood with 27 officers and 614 men. The following day final preparations were made and at 0130 hrs on the 25 Sep a final ration of hot coffee, possibly laced with quartermaster's spirits, was distributed before a silent move to assembly areas where everyone was in position by 0340 hrs. British and German artillery opened the proceedings and at 0410 hrs the advance began. Within ten minutes of rifle fire and some hand to hand combat, the 4th Gordons had found their way through gaps in the wire and were in possession of the German trenches. C and D(U) Companies pushed on to their objectives as far forward as the German 3rd line. The German artillery launched a vicious bombardment on their own recently vacated trenches and with many others Sgt Forbes was killed.

The Germans concentrated north of the Menin Road then launched repeated, and probably well rehearsed, counter attacks from the north and north east, probing through the maze of trenches and over the open ground pushing the Gordons back through the 'wood' to their starting positions. The counter attacks together with accurate artillery and mortar fire made communications with, and resupply to, C and D companies impossible and they were for a time cut off from their comrades. On its return to the billets at Ouderdom the 4th Gordons discovered that they had suffered 334 casualties (killed, wounded and missing). Less than half their starting strength of 641 was available for further operations. A high proportion of the Battalion's losses were from C and D Companies.

On the 27 and 28 Sep the surviving Student Soldiers and their comrades were addressed by their Corps Commander Allenby and their Divisional Commander Haldane. Allenby would later command Lawrence of Arabia and many others in the successful campaign against the Turks in the Middle East. His forces would rely heavily on Principal George Adam Smith's maps of the Holy Land.

Haldane was a fellow Gordon Highlander, relative of the man who had established the TF and the OTCs, and a co-conspirator of University Rector Winston Churchill for the escape from the Boers in Pretoria. Both senior officers complimented the men on their efforts and emphasised the necessity of containment operations if the main attack at Loos was to succeed.

Loos did not succeed. It proved to be a tragic costly disaster that killed thousands, a high proportion from Scotland. The Germans were so moved by the scale of British losses that they ceased fire long enough for survivors to be helped back to their own lines. In German military folklore the battle became *Der Leichenfeld von Loos* (the corpse field of Loos). The battle had serious military and political repercussions, and led to the appointment of Douglas Haig as the Commander in Chief of the British Expeditionary Force on the Western Front. With the benefit of perfect hindsight it has also been calculated that the Germans held their line at Ypres using only local reserves which would probably not have gone to Loos in any case.

The old U Company, whether designated 'D' or not, effectively ceased to exist at Hooge in late September 1915. The surviving University element became diluted with incoming casualty replacements. Many Student Soldiers went on to serve in other units often as commissioned officers. Some after recuperation returned to their studies in Aberdeen. Some of those who survived the war reappear in the AUOTC story. For much greater detail on U Company and its Student Soldiers read John McConachie's excellent book, the details for which appear in the Sources Appendix.

The following tribute appeared in *Alma Mater* some months after the battle:

Memories of 'U'

Gaily we've marched on the winding road
Singing a rollicking air
Laughingly tumbled through hedge and copse
In England's fields so fair
Boyishly pranked in billet and out
Never a cloud in the sky
Jestingly talked of the task in front
Gradually drawing nigh

Plodding along on the cobble stones
Singing the old refrain
Ploughing the path to a Flanders trench
Mud, and bullets, and rain
Eating and sleeping, fighting and digging
Our home the sandbagged wall
Sharing our labours, our joys, our woes
Comrades and brothers all

O many sleep on in the little farmyard
Nigh Kemmel's wooded hill
And many more by the Menin road
Are lying cold and still
Soft be your pillows, O brothers dear
Heavenwards your spirits soar
Comrades in billet, in field, in trench
Our comrades evermore.

The OTC

Principal Smith was a sad man when he chaired the Nov 1915 MEC meeting. His eldest son, who had been an OTC Cadet Sgt before being commissioned in the Gordons, had been killed in action 6 weeks previously, serving with the 2nd Gordons in the Loos offensive. (His second son, the pre-War U Company member and Regular Indian Army officer with the 33rd Punjabis, was killed in East Africa in a German ambush in 1917).

The MEC noted that Lt Kinloch had been promoted Capt. The meat of the agenda lay in the implications of The Derby Scheme, a voluntary recruitment policy created earlier in 1915. Men who voluntarily registered their name would be called upon for service only when necessary. Married men had an added incentive in that they were advised they would be called up only once the supply of single men was exhausted. It had been decided that all medical students in the first 3 years of their studies should as a matter of duty join His Majesty's active forces. This meant that all OTC recruiting from Years 1, 2 and 3 of the medical faculty ceased. All such students were, subject to being of military age and physically suitable, expected to volunteer for the combatant ranks and other branches as required. Further, all the current Year 1, 2 and 3 men already in the OTC were to be told that the OTC was no longer considered a substitute for active service. National, military and medical authorities had agreed to the changes which applied to eligible men of all classes and professions without distinction. Those cadets in more senior years of their medical training would continue their studies and on graduation seek RAMC commissions.

CAMP GROUP, O.T.C.

AUOTC During World War One
Pipes and Drums Evident in Front Row

The Derby Scheme, failing to produce enough recruits under what has been called 'a regime of moral conscription', was abandoned in December 1915. The Military Service Act came into force on 2 March 1916 initiating almost universal conscription for the first time in British military history. Men from 18 to 41 years old were now liable to be called up for service in the army unless they were married, widowed with children, or in one of a number of reserved professions. These latter were usually industrial, but also included clergymen and teachers. (It has already been noted that two former members of Aberdeen's Scottish Horse 'U' Troop, one a clergyman and one a teacher, enlisted anyway.)

As the Battle of the Somme raged through its early weeks across the Channel, 3 officers and 64 cadets set off from Aberdeen for the 1916 Camp at Peebles. This was again a joint affair with EUOTC. Attendance had been strictly enforced with only those committed to hospital residency attachments exempted. One 5th Year medic had enrolled in the OTC but never attended a single parade. He was reported to the Military Authorities. Following the Camp, Capt Kinloch stayed in Peebles for an additional 3 weeks of training at the local RAMC Training Centre.

Principal Smith had made a point of visiting the unit camps and acting unofficially as the unit Chaplain. The unit was very pleased when in 1916 he was Knighted and also Gazetted as an Army Chaplain 1st Class with the rank of Colonel. On the invitation of Sir Douglas Haig, Army Chaplain Smith travelled to address Scottish troops on the Western Front during October 1916.

Throughout the year the University and other Colleges continued to contribute to the war effort. In the Materia Medica Department at Marischal College a dozen sewing machines were busy producing garments; 'hospital comforts' such as slings; and dressings. Dressings were filled with specially selected Sphagnum moss. The moss had been used to staunch blood and help wounds to heal for centuries, including by the Scots troops at the Battle of Flodden in 1513. Its use had waned especially in the more controlled conditions of hospitals and operating theatres. The Great War's huge demand for dressings brought Sphagnum back into popularity especially as it was cheaper (in Scotland at any rate) and far more absorbent and comfortable than cotton wool. The humble moss became almost a strategic material. The Red Cross in Canada surveyed their own copious bogs for the plant, but deferred shipping the bulky material to Europe in light of the impact on other priority cargoes, the currently adequate output from Scotland and Ireland, and the threat from German submarines in the Atlantic. Large numbers of workers produced hundreds of thousands of dressings in Marischal College. Students were urged to volunteer to help in the War Work Room, even if only between lectures to serve tea to the workers.

In November 1916 King's College lost one of its 'weel kent' personalities. Dan Dankester, the Sacrist of King's College, died. His influence on students was such that a visiting Canadian soldier on leave had sought his autograph, written on the back of a Chapel ticket, for friends back home. Dankester was the first person new undergraduates met under the arch at King's and the man who hooded them on graduation. He had joined the staff at King's in 1891 after 21 years in the Army. He was 'the very soul of good company and merriment' in his sanctum, regaling visitors of his experiences in Afghanistan. An artilleryman and field medic, he had been involved in the British Army's rout at Maiwand (in the area all too well known to soldiers of the early 21st Century as Helmand). Dankester had brought out panniers of surgical supplies, the only equipment saved from the disaster. His work in the hospital during the Siege of Kandahar was recognised by a transfer to the Medical Staff Corps the forerunner of the RAMC. Thus he had a natural affinity with the aspiring military medics of the OTC.

In the same *Alma Mater* edition as the tribute to Dan Dankester, a note was made on the recent publication of *Student and Sniper Sergeant*, the posthumous biography of U Company's JK Forbes killed at Hooge in September 1915.

1916 ended with strict enforcement of attendance at

OTC drill nights from a total strength of 3 Officers and 94 Cadets. All medical students had been investigated in relation to Military service liability. There were seven complete exemptions on physical fitness grounds. All students not yet of military age had been written to and all had agreed to join the OTC. 19 men including an officer had been discharged from the Army and had returned to their studies. The CO met them all and invited them to join the unit.

An Army Instruction clarified an area of some uncertainty by confirming that students in faculties other than that of medicine were not required to join an OTC Medical Unit if that was all that was available to them.

With more trainees and a wartime need for even higher training standards a bid was made to the War Office for a SSgt RAMC.

On Saturday 1 Feb 1917 a War Fete was held in the Marischal Union with proceeds going to the University's War Work. A Gordon Highlanders military band entertained those who had paid one shilling for admission, teas and amusements.

The cycle of recruitment, drill nights, lectures and social events continued through 1917 with *Alma Mater* publishing jokes about attendance records and lack of promotion. Memorial Numbers of *Alma Mater* had been sent to the Rector Winston Churchill. He acknowledged receipt in typical style: '*The extraordinary reputation acquired by the Scottish Divisions in our Army, which was already representative of the flower of our race in all parts of the world, was due in no small degree to the astonishing military and personal qualities of the young Scottish gentlemen who hastened from their universities to command and lead their countrymen in the field. Aberdeen University will rightly cherish their memory as its most precious possession'*

Alma Mater also recognised the increasing influence of women in the University, partially due to the absence of men on military service except for the very young and the senior medics. Between 1916 and 1918 women would outnumber men in the University. Special *Alma Mater Women's Numbers* did however note decreasing numbers of ladies in the Arts Faculty and stressed the opportunities for them in other faculties.

In March 1917 the OTC held a Reception in Mitchell Hall in order to give a hearty send off to those about to leave for military service. An hour of whist in the picture gallery was scheduled before dancing commenced with 'pretty partners'. During the interval Principal Smith addressed the men leaving, reminding them of the greatness of the cause and the glorious record which the University already had in this world's conflict. He wished them all God's Speed. Capt Kinloch thanked Smith on behalf of those present before eightsome reels and other dances recommenced. Before the planned end of dancing, two busybodies accompanied by a Police Sergeant invaded the hall to state that they would countenance only twilight dancing. Quickly recognising that the looks developing on the revellers' faces forecast nothing but escalating trouble the delegation retreated. Dancing continued apace until Auld Lang Syne was sung with gusto and emotion at 11pm. All present hoped that the event could become an annual one for the contingent, hopefully someday with happier causes.

Annual Camp was at Gailes being attended by 2 officers and 85 other ranks from Aberdeen together with similar numbers from Edinburgh OTC's Medical Unit, and many medical students from Glasgow OTC's Infantry Unit. 7 medical students from St Andrew's and 10 from Durham completed the combined contingent under the command of Major Littlejohn from EUOTC. The now formally appointed Chaplain, Principal Sir George Adam Smith, attended the second week.

Gailes, on the coast just south of Irvine in Ayrshire, was well equipped to support a summer camp and was already well known to many University men. Gailes was home to two Officer Cadet Battalions.

In February 1916, a new system of officer training had been introduced, after which temporary commissions could only be granted to men who had been through an Officer Cadet Battalion. Entrants needed to be aged over 18 and a half, and to have already served in the ranks or with an OTC. The training course lasted four and a half months. An Officer Cadet Battalion could train 400 cadets at any one time, although this was raised in May 1917 to 600. More than 73,000 men gained infantry commissions after being trained in an OCB, with increasing numbers coming from 'the ranks' as the war went on. There were ultimately 24 Officer Cadet Battalions throughout the country, some on Oxbridge College campuses, and two, the 9th and 10th in Scotland at Gailes, From there and throughout their service officers would attend special to arm schools and many training schools and facilities in Britain and behind the lines in France, Flanders and the other theatres of war. Specialist courses on tactics and technologies such as the machine gun and poison gas were developed, and all officers were regularly withdrawn from the line in order to attend. These courses updated officers on developments, and provided a welcome respite from the strain of front line command.

For the nearly 250 Scottish OTC officer cadets at Gailes, there for only a fortnight at least on this visit, training concentrated on their RAMC role. The Inspection report noted real progress since 1916 but did ask that cadets should actually take the trouble to read their pamphlets on RAMC Duties in the Field and in Quarters. The OTC officers' riding skills were found sufficient for duty as mounted Medical Officers. The £50-00 paid annually from OTC accounts to the Aberdeen Riding Academy was thus well spent. Ambulances and wagons loaned for the camp were well maintained and the horses properly groomed and fitted with good harness.

In the Autumn of 1917 the MEC considered the effects of the temporary withdrawal of rules restricting membership to the medical faculty. It observed that War Office accountants had noted the healthy financial balances achieved by the OTCs' careful management and promptly reduced the grants being made. It was therefore not a surprise for the committee to hear that a bid for £100 to equip a new Orderly Room and Store had been refused.

Haldane's 1908 Act had allowed for a Junior Division of the OTC to exist in the public schools. Not all schools had got round to forming their own contingents and the Rector of the then fee paying Aberdeen Grammar School asked the MEC to consider if some of his senior boys could join the University's OTC contingent. This request was refused. The unit was already considerably over established strength and saying yes to one school would open the door to all the others. The Grammar it was thought should rather apply to form its own Junior Division OTC Contingent.

In July 1918 the acting CO Capt Kinloch departed for a 5 month tour of duty with a Mobile Hygiene Laboratory in

France. During his time overseas he was mentioned in dispatches twice. His two 2nd Lts, Messrs Anderson and Walker, took up the reins with a Col AW Mackintosh in nominal command.

In the early summer of 1918 AUOTC's Chaplain and founding father, addressed 127 public meetings and conferences in 39 cities across the USA on the topic of the moral war aims of the Allies. The USA had declared war on Germany in April 1917 and by October of that year American troops were in the trenches. To help explain allied war aims and bolster the American war effort, the British Foreign Office and the National Committee of the USA had sought the help of Aberdeen's Principal Smith.

Back in Scotland all OTC members less those with hospital duties would attend the 1918 Summer Camp under canvas at Barry Buddon just outside Carnoustie. This was the old 19th Century Volunteer training ground, with rifle and artillery ranges, bought by the War Office in 1897 and a frequent venue for Aberdeen's Volunteers including the pre-war 'U' Coy. With a distinctive, often nasty, micro-climate of its own, Barry would be visited by the AUOTC many times in the future earning it latterly the alternative title, 'Barry Butlins'.

At Barry the syllabus included lectures by the CO on the complexities of packing medical stores in the correct parts of wagons, and on the adjustment of Thomas Splints 'by numbers' under the sharp eye of the Warrant Officer. Introduced in 1916 this traction device had reduced the mortality rate from femur fractures from 80% to less than 8%. Other lessons included water purification and the detection of poisons in water sources. The collection of wounded and the loading and unloading of wagons were repeatedly practiced.

Traditional Army humour kept everyone amused. A QMSI sent a new cadet to the Edinburgh Quartermaster for some striped paint required to freshen up 'the Last Post'. Edinburgh's QM played along by refusing on the grounds that they needed it themselves. After duties, the nurses of the local hospital were the principal distraction. One unfortunate who had been separated from his companions while out on a local 'straffe' to the pubs was later found 'in a state of physical weakness and covered in stains'.

By 30 August 1918 the Second Battle of the Somme was well underway with the British Empire's army, having recovered from the German Spring Offensive, starting its war-ending advance into German held territory. Not everyone was pulling together. On that day London's Metropolitan Police went on strike for pay increases and union recognition. They gained the former but not the latter and shocked Prime Minister Lloyd George sufficiently for him to assess that Britain had never come closer to Bolshevism. Many thought he exaggerated the danger but the spread of Revolution from Russia would be a concern for many years while Britain went through hard economic times. Four months after AUOTC's first Barry 'experience', the Great War ended.

In Memoriam

Principal Smith had personally maintained four provisional rolls of service during the war. Editor Mabel Desborough Allardyce led the huge effort to bring everything together into the University of Aberdeen Roll of Service in the Great War. In his foreword, the Principal praised the efforts to record the service of graduates, alumni, students and staff. Some he noted had already been in the Regular Forces at the outbreak of war, a few as combatants, many more in the medical services of the Royal Navy and Army. Still greater numbers he noted were members of the Territorial Force, mainly in U Company of the 4th Gordons, but also in many artillery and medical units. Of the rest the majority were volunteers and the remainder conscripts.

The In Memoriam Roll recorded the 341 who had given their lives, 335 of them with photo portraits. The Roll of Service listed 2,852 who had served in the Navy, Army, Air Force or in work of national importance. The last category covered a wide range of occupations including work with the YMCA facilities in France, and even service as a Special Constable in the Glasgow Police.

The University's professors and other staff, if not on active service, had all devoted their specialist knowledge to the war effort in fields as diverse as intelligence, food policy, agriculture, medicine, munitions and the running of TF Associations, recruiting and other public bodies.

As Rector from 1914-1918, Winston Churchill gets a mention too, giving his service as First Lord of the Admiralty from 1911-15 and a brief tour as the CO of an infantry battalion in the trenches.

The following men, who pursued a medical education at Aberdeen University, are listed as having served in the OTC, and who died in the Great War, are remembered in the University's Roll of Honour as follows:

2ⁿᵈ Lieutenant Edgar George William Bisset, Royal Flying Corps.

Son of James D. Bisset, bank agent; born Inverurie, 30 July 1896; educated Peterhead Academy; matriculated Aberdeen University 1914, student in Medicine, 1914-15. He joined the Boy Scouts in 1909, and in the first months of the war he did good service in charge of a troop assisting the Coastguard at Cruden Bay. At the University he joined the Officers' Training Corps, and when it was decided that all first and second year medical students should join up he obtained a commission in the 5th Gordon Highlanders, in December 1915. After training at various camps in England he was sent to France on 1 July 1916, and went through the first Battle of the Somme. In October of that year he joined the Royal Flying Corps as an observer, and was just up for his last flight to obtain his "wings" when a bullet from an enemy aeroplane rendered him unconscious, and he died in hospital soon after, 7 January 1917.

Lance Corporal Douglas Gordon Bonner, 1st Bn Gordon Highlanders.

Son of Alexander C. Bonner, wholesale druggist; born Aberdeen, 9 August 1899; educated at Aberdeen Grammar School; matriculated in Medicine in 1916 and served with the University O.T.C. On 13 August 1917 he became a Cadet in the Royal Flying Corps; was transferred later in that year to the 14th Battalion London Scottish, with which Battalion he served in England until May when he was sent to France, and there served with the 1st Battalion Gordon Highlanders. Bonner was in hospital for a time with trench fever, but rejoined his Battalion on 24 September and was killed in action at Havrincourt on 27 September 1918.

Captain Austin Basil Clarke MC,
Royal Army Medical Corps

Son of Dr. A. B. Clarke ; born Shebbear, North Devon, 9 July 1892 ; graduated M.B., 1915. A foremost member of the OTC, Clarke, on graduation, at once obtained a commission in the RAMC. After a few months in training he proceeded to France as Medical Officer to the Queen Victoria's Rifles, a Battalion of the London Territorial Division. For three years he remained with this Battalion, was in all their hard-fought engagements, and by his zeal and devotion to duty endeared himself to every officer and man, gaining the Military Cross for his valour. He refused an offered Staff appointment, stating that his duty was to remain with his Battalion. And so serving his country he met his death on the Bapaume - Cambrai Road on 23 November 1917. The letter written by his Colonel is one of the finest appreciations of service it is possible for a man to have had : "He deserved a decoration every time he went into action. Only the day before he was killed he went out into 'No Man's Land' and carried back a wounded airman into our lines—but I could fill pages with his bravery." His Divisional Colonel wrote : "You know how your son loved his men and how he would dare all for them, and they just worshipped him—no Doctor was like their

76

Doctor. . . . Professionally he was the beau ideal of a brave Regimental Medical Officer."

Captain Robert Scott Cumming MC
Royal Army Medical Corps

Son of Robert Cumming, advocate ; born Aberdeen, 22 July 1893 educated Aberdeen Grammar School ; M.B. (Hons.), 1915 ; one of the most distinguished students of his year, gaining the John Murray Medal and Scholarship and Matthews Duncan Gold Medal. He was a member of the University O.T.C., and was commissioned in the R.A.M.C. (S.R.), May 1914. Immediately after graduation Cumming was commissioned in the Regular R.A.M.C., 24 July 1915, and was attached to the 93rd Field Ambulance, 31st Division. After some months training in England he went to Egypt where he served from December 1915 till February 1916, and then in France from March 1916 till February 1918 when he was invalided home. He saw further service in India and Mesopotamia, but, never completely recovered from the illness contracted through exposure on the battlefield, he died in the 3rd British General Hospital, Basra, 14 March 1921.

The ability which had earned him distinctions at the University won him awards in the Army ; he gained the Military Cross, 3 May 1917, and was mentioned in dispatches, June 1917.

Lance-Corporal John Mitchell Duthie, 5th Bn Gordon Highlanders

Son of James R. Duthie; grocer, Fraserburgh ; born Aberdeen, 12 February 1898 ; educated Fraserburgh Academy; student in Medicine, 1915-16. He served in the O.T.C. whilst at the University and enlisted under the Derby Scheme at the close of the summer session 1916, joining the 5th Battalion Gordon Highlanders. After training at Ripon he left for France in February 1917 and fought on the Belgian frontier, until he was killed in action near Ypres, 31 July 1917.

2nd Lt Edward White Irvine, Royal Field Artillery.

Son of Rev. John A. Irvine, Aberdeen ; born Liverpool, 30 September 1897 ; educated Aberdeen Grammar School ; student in Medicine, 1915-16. Irvine served with the Aberdeen University O.T.C. from 1915 -16, and with the Edinburgh University O.T.C. from 1916-17 ; he was commissioned in the R.F.A., June 1917, gained special distinction in signalling, and proceeded to France early in the following year. His military career was all too short, for after seven weeks in France he fell near Morcourt-sur-Somme, at the head of his guns, leading them into action, 27 March 1918. During all the previous seven days of almost continuous fighting his cheerful courage had never failed.

Capt Eric Newton,
Royal Army Medical Corps.

Son of Isaac Newton, Captain, Indian Medical Service ; born Umballa, Punjab, 28 February 1889 ; graduated M. B., 1915. A noted athlete, he achieved the feat of gaining a triple blue in hockey, tennis and cricket. In hockey he achieved wider fame, being chosen to play for Scotland in international matches in 1912, 1913 and 1914. After graduating Newton at once joined the Army, receiving a commission in the R.A.M.C. on 1 August 1915. He served in Egypt and then in East Africa where he rose to the rank of Captain. He was killed in action at Nanyati, East Africa, on 5 August 1917.

2nd Lt John Dean Riddel
5th Bn Gordon Highlanders.

Son of George Riddel, farmer, Kininmonth, Longside ; born New Deer, 8 September 1893 ; educated Kininmonth Public School and Peterhead Academy, gaining the Medal for Classics. He entered the University in 1914, with a view to qualifying for work as a Medical Missionary in China. As a student Riddel was in the O.T.C. He enlisted in the 5th Gordons in 1915 ; after a year's service first as Private and then as Corporal and Musketry Instructor, he was gazetted to the 4th Reserve Battalion and posted to the 5th Battalion Gordon Highlanders. In January 1917 he left for France, where he served till his death on 17 April 1917 from wounds received in action near Arras ten days previously

2nd Lt William John Campbell Sangster
4th Bn Gordon Highlanders (U Company)

Son of William Sangster, draper ; born Aberdeen, 1 January 1896; educated at Aberdeen Grammar School ; Christ's College, Blackheath, and Aberdeen University ; graduated M.A., 1914, and was studying for a medical career. He had belonged to the University O.T.C. and when war broke out he immediately joined the Army, receiving his commission as 2nd Lieutenant in the 4th Gordon Highlanders, 3 October 1914. After training at Aberdeen, Bedford, etc., he crossed to France 24 June 1915. In the ensuing three months, he proved himself the type of officer who is beloved and trusted by his men. On the fateful 25 September 1915 Sangster fell. He was detailed with a platoon to capture a portion of German trenches, which he did successfully. With great courage he and his men held on to the position, later it was re-captured by the Germans, the fighting was fierce, and the traditions of the Gordons were upheld.

Lt William Leslie Scott
5th Bn Gordon Highlanders

Son of William Leslie Scott, solicitor. Born Peterhead, 24 December 1892; student in Medicine, 1911-14. As a 4th year Medical student, Scott had every right to consider himself entitled to finish his course before joining the Army, so he returned to College in October 1914, but the desire to take an active part in the fighting was too strong for him, and he obtained a commission in the 5th Gordons in December 1914, having previously served in the O.T.C. After a few months training at home, he was sent to France where he was in charge of the bombing section of his Battalion. In the very short time which elapsed before his death, he showed himself a leader of dauntless spirit, regardless of personal danger. A fellow-officer wrote; "He made a magnificent officer, and a very cheery trench companion". He was killed at Festubert while entering a German trench with a party of bombers on

16 June 1915.

2nd Lt George Buchanan Smith
2nd Bn Gordon Highlanders.

Eldest son of Principal the Very Rev. Sir George Adam Smith. Born Aberdeen, 18 October 1890; educated Glasgow Academy; Glasgow, Aberdeen, Edinburgh Universities; M.A. (Glas.), 1912; LL.B. (Aberd.), 1914; Sergeant O.T.C. Commissioned S.R.O., 4 August 1914; attached 3rd Gordons, Stoneywood Wireless Station, till he conducted a draft for the 1st Battalion to Kemmel. On 14 December he led two platoons against the German lines, and having lain all day under fire, severely wounded, brought back the survivors, his C.O. testifying; " Your gallant conduct in the field has been reported to me, and I have had much pleasure in bringing it to the notice of higher authority". After three months in hospital and on garrison duty till 8 August 1915, he joined the 2nd Gordons, engaged in manoeuvres and trench-construction, and was promoted second officer of "A" Company on the fighting line. After a night of cutting wire before "The Silesian Sap " he led the guiding platoon of the regiment against the German position between Vermelles and Hulluch and there fell 25 September 1915. His capability as an officer is shown by the fact that "he had so instructed his N.C.O.'s that they were able to carry out orders and made good even after their officer fell".

Surgeon Probationer Alexander Ledingham Strachan
Royal Navy Volunteer Reserve.

Son of Alexander Strachan, chemist; born Aberdeen, 29 November 1894; entered the University October 1913; student in Medicine, 1913-16. Whilst at the University Strachan joined the O.T.C., and when an appeal was issued for Surgeon Probationers for the Navy he at once volunteered, was commissioned March 1916, and appointed to H.M.S. "Genista", a mine-sweeping vessel. There were few dull moments in Strachan's brief service career: on his way to join his ship he reached Dublin in the midst of the rebellion, and took charge of a hospital there ; later the "Genista" saved the lives of the officers and crew of a ship which was found in a sinking condition, and Strachan received a special letter of thanks along with a presentation for his good services on the occasion. On 23 October 1916 he went down with his ship in the Atlantic, after a successful U Boat torpedo attack.

<u>Private Alexander Forbes Stuart,
Royal Army Medical Corps</u>.

Son of Rev. F. W. Stuart, U.F. Church Minister, Gartly, Aberdeenshire ; born there, 5 March 1898 ; educated Central Public School, Gartly, and Gordon Schools, Huntly ; student in Medicine, 1915-16. He was the fourth member of this family to enter Aberdeen University. As a schoolboy, Stuart was an enthusiastic Boy Scout and had done service in the Cruden Bay neighbourhood before coming up to the University, where he joined the O.T.C. On 14 October 1916 he enlisted in the R.A.M.C. and after training was drafted overseas, serving first at Salonika and then at Malta. While at Salonika the illness which later proved fatal, manifested itself and after some time he was invalided home and discharged on 8 March 1919. He died at Noranside Sanatorium, Forfarshire, on 21 April 1919, of illness contracted while on active service.

Chapter 3

SLUMP AND RECOVERY
THROUGH THE ROARING TWENTIES
1919-1929

Following the Armistice of November 1918, the Army Council announced that unless there was some unseen change in military circumstances, and in the interests of education, there would be no further need for fulltime training in the Senior Contingents of the OTC. The Council noted that OTCs had much improved over the war years and Universities were asked to continue supporting the Corps. *'The OTC was formed for such a war as the present one and its foundation has been more than justified by results....the Council know this has only been possible with the support of the Universities'.*

In particular it was recognised that Medical OTCs had produced the necessary blend of military administrators and good doctors. The war had exposed significant differences between those young Medical Officers who had trained in OTCs and those who had not.

In February 1919 Aberdeen's MEC suspended OTC parades for the rest of the term but emphasised that regular attendance during the Summer term would be required of those wishing to attend Summer Camp. On the perennial topic of 'Efficiency', cadets who had been subject to intensive training during the war were permitted to attend half the number of normal drills and still be deemed 'Efficient'. Training for those wishing to gain Certificates A and B would continue

Instead of the usual parades, a series of illustrated

87

lectures would be given for OTC members and others. It was emphasised to medical students that future practitioners would be working in communities with large numbers of men disabled by the war to one extent or another. Many of their patients would still be suffering from diseases contracted in the various theatres of that war. The OTC lectures would give all medics a well informed introduction to these challenges.

On Thursday 8 January 1919 the Union Dining Room was the venue for a grand reunion dinner for survivors of the 4th Gordon's old D, E and U Companies. These pre-war companies took volunteers from current and former members of the University and its two main feeder schools, Aberdeen Grammar and Robert Gordons. Four months later U Company veterans held their own dinner which was reported as a *'howling success'* with some postprandial *'nasty knocks'* for the participants.

The Great War had changed British society for ever. At the end of the Summer term 1919, many detected a listless atmosphere in the college quadrangles. Men returning from four years of war or just up from school were, it was thought, entering a Varsity which had *'degenerated into a mere place of learning'*. The old corporate life had gone with the 'shaky ladder' between King's and Marischal now broken altogether. *'The Medical believes that Arts is a moribund concern, the Arts man thanks his God sometimes that he is not a Medical. The Science people stand gloriously aloof from both. These are the students but the student body has ceased to exist'.*

The MEC considered a proposal to form a central association of University MECs from across the country in order to discuss and properly represent to the War Office matters of mutual interest and concern. Aberdeen's MEC was distinctly lukewarm about the proposal being in general happy with their direct War Office relationship and perhaps wary of the creation of a new level of bureaucracy. In September 1919, 'The Central Organisation of Military Education Committees of the Universities of the United Kingdom' was established following a conference of representatives drawn from the MECs. This organisation still exists today as the Council of Military Education Committees (COMEC). The major function of COMEC as envisaged in 1918, is to serve as a single point of contact to represent the views of MECs to the MOD and as a channel of information between the universities and the MOD.

The War Trophies Committee wrote to AUOTC informing it of the allocation of a German Field Gun as its very own trophy. It would, it was hoped, help future generations recall the part played by officers and cadets in preparing candidates for commissions during the Great War. Some months later the gun was duly delivered and temporarily placed in the Marischal College Quadrangle while a permanent location was sought.

The recurring question of an Infantry OTC unit for Aberdeen surfaced again but was put off to a later date when circumstances might be more appropriate.

In the Autumn of 1919 AUOTC's safely returned 'real' CO Capt Williamson faced some thorny problems. Capt Kinloch who had acted as CO for most of the war wished to resign to better pursue his career in Public Health. The two Subalterns Anderson and Walker had resigned and the unit was short a Sergeant Instructor. Capt Williamson's recruiting efforts amongst students had been met with hostile opposition to drills or parades. It was realised that reviving interest in the unit would be very difficult. There was little comfort when during a visit to Aberdeen, Colonel James, the General Staff Officer responsible for OTCs, told the MEC that the situation was bad everywhere, with OTC contingents existing merely on paper to maintain the flow of War Office grants.

The whole Volunteer environment around the OTCs had been in rapid decline since the Armistice with TF units disbanding. The Territorial Force (TF) reconstituted in February 1920 and became the Territorial Army (TA) in October of the same year.

During the Winter Term of 1919/20 Captain Williamson gave a series of three lectures in lieu of parades in an attempt to stimulate interest. Out of a nominal strength of 113, lecture audiences dwindled from 45, to 25, to 10. There would be no further lectures for the meantime and any notion of a successful Spring Camp was abandoned.

Against this depressing backdrop the question of an Infantry Unit was yet again discussed. It was now clear that the absence of an Infantry Unit had disadvantaged many students in their progress towards wartime commissions in arms and services other than the RAMC. It was thought that the absence of an Infantry unit had led to a waste of potential officers and talented manpower, best epitomised of course by the unique story of 'U' Company. True as all this might be, it was considered futile to pursue the issue in the current unhappy circumstances. There might be some hope for an Infantry unit in the future. For this reason it was decided in 1920 not to support an application by the CO of 4th Gordons to reform a 'University' Company within his Battalion. Students would still be allowed to join the TA on the understanding that they could leave, without penalty, to join an AUOTC Infantry Contingent, if one was ever established. In November 1920 OC D Coy of the 4th Gordons, himself an Aberdeen graduate, invited students to attend recruiting meetings scheduled at the King's College Pavilion and at the Union Debating Hall in Marischal College.

Principal Smith was still concerned about the war weariness in the student body which included large numbers of Great War veterans who wanted nothing more to do with uniforms, drills and parades. He thought a delay in resuming normal OTC activities might need to extend as far ahead as October 1922. Colonel James from the General Staff indicated that, while Dublin and Belfast had resumed training, Edinburgh had only 44 cadets and Glasgow had 30. The Cambridge and Oxford Contingents were more or less moribund.

The War Office resurrected its support for Cert A and B training in 1921 and some inducements existed for RAMC Cert B holders to join the Special Reserve of Officers (SRO) particularly now that the War Office had stipulated that no future emergency temporary commissions in the RAMC would be granted to anyone outside the SRO or the Territorial Army (TA).

The depressing news came that 60 sets of kit were unreturned and possibly lost forever. In this generally unhappy period, Aberdeen sent no representative to the COMEC meeting in London in June, and still hesitated to write to the War Office regarding the formal suspension of OTC activities. Successful stalling might lead to better times.

4th Gordons had not given up in their quest to re-establish U Company. The Battalion's Adjutant wrote to *Alma Mater* from the TA Drill Hall at Woolmanhill. He informed readers that prior to 1914 one of the Battalion's eight companies had been reserved for the University. The four company organisation formed during the war, and still in operation, had designated D Company for volunteers from the University, and for former and current pupils of the Grammar School and Robert Gordon's College. D Company, formerly the strongest and best, was now less than half the size of the other companies. The 'working classes' of Aberdeen had made a good response but a further 300 recruits were needed. Acknowledging that 'veterans' could not be asked to do more he asked those too young to have served in the Great War to come forward. If numbers were sufficient he would ensure that drills were again held in the afternoons to facilitate attendance at lectures and other college commitments. Without new University volunteers, he feared that open recruiting would bring to an end a tradition stretching back to 1897.

In December 1921 the War Office wrote to Aberdeen informing them that it was considering the future of all Senior Division OTC contingents. In Aberdeen's case they had noted that in spite of the fact that the war had ended three years ago, the unit, even on paper, was below the minimum strength of 30 set out in OTC Regulations. Captain Williamson's command did indeed only amount to 26 and he couldn't really depend upon all of them. Given these facts and the need for financial stringency the AUOTC was given until April 1922 to avoid disbandment.

Throughout the period 1921/22/23 all Government expenditure was cut drastically under the 'Geddes Axe' in an attempt to address soaring National Debt. For the TA this meant units were being reduced in establishment, amalgamated or disbanded completely.

Principal Smith, the champion of AUOTC from its birth, stated that apart from real sadness about losing one of the earlier OTCs, the lack of opportunity to gain Cert A and B qualifications would be a serious career disadvantage to any of his students who wished to serve in the Territorial or Regular forces. Thus all steps must be taken to save the unit. As he battled for the continuance of the OTC, Smith retired as Contingent Chaplain in 1921 having exceeded the age limit for such posts.

The University Medical Society arranged to present the benefits of OTC membership to students. It was thought that perhaps the appointment of their lecturers as officers might further enhance recruiting and, with Kinloch leaving the unit, two out of three officer posts would be gapped. Douglas Fraser, was a possible Captain and Robert Lockhart a potential Lieutenant.

While the MEC considered how to avoid disbandment, the War Office, unconvinced that the Great War had been 'a war to end all wars', was seeking input on how senior division contingents of the OTC could convert automatically to Officer Cadet Units (OCU) in the event of a General Mobilisation. The universities and contingents were asked to submit plans for estimated strengths, training grounds, accommodation, messing, recreation, ranges, stores, and armouries. The Scottish Universities all submitted their plans based on a blueprint drawn up by Edinburgh.

By the time the MEC met in June 1922 disbandment had been avoided but with Kinloch joining the Reserve, and the hope for two potential lecturer/officers having come to naught. Williamson was once again, as in pre-war days, the only officer.

Thus AUOTC barely survived its post Great War

slump and in the summer of 1922 set out for its first Camp since Barry Buddon in 1918. The Contingent's 'return from the dead' was saluted by a 'guard of honour' of Glasgow and St Andrew's cadets who presented arms (with beer bottles on canes) when 68 Aberdeen men arrived at Fleetwood near Blackpool. Aberdeen had 16 out of 20 Cert A candidates pass the exams and the Inspecting Officer noted that much had been achieved with mostly new cadets, good NCOs and the ever dependable Williamson. It was suggested that an NCO, although technically unqualified for commissioning, should be tried out in one of the gapped posts.

Williamson, his medics and a drum, early 1920s

Thirteen university contingents shared this camp. The usual pranks were executed among the tent lines. The temporary appropriation of shaving and cleaning kits from those labelled as ardent Tories, was put down to 'bolshevism'.

The camp was most memorable for its proximity to the off-duty holiday resort delights of nearby Blackpool. The 'Big Wheel', turning since 1896, could be seen from the camp as could the iconic Tower. Overcrowded charabancs took cadets to the dance floors of the Winter Gardens. Others travelled into town by tram, noting the girls in the lineside tennis courts.

Principal Smith again made a point of visiting the contingent at camp, the only principal of a possible thirteen to do so. The Bristol and Aberystwyth contingents asked to attend Aberdeen's open air church service on the last day, thus taking the opportunity to hear the famous George Adam Smith speak.

Beginning to thrive once more the OTC followed its usual round of lectures and drills throughout the 1922/23 Session. In the first hours of daylight on one June morning in 1923, seventy five men of the Medical Contingent marched from the Marischal Quadrangle to the Station on their way to Summer Camp. The destination was for the first time overseas, at Ramsay on the Isle of Man. The Glasgow and St Andrew's joint welcoming guard of honour this year saluted Aberdeen's great fishing heritage with fixed bayonets. Each bayonet was topped with a pungent smoked haddock or 'haddie'. The sarcasm was duly repaid with night raids on the offenders' tents. Ramsay was the last camp where Aberdeen OTC was represented by Medics alone.

The student members of D Company were at their annual camp at Montrose with the rest of 4th Gordons. Although only 32 in number they were again excelling in all battalion military and sporting activities Like the OTC, D Company would experience great change in the next year.

In expectation of a big announcement, a joint OTC

and D Company smoking concert was held in November 1923 in the Debating Hall. A 'men only' affair, participants were asked to bring their own mugs and be prepared to contribute to the entertainment programme, 'the more celebrated the artiste, the freer the admission'. The night's conversation concluded among other things that the 'knock kneed' looked best in the OTC's RAMC breeches and puttees, the 'bow-legged' in the Gordon kilt.

In late 1923 the local Territorial Army Association agreed to support the University's bid to the War Office for an Infantry Unit to be established. The Association promised that any student currently serving in a TA unit would be allowed to transfer to the OTC's Infantry without penalty. Local support assured, the MEC sent off the official request.

Also to the War Office went an undertaking that the University would accommodate a mobilisation Reception Unit. It was however pointed out that such a unit should operate for the Gordon Highlanders rather than the Argyll and Sutherland Highlanders. The latter had been suggested by a War Office staff officer, obviously lacking awareness of Scottish geography and regimental sensitivities.

October 1923 saw the first radio broadcast by BBC Aberdeen, one of the initial locations to bring a new form of entertainment to the British people.

Principal Smith in December 1923 announced that at long last, after several attempts since 1911, an infantry unit was a real possibility, one which would fill a *'long felt need in our academic life'*. A successful bid however would depend on sufficient numbers coming forward. D Company members were told that they could transfer without penalty or stay with the 4th Gordons. Smith appealed to all non-medical students who had at heart the interests of their Nation and their University. Successful recruiting would mean the new unit would go to Summer Camp in 1924 and train with infantry contingents from other universities. Smith intimated that the new unit would hopefully be commanded by a TA officer of great war experience.

The unit would also now share with Glasgow a Regular Army adjutant who would be based in Glasgow. The first incumbent was Capt RA Grant-Taylor OBE MC of the Royal Scots Fusiliers. After a splendid record of service during the Great War, Grant-Taylor had gone with his battalion to Ireland in 1921 into the chaotic situation of the closing months of the Irish War of Independence. Here he was involved in highly dangerous undercover intelligence work against the IRA. His efforts in Glasgow and Aberdeen were key to the rebuilding of both contingents after the post war slump.

Christmas not being an official holiday in Scotland, the MEC met on Boxing Day 1923 to hear the good news that Major John Boyd Orr DSO MC had expressed his willingness to command the new Infantry Unit.

Boyd Orr, from Ayrshire, and a product of Glasgow's Arts and Medical faculties had progressed through school teaching and general medical practice to pre-eminence as a research scientist. He had arrived in Aberdeen in April 1914 to establish from scratch a new institute for research into animal nutrition.

At the outbreak of War, his experimental farm being given over to food production, he had been released for service with the RAMC. He had first worked with a specialist unit to improve hygiene and health standards in the many temporary, large and sometimes unsanitary training camps scattered across the country. He was then appointed as

Medical Officer to the 1st Sherwood Foresters. His courage and medical competence gained him an MC at the Somme and a DSO at Passchendaele. He ensured his battalion fed well with supplements of fresh vegetables liberated from abandoned farms and gardens near the trenches. He also increased every man's boot size, thereby largely avoiding the debilitating trench foot so common along the muddy, wet, unsanitary and cold Western Front.

Since he was still technically a civilian surgeon the Army reluctantly released Boyd Orr to the Royal Navy where he thought he would have a better chance of keeping up with, and contributing towards, medical and nutritional advances. He worked in Chatham's Naval hospitals before joining a ship. At sea, Boyd Orr, as he had hoped, found his duties much less onerous than that of an infantry MO, and he got on with his nutrition science studies. He finished his war service researching the health, physique and energy expenditure of infantry recruits.

After the War, Boyd Orr returned to Aberdeen and succeeded in forming the institute in purpose-built and rather grand buildings beside the experimental farm west of Aberdeen. Even Boyd Orr's great capability and drive would have achieved little were it not for his meeting a businessman keen to put to good use some of his considerable war profits. The businessman's name was Rowett and the new Research Institute was opened by Queen Mary with his name in its title. Rowett had stipulated that any discoveries in animal nutrition relevant to that of humans should be pursued. Boyd Orr was very much of the same opinion.

In March 1924 Boyd Orr himself announced that authority had indeed been received for an infantry unit of 120 men. The appropriate authorities of the Gordon Highlanders had approved the wearing of their regimental tartan and it was hoped too that a pipe band would be established formally soon. There would be no drills before the Summer session but recruiting would start immediately. Before long 97 cadets had signed up, including 12 medical students, and as expected D Company's ranks were sorely depleted. It was agreed that the new unit would give preference to arts, science, divinity and law students but that the medics who had already joined could stay for two years before being moved across to the Medical Unit.

The arrival of this new unit created some administrative tension. Williamson was quick to point out that the healthy balance in contingent funds, now to be shared with the Infantry, had been created by 12 years of careful management by the Medical Unit. It was however agreed to create one Contingent account which would for a start support proposals for a joint Camp for both Units.

Boyd Orr had recruited his Head of Animal Husbandry at the Rowett as an additional officer for the new unit. Arthur Crichton had served as an NCO with 'U' Company, and had been wounded in May 1915 and again at Hooge in September 1915. He was commissioned in the 4th Gordons in 1918. Returning to his studies he had graduated BSc in 1920. He had represented the University in swimming and football. His wartime experience, as an infantry soldier and officer, and his understanding of the pressures of student life would be invaluable for the new unit.

Boyd Orr now considered how to clothe his young infantrymen. They were to wear the same University Crest as the Medical Unit. Tunics and Kilts would cost £402 and sporrans £90 more. The Principal undertook to organise subscriptions to fund the latter. The Infantry Unit Orderly

Room was to be at King's College, Old Aberdeen.

In 1924 Aberdeen's medics and infantrymen went to camp together. The senior medics were delighted to be returning to Fleetwood again. The camp was to be shared with all the Scottish OTCs, the Belfast Contingent and some units from south of the border. A great rapport was enjoyed with the Belfast men with singing and dancing sealing a strong alliance during the traditional escapades between units. Durham cadets stayed up in their boots all night until the best raiding time, in the small hours, when they collapsed whole rows of Aberdeen tents. After the last parades and drills of the day everyone made the best of Blackpool's Winter Garden dance halls and restaurants. Aberdeen's men wished that their own Granite City had something quite as good.

In Autumn 1924 the question of military relationships with the University's two main City feeder schools, Aberdeen Grammar and Robert Gordons, again arose for MEC consideration. The two schools were seeking MEC support for their bids to create Junior Division OTC contingents. Boyd Orr was concerned about any impact on his recruiting and would prefer opening his unit up to senior boys. Williamson disagreed and wanted the schools to form their own contingents as they desired.

The pre-Christmas MEC of 1924 heard of continued wrangling with local tailors over the price and quality of tunics for the Infantry. It was agreed that the Medical Unit Orderly Room in Marischal would also act as the overall Contingent Orderly Room.

MEC members heard from the War Office that technology had sufficiently matured to allow officers to join the Tank Corps without an engineering degree.

Mobilisation plans were again discussed with

University Secretary Major Harry Butchart who was nominated for command of any Reception Unit established in an emergency. He had visited the Gordon's Regimental Depot at Castlehill Barracks and Army HQ in Perth to find out what his mobilisation role might entail. He sought nominees for an Adjutant and Quartermaster to support him. He was no stranger to military staff work.

Butchart would be a legendary Secretary of the University until 1952. He would serve as Law Agent until 1967 conducting all the wheeling and dealing necessary to secure buildings and ground for the expansion of teaching, residential and sports facilities in Old Aberdeen. A champion of the OTC throughout his life he deserves an extended mention here.

In his youth Butchart played rugby for Edinburgh Wanderers and many NE clubs narrowly missing a 1901 fixture against the All Blacks due to work commitments. In his later years he would be seen in his kilt at King's playing fields, shouting on the Aberdeen team from the sidelines. Rugby 'skills' extended into his working life. His 'robust' management style is said to have included under-table shin scrapes at meetings and the pressing of junior staff against walls to emphasise his displeasure at their actions. He is commemorated by the Butchart Building, originally a sports and exam hall, in University Road. A founding member of the Scottish Ski Club in 1907 he became its president in 1950. A particularly good snow holding corrie at Glenshee bears his name to this day.

Butchart's military career was extensive. Educated at Aberdeen Grammar and Aberdeen and Edinburgh Universities, he graduated in Law in 1905. While at Edinburgh in 1905 he joined a Mounted Infantry Company, of the Queens Rifle Volunteer Brigade (Royal Scots). Back in Aberdeen he was commissioned in the pre-Haldane 1st Volunteer Battalion, Gordon Highlanders in 1907 before moving to the Scottish Horse. In this unit he led his men *'over mountain and down ravine'*. He formed his own law partnership in 1908 but was mobilised in 1914. He served with the Scottish Horse, Australian and New Zealand cavalry regiments, and as a divisional staff officer during the defence of the Suez Canal, Allenby's Beersheba and Jerusalem campaigns, and later in France and Belgium. He finished the war with the DSO, the Star of Roumania (Officer Class) and two mentions in dispatches.

Not everyone was a fan of the OTC. In December 1924 a contributor to Alma Mater disapproved of the use of Mitchell Hall for an OTC Dance. He believed that this demonstrated unwarranted special treatment for a body that was not unanimously held to be a desireable feature of University life. Nor, he proposed, was it a 'society' like the others formed by students for various pastimes and sports. The correspondent, dubbed the 'Honorary War Correspondent on the AUOTC', and President of the University's Labour Club, struck again the following year. He complained that the OTC which *'left rifles lying about in the King's Quad'*, seemed to be protected from all criticism in a most undemocratic manner. If such things happened in Prussia, he suggested, everyone would have a name for it.

As a measure of progress since the lean years following the Great War, the 1925 AUOTC permitted establishment and actual strengths were as follows:

Unit	Establishment	Actual
Medical	1 Major	1 Major
	1 Captain	1 Captain
	1 Subaltern	
	90 Cadets	74 Cadets
Infantry	1 Captain	1 Major
	1 Lieutenant	2 Lieutenants
		1 2nd Lieutenant
	120 Cadets	120 plus waiting list

The 1925 Camp was held near the North Wales coast, well away from the delights of Blackpool, in Kinmel Park outside Abergele. Kinmel had been a big World War I training camp, with practice trenches still in evidence. In March 1919 it had been the scene of riots among some of the 15,000 Canadian troops stuck there and frustrated by delays to their repatriation to Canada. They were overcrowded, on half rations, short of coal for the hut stoves, and missing pay. They were unaware that shipping strikes were causing some of the problems. Conditions were much improved five years later for AUOTC's medics and infanteers.

After Summer Camp the cadets heard bad news about one of their new and key officers. Major Boyd Orr having achieved the great success illustrated by the figures above, resigned from command of the Infantry Unit due to pressure of work at the Rowett. He would go on to achieve a Knighthood in 1935, be a wartime food planner for Churchill, and an MP for Universities. He would be Rector of Glasgow

University, and in 1949 would receive a Nobel Prize for his contributions to Nutrition Science and World Food Policy. In the same year he was elevated to the Peerage as 1st Baron Boyd-Orr.

George Williamson
AUOTC's first Commanding Officer.
Post World War One pose between the guy ropes.

Perhaps reacting to the University's nomination of Major Williamson as overall Contingent Commander, the War Office pointed out that he had been in command of the Medical Unit continuously since 1919. Thus he was considerably exceeding a normal 4 year command tour. He would not be extended in post beyond October 1925 and a change would, it was said, do him and the unit good. Williamson was duly dined out in style at the Palace Hotel on Saturday 7 Nov 1925. Speeches reminded everyone that he had first raised the unit in 1912 and nurtured it until 1914 when he deployed overseas. After the war he had seen it through its post-war crisis before managing the formation of the Infantry Unit. He had effectively commanded the whole enlarged contingent for two years and had, throughout his OTC service, overseen all parades, Cert A and B training, and Annual Camps, often single-handedly.

Thus 1925 ended with Capt Fowler commanding the Medical Unit and Lieutenant, soon to be Captain, Crichton the Infantry Unit. Major Butchart, filling the Major's post in the Medical Unit, would be overall Contingent Commander.

Presumably because of some issues elsewhere in the British OTC network, Aberdeen was reminded by the War Office once again to recruit only British Subjects of pure European descent.

Although the Medical unit had included pipers and drummers from the start, 1925 saw the formal establishment of the Pipe Band. This was made possible by the kind donation of instruments by a Mr James Leith, and the allocation of £93 from unit funds. The Band, later behind a mace spinning Drum Major Tom Nicol, would soon be leading the contingent down Union Street on return from camp to mark the end of the University session. The Pipe Band became one of the most popular features of the unit, a key part of *esprit de corps,* social life and 'public relations'. A home from home for those who arrived at University as competent pipers from the highlands, lowlands and islands, it would also contribute at least its fair share of officers to the

TA and Regular Army. Aberdeen's pipers would in many cases go on to play significant roles in the development of band and solo piping. More Band history is presented in an Appendix.

It was further decided that in line with requests from the Medical cadets and with practice at other Scottish Universities, the whole Contingent would wear the kilt. The cost of putting the Medical Unit in kilts was estimated at £450.

Financially, in the mid 1920s the enlarged AUOTC's annual accounts showed income and expenditure at around the £2000 to £3000 level. Typical financial activities of this time are illustrated by the following examples from the 1925/26 Audit Report.

Public Account.

Receipts

Efficiency Grants	£758
Camp Allowances	£1492
Allowance for cadets to Aldershot	£62

Expenditure

HQ Costs	£66
Ranges	£14
Ammunition	£7
Clothing	£704
Post and Stationery	£19
Permanent Staff payments	£18
Camp Supplies and Rations	£560
Railway travel to/from Camp	£560
Shooting team travel	£9

Expenses at Fort George	£1
Expenses at Aldershot	£23
Band	£93
Kit deficiencies	---- / 16 Shillings

Private Account

Balance brought forward	£316
Interest	£24
Cadet Deposits	£20

Major Butchart suggested that in order to avoid a diary clash with the Summer Term Gala week a short training and musketry camp should be held in the Easter Vacation. This was duly done at Montrose in Easter 1926 with 4 officers and 68 infantry cadets and 27 medics. At the end of the year another officer joined the infantry unit in the form of Aberdeen Law graduate and former Indian Army Captain, Lt George Williamson BL.

For nine days in May 1926 the country experienced a General Strike of miners, railwaymen, dockers and steel workers with the miners staying out until November. The Armed Services and volunteers were deployed under Government emergency powers to avoid complete paralysis especially in the supply of food and other essentials. At the height of the Strike, Aberdonians were warned to stay off the streets to avoid baton wielding policemen. Aberdeen police did indeed baton-charge a crowd of more than 6,000 who were smashing the windows of any local transport daring to move, some of it being driven by student volunteers.

Months of planning for the Government reaction to

this serious disruption, if not actual revolution, had included the cancellation of OTC camps. Universities were seen as an important source of volunteer workers to break any strike action affecting transport and power stations. Thousands of Scotland's students enrolled as volunteer workers. Former soldiers and members of the TA were encouraged to join auxiliary constabularies to maintain order if the need arose. All serving personnel were readied to support the Civil Powers.

Revolution may briefly have been in the air but for the OTC the key question of the uniform change for the medics rumbled on. The cost was now estimated at £485 for 100 sets of jackets, kilts, Glengarries, spats, hose, kilt aprons, sporrans and badges. Costs had risen because the old RAMC jackets could not be altered sufficiently to match the kilts. New tunics were thus required.

1927 saw the unit have a short Spring Camp, again at Montrose, with similar numbers as in the previous year. A new impetus to physical training and sport was given by the attendance of the University's Director of Physical Training and Sport, Capt Arthur W Brocks formerly of the Worcestershire Regiment (Military Cross 1916 Gallipoli; 1917 Brigade Physical and Bayonet Training Supervising Officer), whose important contribution to camps would become a regular feature of OTC life. A gymnast, fencer and boxer, his contribution was recognised in *Alma Mater* as follows:

Ode in Praise of Captain Brocks

Ye'll a' hae heard tell o' our freen' Captain Brocks
O Captain AW Brocks !
He's as stieve as a stane
And as teuch as a bane
Wi' a fist that would knock out an ox.
He's nearly as braid as he's lang,
But as lively as ony 'whiz-bang'.
In spite of his size
he's remarkably wise
He's just five feet six in his socks,
He's a really great fellow our Brocks.

Annual Camp 1927 was held at Blair Atholl in conjunction with St Andrew's, Glasgow and Edinburgh. The medics' Advanced Dressing Station and the infantry's 'great dash' in the attack were noted in the inspection report. Practical exams for Certs A and B were as usual part of the Camp programme and written exams were scheduled for November. It was now thought that the Cert B practicals were being set too high at Company Commander level. They should be limited to Platoon level albeit with knowledge of how all arms operated and cooperated on the battlefield. The three written papers for Cert B were General Tactics, Special to Arm Tactics and Organisation and Administration. Given the very limited experience of candidates the last paper was replaced with a wider examination of cadet knowledge on issues relating to 'Imperial Defence'.

The Infantry did not do so well as usual in the drill competition. They put this down to a lack of practice on long marches to 'watering holes', to which they had become accustomed when on Camp near Blackpool or Scarborough. The Tug o War team coached by Sgt Smillie did however triumph.

Unit officers had always received equitation training and cadets asked to join them on horseback. No Government funds were available for this but the MEC approved the following policy. Cadets who passed their Cert A would receive riding lessons at one quarter of the cost. This contribution would be refunded to them on completion of Cert B. Arrangements were duly made with the local TA Royal Field Artillery brigade riding school. £28 would give 12 students a course of 20 riding lessons.

Whether able to ride or not, it seemed, as had been the case since the end of WW1, that few cadets were applying for commissions, Regular or TA. This was perhaps understandable for the medics, as at present there was no local TA RAMC unit for them to join. It was disappointing however that more Infantry Unit graduates were not finding their way into the many infantry and other Territorial units in the City and Shire. During the 1920s it was recognised by some that with the OTC not represented on the TA Association (it was of course at this time not part of the TA) and little cooperation between the OTC and the TA for example in integrated training, opportunities were being missed. With more joint training cadets might have been given a chance to experience section and platoon leadership while the TA could assess them for Commissioning potential and encourage them accordingly.

Optimising the OTC/TA relationship would be a subject of recurring debate for decades to come. Fostering closer training relationships with the TA would be repeatedly considered and implemented to one degree or another, generally in a limited and infrequent manner. There were however administrative and practical problems associated with the idea. The OTC was a self contained little 'family' and soldiering elsewhere did not appeal to most, at least while they were at University.

Shortly before 1927 Camp, Lt Eric Linklater MA rejoined the unit. Linklater had joined the University as a medical student in 1916. He left his studies to do his bit in the Great War serving on the Somme and elsewhere on the Western Front before receiving a serious head wound and being hospitalised for months. In 1919 he recommenced his studies in medicine and English. He soon realised his true calling, dropped medicine and concentrated on English. During this second period at University he was the Cadet Company Sergeant Major (CSM) of the new Infantry Unit. He graduated MA in 1925 and went to work in Bombay as a journalist for two years. He returned to Aberdeen, via Persia and the Caucasus, to work as an Assistant in the University.

A new Adjutant, again to be shared with Glasgow and based there, arrived in Oct 1927. Capt Grant-Taylor of the Royal Scots Fusiliers handed over to Major Peploe of the Highland Light Infantry. Peploe would prove to be a very industrious and popular member of staff and a memorable OTC character of the late 1920s. Grant-Taylor, after surviving the Great War and the best efforts of the IRA, would be accidentally killed by aircraft gunfire in England in 1942 during a ground support demonstration.

It was believed that holding the 1927 Annual Camp at Blair Atholl, rather than somewhere more exotic in England, had adversely affected attendance. War Office funds in general were not in a very good state and it was thought likely that camps for the foreseeable future would be restricted to

111

Scotland in order to reduce travel costs. However Peploe immediately set to work to secure a more exotic location, outside Scotland, for the 1928 camp

Butchart was looking rather enviously at the permanent HQs, drill halls, stores and offices enjoyed by other contingents such as Glasgow. With unit funds in a fairly healthy state he thought Aberdeen should now start to catch up with the others.

Since the end of World War 1, unsurprisingly, Britain's defence budget had been reducing rapidly. As ever, defence spending was the subject of intense political debate. In 1919, the 'Ten Year Rule', had been adopted by the Government. The Services were required to construct their annual spending estimates on the assumption that the Empire would not be engaged in any 'great' war within a ten year horizon. In 1928 Churchill got the Cabinet to agree that the rule be self perpetuating until specifically withdrawn. Some, including Prime Minister Ramsay MacDonald, thought the Rule was dangerously out of kilter with the international situation and wished to abolish it. The rule stood fast through most of the inter-war years until rising concern about Continental Fascism and Nazism indicated a policy change would be prudent.

The MEC wrestled with smaller scale finance. A lodging allowance supplement of £10 per annum was granted for the Sergeant Instructors to bring Aberdeen into line with practice in Glasgow. There were no available Married Quarters at Castlehill Barracks. A Sergeant Instructor with the Medical Unit had taken a posting to the Colonial Service. His nominated replacement had found no Married Quarters in Aberdeen and promptly negotiated a posting to Edinburgh instead. The Med Unit post remained gapped until another

Sergeant reported. This quartering problem would continue into the 1930s. The Adjutant, Peploe, brought Glasgow's solution to Aberdeen. In 1930 two Aberdeen Council houses at 148 and 152 Hilton Avenue would be rented permanently for the use of OTC Sergeants. This would allow the unit to retain accommodation during any gaps between postings, initiate a system for furnishings, and properly manage any assistance with fuel and light charges. By 1932 the Sergeants' concerns would move on to a lack of compensation for the high bus and tram fares incurred getting between home, Kings and Marischal. The MEC solution was to purchase and issue two bicycles.

Despite financial fears, the OTC lines in the defence budget obviously eased a little because the Spring training at Montrose did receive Government grants. Cadet contributions, already collected, were redirected to the Sport Fund. Also the news came that the Contingent would indeed escape Scotland and hold its 1928 Camp at Scarborough. This great news was immediately included in recruiting articles in *Alma Mater*.

OTC members, particularly the senior year medics, did at this time seem to have a grip on most key positions on the paper's staff. Whole editions were dedicated to the Contingent. Criticism was published however. In a letter to the Editor, an opponent of the OTC held forth in such style that it deserves reproduction here:

"Dear Sir, I notice that the OTC are again appealing for recruits from the student body. Blatantly, Scarborough women are held up as incentives. This toy soldier contingent, while it appears to be a step advanced from the Boys Brigade (it gets kilts and, on occasion I believe, a gun) is animated by slightly different ideals. So far as I can ascertain, these

113

ideals range from 'For King and Country' to 'Come and have a good time', good being liable to a variety of interpretation. Which ideal strikes most deeply the heart of the embryo Wellington I do not know. I was amongst those who objected to your OTC Number [of Alma Mater] on mere principle. Now I should like to protest against the Church Parade of the OTC. Why should they be honoured by a special Sunday parade in Chapel? Chapel is for the use of students and of no military organisation. If the members of that organisation desire to attend as students, let them. If not, why worry? - Yours etc Mount Street"

In the same *Alma Mater* another knock was delivered against the OTC, perhaps unknowingly. A correspondent, under the nom de plume, 'Bangor', drew attention to the AUOTC's War Trophy, the German Field Gun delivered to Marischal College nine years previously. It was now at King's, an eyesore to some and still there despite SRC requests to the Senatus to have it removed. Truthfully or not 'Bangor' stated that he was unaware of its associations but felt that it certainly appeared to be nothing more than a useless collection of old iron, fit for the dump heap. It certainly did not fit in with the green lawns and grey walls of King's College. Perhaps in partial defence of the object 'Bangor' noted the gun was aimed point blank at the Latin Department. The author has been unable before publication to confirm the ultimate fate of the OTC's German Field Gun. Removal as scrap, perhaps during the frantic gathering of anything metal during the Second World War, seems likely. The trophy after metamorphosis by the munitions industry may even have found its way back to its Fatherland. Many institutions, barracks and villages received war trophies of this sort. German guns (each usually marked up with which unit had captured it, where and when) were removed and dumped in local quarries and ditches. These actions stemmed from a combination of teenage high jinks and real local dislike for such items in places where significant proportions of the male population had been killed or maimed by such weapons.

The magic of 1928 Scarborough was enjoyed by 125 Aberdeen cadets and others from Edinburgh, Glasgow, St Andrew's, Durham and Leeds. Attendance statistics as a percentage of established strengths were most pleasing to AUOTC's officers:

Aberdeen 93%, St Andrew's 66%, Leeds 46%, Durham 38%, Edinburgh 33%, and Glasgow 32%.

Perhaps because of greater numbers, Aberdeen won the sports competition, once again organised by the unpaid Capt Brocks whose expenses were duly defrayed by the MEC.

The Inspecting Officer at Scarborough was no less than Aberdonian, and Chief of the Imperial General Staff, General Sir GF Milne. His comments were generally positive except for mentions of a need to improve cadet ability to take charge of drill; off-parade discipline that was 'not on the whole satisfactory'; and the usually excellent demonstration of a Dressing Station being marred by a few unshaven medics.

Contingent Officers, Scarborough, 1928.
CO Harry Butchart seated second from left
Principal Smith, seated third from left
Eric Linklater standing second from left
Arthur Brocks standing third from left

Briefing above Scarborough, 1928. Butchart nearest camera.

General Milne had seen active service as a Gunner officer on the Nile and in the Second Boer War where he had earned a DSO. During the First World War he had risen rapidly to command the British Salonika Army on the Macedonian Front. He would be CIGS from 1926 to 1933. The year before his visit to the OTCs at Scarborough in 1928, Milne had managed to convince one JC Fuller to withdraw his resignation. He had told Fuller that the Army would indeed be modernised in line with the doctrine for mechanised warfare that he and Liddell Hart were championing. Liddell Hart had already resigned in 1924 and was carrying on the campaign for modernisation as British journalism's only full time military correspondent. Continued severe constraints on defence spending would mean that things did not quite turn out the way that Milne promised or hoped. Milne was promoted Field Marshal later in 1928 and became Baron Milne of Salonika and Rubislaw in the County of Aberdeen in 1933. He died in 1948 having lived to observe, from retirement, mechanised warfare on the grand scale of World War Two.

For Aberdeen OTC a successful camp was followed by a disrupted return to Aberdeen due to the 'gross carelessness' of the Railway. The goods van with everyone's kit was wrongly detached from the special train at Edinburgh. Everyone had to hang around Aberdeen station from the early hours until 2pm when another train brought in the missing wagon. OTC admin staff noted that this was the fourth occasion that the Railway had caused great inconvenience to the unit. A claim for damages of £25 was lodged with the Railway's management. Having deducted a counter-claim of £5 for 'damage to rolling stock', the Railway parted with £20, which was put to good use in the cadets' recreation fund.

1928 saw a new addition to the training programme. A 'Tactical Tour' (what might be known in later times as a Staff Ride with aspects of a Tactical Exercise Without Troops or TEWT) had been conducted in the local area for 50 cadets. It had been deemed by all as most worthwhile and, despite the costs of buses and haversack rations, it was agreed that it should be repeated in following years.

Lt Linklater left for China and the USA on a Commonwealth Fellowship in 1928. He would progress through an excellent career as a writer and military historian, and was Rector of the University 1945-48.

Linklater was replaced by Lt Roy Strathdee, an Assistant in the Chemistry Department and a former Cadet Sgt in the Infantry Unit. Strathdee had served in the 4th

Gordons and 5th Gordons during World War One gaining experience as a private soldier and, after commissioning in December 1917, as a junior officer. He would play a key role commanding the Contingent during the next World War.

On 11 Nov 1928 the University War Memorial in King's Chapel was consecrated. Designed by Aberdeen architect William Kelly in 1922 it included The War Memorial Window made by another Aberdonian Douglas Strachan in 1920-1.

At the end of 1928 the MEC, with Principal Smith still in the Chair, contributed to War Office deliberations by recommending that a University candidate for commissioning with a 1st or 2nd Class honours Degree and Military Qualifications should receive three years ante-dated seniority.

Due to insufficient interest there was no Spring Camp in 1929 but the Summer Camp at Peebles 6-20 July, despite being in Scotland, was a great success. It was of a different nature than before, employing a *modus operandi* that would be repeated. It was a joint camp with Glasgow OTC who of course shared Major Peploe with Aberdeen. He ran all the training and exams for both contingents. The site was the town council owned Hay Lodge Park on the left bank of the River Tweed. The regional Royal Engineers had supplied this 'virgin' site with water supply, sanitation, ablutions, kitchens, and messes. Duckboards kept boots out of the heavy clay soil in and around the tent lines. Ordnance stores from the Stirling depot and civilian contract caterers completed the infrastructure to support the following people:

		Offrs	Other Ranks
Aberdeen	Infantry	3	92
	Medical	3	64

Glasgow	Infantry	4	116
	Medical	3	53
	Engineer	2	66
Camp Adjutant			
(from Cameronian Depot)		1	
RE Officer		1	
Camp Medical Support		1	3
TOTAL Military		18	394

Peebles extended a warm welcome to the students making available the facilities of the town's clubs. Only one cadet, from Aberdeen's infantry, let the side down. He was sent home in disgrace for 'conduct unbecoming'. The usual infantry and medical schemes were conducted but this time with the added excitement of the construction of a trestle bridge across the Tweed by Glasgow's 'Sapper' cadets. The usual running tracks and sports pitches were laid out by Capt Brocks for the inter-unit competitions and bathing was permitted in the Tweed. Brocks was paid this time, being put on Glasgow's strength as a Lt. The Very Reverend Principal George Smith again visited the proceedings. One Aberdeen cadet broke his leg during football for which the unit made a compensation claim to Scottish Command to no avail. Football, even at Annual Camp, was deemed not to be Military Training.

Fancy dress opening of Glasgow OTC's trestle bridge across the Tweed. Hay Lodge Park, Peebles, 1929.

MEC accounts this year included £8 spent during a visit by the Prince of Wales to Aberdeen. A proper location at Marischal College for the Medical Unit HQ was still being sought. The plans for Belfast's and Glasgow's OTC HQs were being studied as to what should be aimed for.

In 1929, British forces finally left the Rhineland which they had occupied since 1919. Thus ended the first British Army Of the Rhine. There would be another BAOR, which would last five times as many years, defending rather than occupying German territory.

At home, although Britain's economy had never properly recovered from World War One, the change of decade was marked with a plunge into deeper economic depression.

Chapter 4

GUNFIRE UNDER ELPHINSTONE HALL
AND RUMOURS OF WAR
1930-1939

In January 1930 Lt Col Butchart briefed the MEC on COMEC business. The gathering of representatives from all the UOTCs had heard about plans to have Certs A and B recognised by the forces of the Dominions (in 1930 these were Australia, Canada, the Irish Free State, Newfoundland, New Zealand, and South Africa). The creation of an Officer Cadet Reserve and the OTC Tentage Allowance were also hot topics. Aberdeen's MEC moved on to discuss the provision of Blue Patrol Jackets and Trews for the Sgts.

In 1930 Butchart was granted an extension of his command to Oct 1931. He would be required to transfer back into the Reserve and be 'attached' to the OTC. This would free up promotion prospects within the Med Unit for Capt Fowler and Lt Fraser. Butchart was now nominally filling only a Lt post and getting only that rank's pay and allowances at camp and on courses. The MEC decided it only fair to make Lt Col Butchart's conditions up to that of a Major using Contingent private funds. Other expenditure in 1930 went towards linoleum flooring and furniture for the OTC Common Rooms at Marischal and King's.

At King's the makeover concentrated on two rooms adjacent to the new shooting range under the newly completed examination space, Elphinstone Hall. Improved electric cabling, and electric radiators, would make life more comfortable and fight off the damp prevalent in the rooms. A picture hanging mould on the walls, a clock, rugs and door mats would greatly improve the rifle store and office. Four new match rifles would join others in the store at a cost of £30.

The 1930 Camp was held on virgin ground at Delnies outside Nairn with similar numbers from Glasgow and Aberdeen attending as in the previous year. This time though Glasgow brought its Artillery Unit with its section of guns. The District RE authorities again engineered water for the camp area. Ablution water came from a spring fed cistern. Drinking water was led from Nairn's town system. On this occasion clearly all the administrative 't's had not been crossed and after threats to do so, the water authority turned off the supply. If this situation had continued the camp would have been terminated since the OTC did not have water carts or the horses to pull them. Representations to the local authorities resolved the issue and the 17 officers and 392 cadets could drink again.

All the units present could learn and practice a multitude of tasks in the training areas around the camp and on the Moray coast a mile or so away. Attachments from the RAMC and the Seaforth Highlanders kept the medical centre and camp admin going. Regimental Aid Posts and Advanced Dressing stations were again set up to delight the Inspecting Officer. The Infantry it was thought should have made better use of the training areas available particularly in developing their understanding of the use of Machine Guns.

Too much time it was suggested was being spent on Certificate training and practical exams. OTC staff must have thought they were damned if they did and damned if they didn't. In any case Aberdeen achieved an 80-90% pass rate across the board.

Aberdeen and Glasgow Officers - with a map ! Nairn, 1930.

In addition to the traditional athletics and team games, a swimming gala was held in Nairn's Swimming Pond. Church parade was held in Nairn's Old Parish Church by the Rev Professor Archibald Main of Glasgow. At the end of the service inadvertent humour came in the request for 'worshippers to remain seated while the Corps leave the church'. Although perhaps not all true worshippers, the contingents apparently contained few real sinners with only one cadet, this time from Glasgow, being sent home for drunkenness.

The OTC grip on the weekly *Alma Mater* was increasing with the commencement of a regular OTC page in each edition. OTC members were still dominant in the SRC, the Union and in many other bodies such as the Athletics Association. Recruiting adverts would be placed regularly emphasising that, with the new HQ at King's nearly ready, joining the Contingent had never been so attractive. Those interested were encouraged to seek further information from the Sgt Instructors at either the King's or Marischal HQs.

To illustrate the OTC's weekly page, contributions of photographs from camps were called for. Prints were to be classified as '1. Publishable', or '2. Unpublishable' and sub-classified as 'a. amusing, b. interesting or c. beautiful'. The Editor reserved the right to retain all Class 2 specimens for his own purposes

The new miniature range under Elphinstone Hall was to be the venue for weekly shooting competitions leading to the award of the Strathcona Cup, a grand trophy on display in the Reading Room of King's Library. The Cup formerly belonged to the pre-war U Company. Four teams would be organised on the basis of the University's 'Four Nations', Angus, Mar, Buchan, and Moray. Before the Strathcona Cup Competition got underway OTC members would need to ascertain their 'National' allegiance. The range was officially opened with a competition between officers, SNCOs, JNCOs and cadets.

The ancient universities of Scotland divided their student bodies into nations for the purposes of Rectorial elections. The election of a Rector also traditionally involved fierce battles between opposing supporters, with savage grappling and bombardments by flour and soot bombs. Battlefields ranged from university quads to key road junctions such as Queens Cross. A battle of late 1930 can be viewed online at the British Pathe News archive by searching for 'Aberdeen University' and picking the clip entitled *'Not So Quiet On the Students' Battlefront'*. A piper, more than likely an OTC one, is seen leading out the combatants.

Like other University clubs the OTC held an AGM where the proposed programme of activities, the committee, and accounts were presented for approval. This year the AGM was held in the Debating Hall at Marischal and with AGM business complete, Butchart showed films taken at the Peebles and Nairn Camps.

In November 1930 the War Office promulgated its plans for reorganising the Senior Division of the OTC. OTC establishments would align with mobilisation regulations, and better use would be made of technical resources especially where Universities included Engineering Faculties. The control of contingents with four or even more different arms represented would be improved, by properly establishing the posts of Commanding Officers. Above all, the new arrangements would save money.

The only real implication for Aberdeen, apart from getting a proper CO post, was that its Infantry 'Company' would lose one of its four rifle platoons in order to create a machine gun platoon formed from senior cadets. This new structure would come into being in early 1932 but before then some preparatory machine gun training would start.

The end of 1930 was celebrated with the annual 'smoker' held at the Royal Hotel in Bath Street, where films of camp were again shown to add to the mirth of the crowd. Adjutant Peploe came up from Glasgow for the occasion. A few weeks later the start of another year's training was marked by, with ladies present, the rather more civilised annual dance in Mitchell Hall where cadets were asked to wear uniform.

127

In March 1931 the miniature range closed while Sgt Instr MacDonnell was away at Woolwich on a course. The Clubrooms remained open but the temporary closure didn't help dispel the general apathy regarding the Strathcona shooting match fixtures programme.

Glasgow OTC was reported to be at full strength so Aberdeen's recruiting efforts were renewed. Students were advised that, if selected, the joining fee was only ten shillings as a deposit against their uniform which was, apart from shirts, all issued free. Two shillings and sixpence would be levied every year to cover sports equipment costs. Summer Camp was free with travelling expenses to and from Camp being claimable.

The OTC was not, they were reminded, part of the TA and cadets were not paid. However there was nothing to be gained by *glossing over the real purpose of the Corps and defending it only on the ground of its merely incidental attractions. As the Americans have it 'a girl may wear a golf skirt and not play golf; or wear a bathing suit and not go near the water; but when she puts on a wedding gown, kid, she means business'. Putting on the King's uniform means business"*.

The unit drilled regularly in preparation for its Annual church parade held in March or April. In May, tactical tours were held on the same lines as the previous year, taking place this time over the Cairn O'Mount and as far south as Brechin, and around Strachan and Potarch.

At national level there was increasing concern that the forces were falling below the 'safety point'. However at this time, and right up to the start of World War II, the North East had better TA recruiting figures and unit strengths than most other areas. The OTC needed more recruits if it was not to fall behind the demands of the 'market place' for those of its products who chose to seek a TA Commission. OTC recruiting had been steady but slow with too many employing a well known dodge of joining just before the attractions of Annual Camp. Such dodgers avoided all the previous drill commitments. Students were again reminded of the unrivalled opportunities to know one's fellows in different settings. Knowledge of one's fellow men from Aberdeen and other Universities was, it was said, an essential complement to intellectual training. With this in mind OTC members discussed the pros and cons of different Summer Camps in previous years. The attraction of a fortnight near resort towns such as Blackpool, Scarborough and even Rhyl were undisputed. However the Peebles and Blair Atholl camps, where the quieter surrounds had necessitated more self generated camaraderie and fun, had been huge successes. Some thought that the fact that Camps were held in Scotland was not the real issue for recruiting. Camps shared by only two Scottish contingents were it was thought too small. Glasgow and Aberdeen may have grown to be too friendly. Camps for all four Scottish Contingents, in Scotland or England, would lead to more sport, inter varsity ragging, and entertainment while also reducing any individual's appearance on duty and guard rosters. Big joint OTC camps were not unreservedly welcome in the neighbouring communities. Nocturnal inter-contingent competition would escalate from prize collections of local brass door name plates through to large advertisement hoardings.

Dunbar was the venue for the 1931 Annual Camp, in tents on the old race course of the Hedderwick Hill estate. It had been billed as being better and brighter than any before.

It would combine the positives of Scarborough 1928 (heat, sunburn, aircraft demonstrations, South Beach) and Peebles 1929 (cricket, pipers playing for eightsome reels on the village green, sport, town strolls, swimming in the cool of the evening) but be without the negatives of the less popular experience at Nairn in 1930.

In anticipation of their new organisation the Infantry Unit trained with 5 machine guns loaned by the 6th Seaforths and 6th Gordons. The Medics' training was enhanced in rather less exciting fashion by the temporary issue of a proper RAMC water cart! Glasgow was again at camp with Aberdeen, this time without their Gunners. Church Parade was at Belhaven led by Principal George Smith of Aberdeen. With swimming at the adjacent beach banned due to dangerous tides, the swimming gala was held at Dunbar pool. The senior visitor to Dunbar and a long serving champion of the OTCs, was the outgoing Glasgow MEC (1909-1931) and COMEC (1919-1931) Chairman, Professor of History, Dudley Julius Medley.

Dunbar was a successful camp but many still longed for the big camps with all four Scottish universities plus chums from Ulster, England and Wales. The daily routine at Dunbar was :
0600 Reveille; 0630 Tea and Biscuits; 0700 First Parade and Road Run with Brocks; 0745 Breakfast, make up beds and tidy tent lines; Training with lunch break until 1500; Free time or sports with Brocks; 1630 Tea and inter contingent games; 1730 Guard Mount (contingents trying to out do each other in smartness); 2300 Lights Out but cadets allowed to return to camp at any time provided all duties are carried out.

In Autumn 1931 Sergeant Instructor Edgar, Scots Guards, spent 8 weeks on the Machine Gun Instructors course at the Small Arms School, Netheravon, Wiltshire. He was refunded his housing costs for the period of absence and returned to Aberdeen to meet the new Adjutant, Capt Morgan of the Border Regiment. Morgan's war service had been in Africa.

Morgan and the rest of the MEC met in December 1931 to consider the news from the War Office that there were to be no OTC camps in 1932 due to financial constraints. It is often said that 'worse things happen at sea' and the same constraints had led to an ill managed pay and allowance reduction in the Royal Navy. In September 1931 Britain's defence and political establishment had a great shock when members of the Atlantic Fleet mutinied at Invergordon. The consequent financial scare in international markets made things even tighter for the Treasury with the already weak Pound falling further and the Government abandoning the Gold Standard.

Moscow, through its admirers in Britain, was quick to exploit the event. 'The Red Signal' and 'The Soldier's Voice' were respectively smuggled out to ships and thrown over Army barrack walls. These papers called for comrades to prepare for a new Invergordon, and use their military knowledge of arms to overthrow the oppressors and establish 'a free socialist Britain'.

The Security Services soon routed out British communists behind the incitement to mutiny. The Admiralty reacted to overblown fears of naval subversion by discharging one thousand men. The scare also led to the Government introducing the Incitement to Disaffection Bill which to everyone's surprise led to only one prosecution before the outbreak of World War 2. Not just the OTCs were recruiting University men as during the thirties Moscow recruited its top

British spies for the next few decades including the Cambridge Five: Philby, Maclean, Burgess, Blunt and Cairncross.

The War Office intimated that whilst they could not support full OTC Annual Camps in 1932 they would pay for 4 days of musketry training. Aberdeen considered a long weekend camp at Montrose but given the financial situation abandoned the idea. Instead, as had happened in similar circumstances in 1926, a 10 day training package would be based at King's including several days of route marches with bivouacs or overnight billets on amenable local estates.

In 1931 cadets voted to drop the 'Smoker' event in favour of a really good 'Concert and Hop' early in the Spring of 1932. The design and production of a unit tie was proposed but also dropped. Capt Morgan the Adjutant regretted the end of the Smoker pointing out that his other unit, Glasgow OTC, had attracted over 350 to a similar event, including 58 new recruits. Morgan invited queries from anyone considering going for Regular Commissions.

Late 1931 did see some OTC social events however. Forty people attended a successful bridge drive in the Medical HQ at Marischal organised by SSgt Hearnshaw. The Infantry held their own social in their rooms at King's. Poor recruiting of only two for the infantry and one for the medics, was attributed in part to the lack of the lure of a proper camp.

Getting to know the Vickers Machine Gun, 1932

In the early months of 1932 time was allocated to range days at the Black Dog Ranges in the hope that more cadets would take part in the Wapinschaw. At the Black Dog, to the dismay of their instructors, eager cadets often kept firing their new water cooled Vickers machine guns, even as the tripods slowly collapsed. The combination of cadets, guns and live ammunition at the Black Dog and other ranges would cause occasional stress to instructors for decades to come.

With no camp in the offing vacancies at external Army courses were offered. There were places on a machine gun course at Glasgow, and for the medics there were water supply and general medical courses available at Aldershot.

In May 1932, two Saturday Tactical Tours took place. One took 70 cadets to upper Strathdon. A series of exercise papers produced by Capt Morgan addressed problems of attack, defence, and night operations. Some solutions presented in such field exercises and in answers written by cadets during their Certificate exams provided hilarity. Poor knowledge of map symbols, or a lack of regard for such 'detail' in the tactical map appreciations, had notional patrols moving along hedge tops towards excellent harbour positions at the bottom of ponds.

The other tour led 5 officers, 45 infantry cadets and 35 medics, over the Tyrebagger Hill and onto the ground between it and the River Don. These days out in the countryside were a great success and reckoned to be of real value especially given the absence of a full camp in 1932.

The MEC was approached by Capt Crichton for funds to buy a piano for the Old Aberdeen HQ. The MEC asked, from a point of view of investment risk rather than health and safety, for a check to be made as to whether or not the prevailing damp in the HQ was sufficient to destroy a piano.

Even without a two week summer camp, useful training was achieved in academic year 1931/32. A 'Tactical Tour' was held one Saturday in May. Less well attended was a full field exercise day in June 1932 held on the wild slopes of Kincorth by kind permission of the Town Council. The latter was beginning to buy up neighbouring private estates to allow for the city's inevitable housing expansion.

On parade at Marischal College, 1932

To get through the necessary batch of Cert A and B candidates a special training week was held in October's 'Tattie Holidays' immediately before the Winter Term. The week, based in and around King's College, concentrated on Tactics, usually a weak point in the written exams due in November. The 9am to 4pm programme included a sports day and a 'rained-off' tactical scheme before practical Cert exams were held. By now the Sergeant Instructors were making good use of their 'issue' bicycles to get to and from work. The course which was thought good for *esprit de corps*

135

was rounded off in style with a Dance in Elphinstone Hall attended by 220 cadets, staff and partners.

An end of term social was held on 1 December 1932 at the Infantry's Kings College HQ with small bore shooting and whist to the accompaniment of music from the newly acquired unit piano and a gramophone. The acting Drum Major won a 'neatest ankle' competition. Butchart thanked SSgts Edgar and Hearnshaw for their efforts with the Infantry and Medics respectively. He was pleased to note that the Medical Unit was up to establishment and the Infantry very nearly so. Recruiting efforts continued to urge men to join while they could, as the unit was near full strength. Any student pipers not already in the Band were encouraged to do so quickly. Anyone who had still not stocked up with the Unit Christmas Card (4 pence each) was admonished to rectify that, and all were informed that unit ties were finally 'coming soon'.

Over the Christmas and Hogmanay break everyone looked forward to 'the biggest show of the year'. This was another Combined Students' Union and OTC Dance held at Marischal in the Mitchell Hall at the end of January 1933. Organisers modestly enquired in their adverts *'who could resist a University event in the best hall, with the best band and the best buffet, best run by the best people'?*

The range under Elphinstone Hall hosted a shooting competition between the Contingent and the local Police.

To maintain 'cultural' links with Glasgow OTC the travel costs of two delegates to the Glasgow OTC Dance were paid by the MEC. Two weekend return rail fares cost £2-11 shillings, and 'teas' during the journey, 7 Shillings 6 Pence.

Sgt Edgar, Scots Guards and his Small Bore Team, 1932

In the interwar years a relatively low proportion of cadets went on to Regular or TA commissions. In 1932 in an attempt to improve the likely supply of officers in an emergency, the War Office introduced the Officer Cadet Reserve (OCR). Those cadets who passed their Cert A or B written exams in November could consider joining the OCR. Under this voluntary scheme current and former members of the Senior Division of the OTC would have the following 'benefits' in the event of war. Cert A holders would be entitled to enlist straight into officer training units. Cert B holders would be commissioned immediately. By May 1933, Aberdeen OTC had 16 Cert A holders and 25 Cert B holders listed in the Officer Cadet Reserve. Thus very quickly, roughly 20% of the Contingent had joined the new scheme putting Aberdeen second only to Birmingham's Contingent in this respect among all of Britain's Universities. This achievement was set against a general wave of pacifism in student bodies across the country. The OTC weathered any criticism from pacifist quarters and continued to thrive. The 'pacifist' cause continued to be voiced in *Alma Mater* throughout the Thirties. Ripostes from OTC members reminded anti-OTC 'intellects and pseudo high brows' that it was politicians and not soldiers who started wars. They claimed a greater understanding of war would make people in power less likely to start one. Some letters addressed the need to stand up to Hitler and Mussolini, while others accused the OTC of being part of the same militarism. A few correspondents accused the OTC of obsolescence, training for the 1914-18 war that had already been fought. They asserted that the next war would be fought in the air. These views were shared by some in Government and the Army had to fight for resources against the increasingly favoured air force.

Unit establishment and strength in 1932 were:

	Established	Actual
Officers	6	6
Infantry	120	100 (incl MG Platoon)
Medical	90	70

During May 1933, two Tactical Exercises were held, the first in Kincorth and the second, a series of infantry rearguard actions along the Slug Road between Stonehaven and Deeside. At Muchalls, the Medics practiced the set up of a Casualty Receiving Station. They were seen off from Marischal by a large turnout of second year lady medical students leading the cadets to conclude that indeed, 'there's something about a soldier'.

It would still be a couple of decades before women would be joining in as cadets on OTC exercises. Some men thought there was already more than enough female influence in university life. For them the increased civility creeping into traditionally robust Gala Weeks and Rectorial election events was not a trend to encourage. Men were urged to go with the OTC to Blair Atholl to 'get away from women'.

After strong lobbying by the OTCs, annual camps resumed in 1933 with Aberdeen joining Glasgow, at Black Island, an area of ground bounded by the railway and the River Garry, just west of Blair Atholl. (During the Second World War, this site would be the HQ of the Canadian Forestry Corps and have its own railway 'halt'.)

Glasgow brought the Artillery this time, but as a result of the War Office reorganisation the Glasgow Infantry and Medical Units were much reduced. Although Glasgow's newly established CO had taken part in the recces, Aberdeen's Harry Butchart was the Camp Commandant, ably assisted for the fourth time, by Capt Smart of the Cameronian Depot acting as Camp Adjutant and Quartermaster. Glasgow and Aberdeen's shared Adjutant, Capt Morgan, oversaw all training and exams. The District Royal Engineers had again brought limited civilisation to the site but this time latrine construction was poor. The woodwork allowed an unfortunate mismatch in seat and bucket positioning. Resulting conditions were understated in subsequent reports as 'unsatisfactory'.

Field exercises were conducted in neighbouring Glen Tilt and for the inspection Glasgow's medics operated a Main Dressing Station (MDS) supplied with 'casualties' from Aberdeen's two Regimental Aid Posts (RAPs) and Advanced Dressing Station (ADS). Aberdeen's infantry defended a prepared position against determined attack by Glasgow's infantry and sappers. The Inspecting Officer, GOC Scotland, Lt Gen Sir Archibald Cameron, was particularly impressed by all the Cadet NCOs. When not training, cadets could enjoy supervised swimming in the Garry and the usual temporary sports pitches and running tracks. One highlight of the camp was an overhead visit by RAF aircraft dropping and picking up message canisters before communicating with the ground through the wonders of wireless.

A week of training was again held at King's College in October 1933. 86 infantry and 65 medical cadets attended under the supervision of medics Major Fowler, Capt Fraser (another 'U' Company veteran commissioned to the Argylls in 1915) and Lt Whyte; and infanteers Capt Crichton and Lt Strathdee. Capt Brocks was attached as usual to run the physical training. Field exercises culminated with a full Tactical Scheme on Scotstown Moor, then lying well out in the countryside. No practical Cert exams were scheduled this time and the programme covered a broader range of topics and was packed with lectures and visits.

Training Week, King's, October 1933

Major Guiness RE, in charge of the construction of the new Gordons Barracks at Balgownie, gave a talk on his Corps. Capt Hall, Adjutant of the Aberdeen Artillery Brigade, lectured on Gunner matters, and the RAMC was covered by the Contingent's own Major Fowler. The role of the Army Physical Training Staff was presented by Capt Brocks MBE MC who had done so much to enhance Annual Camps and Training Weeks. Cadets spent a morning at Castlehill Barracks at the bottom of Union Street, learning about recruit training, the quartermaster department, mobilisation procedures, and 'the life of a soldier'. Another morning visit was hosted by Fonthill Barracks where cadets

141

learned about the Royal Signals in the Field. The Adjutant, Capt Morgan, lectured on tactics and machine guns, and Capt Farrington of the Royal Tank Corps had come up from Catterick to give a lantern slide presentation on Tanks and Tanks/Infantry Cooperation. Capt Farrington was also able to advise on defensive layouts against a tank threat during the Scotstown exercise. What the cadets were hearing about tanks was truly the current 'state of the art'. At this time the British Army, building upon the doctrines of Fuller and Liddell Hart, was leading the world in the development of armoured warfare. The Germans were particularly interested in the new theories.

One evening a social event was held in the Infantry HQ at King's, which featured the showing of a cine film made at the Blair Atholl Camp by Major Fowler. The week ended with a drill competition won by the Medical Unit, and a Dance in Elphinstone Hall.

The question of a replacement CO still exercised the MEC. The nomination of Major Fowler had been rejected by the War Office due to his belonging to an 'administrative corps' thus not being eligible to command the Contingent as a whole as a Lt Col. Thus despite further private lobbying by Principal Smith and Lt Col Butchart, the latter had to leave and rejoin the Reserve of Officers (Scottish Horse).

Other manning developments were more positive. Aberdeen now had 80 cadets registered with the Officer Cadet Reserve of whom 5 had recently been granted commissions. An ex RAMC NCO had been appointed as 'Storeman'.

Arrangements were made to overhaul the Medical and Infantry Unit typewriters. In these days (2012) it is necessary to recall the state of information technology existing up to the first tentative use of computer word processors, cheap printers and photocopiers in the last two decades of the 20th Century. With no websites or social media (Facebook, Twitter etc) to communicate with cadets, word of mouth, the *Alma Mater* and notice boards at Kings and Marischal were the OTC's media. Written communication was reliant on typewriters, carbon paper and for medium volumes the Banda machine spirit duplicators. The intoxicating smell from the Banda was a feature of offices and unit orderly rooms well into the 1980s. For bigger productions, such as teaching materials and Annual Camp Standing Orders, commercial printers were employed.

The Contingent's social life got off to a good start in 1934 with 150 attending a 'Smoking Concert' in February in the Students' Union. The King's HQ now had the luxury of its own dartboard.

May training included a Church Parade at King's and a Tactical Scheme in the Feughside/Potarch area up Deeside. Four buses set out in the rain with 70 infantry and 30 medical cadets on board. They watched a demonstration of the Kapok Assault Bridge at the Feughside Inn by a section of Territorial Sappers. After crossing the bridge, ambush drills were practiced with musical interludes by an ad hoc tin whistle and mouth organ band. At this time the official band of pipers and drummers was, at 18, bigger and better than ever. The regular tuition, from the Gordons at Castlehill, was paying off.

On 2 June 1934 the Band and the Contingent paraded to 'troop the colour' to mark King George V's Birthday. The unit was also celebrating the fact that official statistics showed Aberdeen to be proportionately the strongest and best qualified contingent in Great Britain.

Summer Camp was held back on the banks of the Tweed at Peebles with the Glasgow Medical and Infantry Units. The War Office, still in dire financial straits, had originally wanted cadets to contribute financially to the costs. After a strong riposte from the Universities, the War Office relented and funded the Camp completely. Special treats were the attachment of a Black Watch Machine Gun Officer to the Infantry and the loan of a water cart and heavy horse ambulance wagon to the Medics. Both units enjoyed a visit to the campsite by a section of Armoured Cars. Despite the adverse affect on discipline by local civilians wandering through the lines, the Medical Unit achieved its highest inspection accolade to date. The War Office's Director General of Army Medical Services wrote to say how pleased he was with the unit's performance.

In Autumn 1934 the War Office agreed the design of Officer Cadet Reserve badges for Cert A and Cert B holders and these were duly ordered and issued.

Two cadets had received Regular Army Commissions in 1934. NS Cowan BSc(Eng) was off to the Royal Engineers and WGS Benzie BSc to the Royal Tank Corps. The Army was taking an increasing interest in officers with degrees and intimated that there would be 80 university candidate places in 1935 and 100 in 1936. Contingents were reminded that any aspiring Sapper candidates would be required to attend the School of Military Engineering for assessment and preparation the summer before they intended applying for their commissions.

In 1934 a new unit cap badge, based on the Boar's Head from the University Founder Elphinstone's Coat of Arms, was approved. It would include the Motto *Non Confundar*. The Latin phrase *'non confundar in aeternum'*

144

originates in Psalm 70 and in an early Christian hymn, the *Te Deum*. It is translated as 'let me never be put to confusion'. The original Latin can also be more loosely translated to 'ashamed' or even 'routed' according to taste or circumstances. The originator of the winning badge design and previous British War Medals, William McMillan ARA ARBS, was asked to prepare the dies for the new badges at a cost of 50 Guineas.

The AUOTC Capbadge
mid-1930s to present day.
Replaced the ladies' WRAC Capbadge in the 1990s

Lt Col Harry Butchart, Secretary of the University and the MEC was asked , to represent the Contingent and the University at the next COMEC meeting.

In 1935 the unit hoped that the War Office would approve Crichton as the next CO, if he passed his promotion exams to Major. Lt Strathdee could then in turn move up the ladder to fill the Captain's post in the Infantry Unit.

The new cap badges were issued and once again the unit entrained for Annual Camp at Dunbar. This time, after study of the tides and winds, sea swimming was permitted at set times under the watchful eye of nominated lifeguards. Glasgow's Engineer, Infantry and Medical cadets joined the training. An RA Field Battery demonstration was laid on and a visit was made to the 1st Gordons at Redford Barracks in Edinburgh. Practical Cert A and B exams were held under the watchful eyes of external examiners from the Gordons and Kings Own Scottish Borderers (KOSB). The laird's private golf course at Hedderwick Hill was made available as a recreation option.

Back in Aberdeen, some improvements to the Medical Unit accommodation at Marischal were in hand. In the Autumn two weeks of training were scheduled, the first week for the Medics and the second for the Infantry. The Adjutant Capt Morgan, an excellent soldier who however had failed to attune to the student mindset, handed over to Lt Stewart of the Black Watch who would spend two years in post before leaving for the Royal Army Pay Corps.

Ceremonial duties this year included lining Castle Street on 23 January to mark the Proclamation of Edward VIII.

The 1936 train to Annual Camp managed to cross the border but only as far as Catterick. There the Aberdeen Contingent was joined by all of Glasgow's sub-units for a programme heavily supported by the Garrison's Regular Army units. Aberdeen's cadets were now being issued with two service jackets, one for normal work and one for ceremonial parades. This major re-clothing of the unit had cost £650. Prior to Camp, the Contingent's officers had attended a Highland Division Tactics Exercise at Gleneagles. This and the additional external support from Regular and TA staff would it was hoped add realism to the Cert A and B training programme. Demonstrations were laid on by tank, signals, and gas units, and by service aircraft. The Infantry Unit was attached to the 1st Bn of the Essex Regiment and the Medics trained with the Northern Command Medical

Services. The mid-July weather was atrocious and this coupled to a poor standard of tentage, may have led to an early example of a litigious society. One cadet suffered from a short illness incurred at Camp and his parents made a claim for medical expenses. Their case may have been helped by the unusual absence of a Medical Officer specifically allocated to the OTC Camp, Catterick Garrison facilities being thought sufficient.

Action packed and 'realistic' as the training at Catterick may have been, the year's Cert A and B results were very disappointing. This drop in performance was put down to there being perhaps too many demos, visits and combined exercises at Camp at the expense of tighter certificate syllabus training. There may also have been a higher marking standard applied and the quality of some of the Contingent's own Permanent Sergeant Instructors (PSIs) was questionable.

Spring 1937 saw 4 officers and 25 cadets make a day trip to No 8 Flying Training School at Montrose. Capt Brocks went off to Aldershot for a short refresher course at the Army School of Physical Training and preparations were made for another Summer Camp at Peebles. The camp, again in Hay Lodge Park by the Tweed, went well and was blessed with excellent weather. Glasgow's Medical, Infantry and Engineer Units joined the fun as did some of the public exercising their right of access. For the 16th year running Messrs Strachan Kerr Ltd provided the catering for all messes. Training at camp concentrated on the Cert A and B syllabi. The CO of the KOSB at Berwick helped run four tactical exercises and a major all arms scheme at the Peebles Annual camp. Instruction included gas warfare and night fighting.

In 1937 Sgt Atkinson, Scots Guards, was posted in. In the opening years of the coming World War, when the Contingent expanded, he would be promoted to WO1 Regimental Sergeant Major (RSM). The Scots Guards would allocate a continuous succession of twenty two RSMs for the Contingent through to 1993.

Glasgow's OTC's Chaplain Archibald Main took Church Parade. The cadets entertained the Provost and other Peebles citizens at a concert in the Town Hall. Lt Col Butchart and the CO 4th Gordons visited from Aberdeen. Major Crichton considered the absentee rate too high. He wondered whether the solemn contracts and obligations involved on joining the OTC were made clear enough to students. Excuses ranged from employment, through participation in the University Jamboree to compulsory attendance by Agri students on potato inspection courses. Absentees would eventually be fined from £3-00 downwards depending on the strength of their excuses.

The medics usual highly competent show of RAMC field procedures was curtailed by a break in the excellent weather and heavy rain. As for the Infantry, the inspecting officer noted that while tactics and the actual giving of orders were good, the time for battle procedure between Company Orders and commencing the attack was excessive. This delay he feared would give cadets an unrealistic impression of what would be required in war. War looked increasingly likely.

Many layers of command above the OTC, politicians and War Office staff officers were observing the Japanese invasion of China with alarm. Concern about these events in the Far East and the previous year's re-occupation of the Rhineland by the German Army, forced the British Treasury to open the taps and begin a long overdue and extensive rearmament programme. There was no shortage of threats across the globe. Hitler in Germany was a direct threat to the homeland. Mussolini sat near the Mediterranean and Suez lines of communication to the Far East where Japan was clearly keen on establishing an empire of its own.

The Army faced stiff competition for resources with the Royal Navy and the Royal Air Force. The latter service, with its influential advocates, ensured that bombers were given a higher priority than the Army. The Army itself was still unclear on tank design and the broader vision of a properly mechanised Army's equipment, organisation and tactics.

Included in all the War Office calculations was the obvious conclusion that whatever type of force was mobilised, more officers would soon be needed by the Regular and Territorial Armies. The Universities, as in the last war, would play a key role in providing them. Reviews of how university candidates could obtain commissions in the Regular and Territorial Armies had been conducted throughout the 1920s and 30s. Regulations for commissioning graduates were published in 1924 and 1934. In 1937 a report was published by the 'Committee on the Supply of Officers for the Army' which had inquired specifically into the shortage of officers being recruited and the serious and demoralising blockages in the promotion system above them. For engineering graduates the War Office would make up to 12 Commissions available annually in the Mechanical Engineering Staff of the Army Ordnance Corps.

In July 1937 Crichton went to represent the Aberdeen MEC at a meeting at the War Office to discuss the syllabi for Certs A and B. The main proposal was for a common all arms Cert A for all cadets before they specialised at Cert B level.

In early 1938 the contingent's strength was good with the Infantry 6 over establishment at 126 and the Medics 13 over strength at 90 cadets. By October 1938 the War Office had ominously authorised significant over-manning in the TA and 20% over-manning in the OTCs. Crichton commanded the Infantry Unit and the Contingent and this was holding back Roy Strathdee's progress. It was decided that subject to War Office approval Major Crichton would hand over the Infantry to Strathdee in 1939. Crichton would command the whole contingent with his current rank of Major but with the pay and allowances of a Lt (the only establishment vacancy). The MEC would make his rates up to those of Major during Camp. The contingent needed new uniforms. The Commander wished every new cadet to receive a new uniform on joining. A complete set of new jackets would cost £185 and these would be reserved for ceremonial use. The old jackets would be worn for routine training.

On another uniform matter, the Colonel of the Gordon Highlanders, General Sir Ian Hamilton, authorised OTC officers to wear Gordon Highlanders Mess Kit with OTC buttons and sporrans. The MEC gave a grant to help officers with the personal expenses involved in implementing this honour.

The 1938 Camp was again at Peebles but this time not in Hay Park. A better site across the Glasgow road meant that the same facilities could be used but that public intrusions would be more manageable. Glasgow's artillery, signals, infantry and medical units joined Aberdeen for the last time in their long lasting grouping. From 1939 Aberdeen was to be grouped with St Andrews. Among other things this required additional office accommodation at Marischal College for the shared Adjutant who would be based in Aberdeen.

At camp TEWTs prepared by a Regular Officer again focussed on the training of the Infantry. The unit's own officers trained the Medics. Aberdeen's Officers at the Camp were Major Crichton, Capt Strathdee, Capt Cottrell-Hill MC Border Regiment the Joint Adjutant, and the RAMC officers Major Fraser, Capt Logie and Lt Gordon. The ever dependable Capt Brocks MBE MC again organised fitness training, sport and recreation. Cadet attendance was better than for 1937 but the obligations of membership still needed emphasising at every opportunity. Apart from one case of Scarlet Fever, health at camp was excellent. The Sir George Adam Smith Cup for Inter Unit Drill was won by the Medics.

A well attended break from training at the 1938 camp was an organised visit to the British Empire Exhibition in Glasgow's Bellahouston Park. West Scotland's industries were at the forefront of the displays which ran from May to October. It had taken 10 months to construct what would be the last showcase for the British Empire. After touring the displays, Aberdeen's cadets doubtless displayed their courage on the many rides in Britain's biggest funfair. Despite the heaviest rainfall for 35 years, over twelve and a half million people would visit the Exhibition.

A new trophy was instituted by the Scottish Volunteer Medical Officers Association for an inter Scottish OTC Medical Unit Competition. Major Fowler RAMC had presented a swimming trophy on his departure to command 153 (Highland) Field Ambulance.

In November 1938, Aberdeen's MEC met to prepare their representative for the imminent COMEC meeting .

151

They wished to raise the issue of OTC officer promotion. They felt that OTC officers should like the Regulars be eligible for promotion based on years of service. For Infantry this meant 2Lt to Lt after 3 years, to Captain after 8 years, and Major after 17 years. For Medical Officers the scheme should be Capt after 1 year, Major after 10, Lt Col after 17 and Colonel after 25 years.

The MEC majority view was still against the recruitment of cadets of other than pure European descent. Outside COMEC business, the meeting discussed the MEC share of costs arising from PSI quartering. It decided to pay all the costs of the Joint Adjutant who would be resident in Aberdeen rather than complicate matters by dividing them out with St Andrews. £9 was granted for the production of a printing block for the Unit Christmas Card.

The OTC has always had to strike the right balance between academic and military pressures on students with the former always having precedence. In 1938/39, second year medical students were told by an overly sympathetic Sgt Instructor not to worry about their impending Cert B exams. He told them just to bring along their books to the exam and copy out the answers. The candidates duly turned up at the Mitchell Hall with their books to be met by their Sergeant Instructor motioning to them frantically that they should hide their books at all costs. The War Office on this occasion had decided to send official observers. The result was that only one candidate from the 60 or 70 actually passed his Cert B. He had done most of it before at his school contingent.

At the end of March 1939 the decision made the previous year to double the TA in size was announced publicly. At the end of April conscription was reintroduced.

The TA divisions would have complete shadow divisions. In the case of the 51st Highland Division this would be the 9th Highland Division. Clearly even the local demand for officers would increase.

The OTC's planning for the momentous year of 1939 had a bizarre twist. The first joint camp with St Andrews was to be held at Tain, from where 'U' Company had mobilised for World War One. In the event, history did not repeat itself for World War Two. With all preparations made for the usual tented camp at Tain, word came down that the War Office had cancelled all OTC Camps. All available tentage, camp equipment and Regular personnel were now committed to the mobilisation and training of reserves. Aberdeen appealed and won a concession on the understanding that there would be no War Office support as regards equipment, assistance or travel costs. Proof of a full training programme would nevertheless be required.

Aberdeen and St Andrews hastily arranged the hiring of tentage from the Boys Brigade and went up the River Dee to Aboyne for their 1939 Camp. The Glentanar Estate gave them a campsite at Craigendinnie, south of the river and only 1000 yards from Aboyne. The site was picturesque, level and blessed with good turf and sandy soil resistant to the flooding threatened by foul weather. Between showers, flies and the dreaded midge did their best to reduce morale. The usual catering company turned out to provide the mess marquees and field kitchens, charging more in an attempt to make up their heavy losses from all the cancelled camps across the country. A 6 bed camp hospital was provided.

Training was conducted on areas provided around Birse by the Cowdray Estate. The 5th/7th Battalion Gordon Highlanders laid on a one day demonstration including the

153

tactical employment of the infantry truck, the Bren Carrier, and the 3 inch Mortar.

Since 1938 OTCs had been allowed to exceed establishment by 20%. The Aberdeen contingent's attendance at camp was 115 out of 145 Infantry Cadets, 96 out of 123 medical cadets and 6 officers. The unit's high standards are illustrated by the fact that 11 absentees from an actual strength of 268 was thought to be too high a rate. Despite the weather and the midges the 1939 Camp seems to have been a memorable and happy affair. Under the management of Capt Brocks, PT parades and football were conducted on the camp site, and Aboyne made available its golf, tennis and bowling facilities. Cricket matches were played on the village's famous Green. A successful innovation in conjunction with the cricket was the provision of a Teas Marquee to which cadet's friends and relations were invited. A successful dance was held under the auspices of the two contingents and the cricket club. No formal inspection was held but Major Rennie visited from the War Office. He discussed, with officers and cadets, the future of OTCs within a national wartime regime of compulsory military training. Among the cadets at Aboyne was Harold Watt, an Arts student who had joined the OTC as soon as he left the Grammar School in June 1938. His bell tent commander was Cadet Corporal John Reid who would one day become CO. Watt spent two years in the contingent before transferring, much to the CO's annoyance, to the new University Air Squadron. This RAF unit would be one of the many great changes to the University's military life brought about by the Second World War.

Chapter 5

WORLD WAR II
THE SENIOR TRAINING CORPS
1939-1945

Britain declared war on Germany on 3 September 1939. For the second time the TA divisions were mobilised and a British Expeditionary Force set off for France and Belgium. Survivors of the BEF's defeat assessed that, although extremely gallant, self-disciplined and quick to learn, they lacked the equipment and training required to match the German Army. Many former OTC cadets, and friends and relations of current members, went with the 51st Highland Division to join a French Army on the Maginot Line. The phoney war lasted until May 1940 when the Germans swept through France. Between 26 May and 3 June 1940, 338,000 British, French and Belgian troops were evacuated from Dunkirk. The railways distributed the survivors as far away as Aberdeenshire.

For the 51st Highland Division, controversially still attached to the crumbling French Army, fighting went on until the 12 June, when hopeless odds finally made surrender at St Valery the only humane option for General Fortune. Some escaped but for most the next few years would be spent in prison camps, mines, and death marches. A second 51st Highland Division, based around the 2nd line 9th Highland Division, with many products of the OTCs in Aberdeen and elsewhere, was resurrected, trained and equipped in time to participate in Montgomery's hard won victories through Egypt, Libya, Tunisia and Sicily. The Division would land on the evening of D Day, liberate St Valery, help the

155

Americans during their 'Battle of the Bulge' in the Ardennes, cross the Rhine, and fight through to Bremerhaven and the end of the war in Europe.

Aberdeen's OTC, now 27 years old, would be required to give basic training to a great deal more people destined for war service across the globe. Students would also join the Home Guard in the defence of Aberdeen.

The North East, like the rest of Britain, prepared for war. Extensive beach defences were constructed as were pill boxes at bridges and road junctions. Many of these are still landscape features over 70 years later. Occasionally, even now, a tree harvesting machine will fall into a brick lined underground hide constructed for the secret 'Auxiliary' units. From these hides sabotage and assassination would be unleashed on an occupying enemy for the 10 or so days the patrols expected to survive. Other preparations were made for secret stay behind communications facilities which could report on German movements and strengths after any successful landing.

The North East would also witness significant parts of the air war. The RAF took over Dyce Airfield which had opened five years previously. With its harbour, ship building, war industries and railway marshalling yards, Aberdeen was an attractive target for raids from across the North Sea. Although not experiencing the devastation wreaked on Clydeside by the Luftwaffe, Aberdeen would be the most frequently bombed Scottish city, suffering many casualties. Twenty eight Luftwaffe attacks killed 169 people and injured 592. Later in the war the North East became home to Beaufighters and Mosquitoes of the famous Strike Wings. The bombers from Banff and Dallachy on the Moray Firth coastline would rendezvous with Peterhead's Mustang fighters, before heading for the Norwegian coast. To evade German radar they would fly low enough to leave a broad wake on the North Sea's surface.

Local industry once more switched to war production. The hardcore from the quarries went out to military construction works. The paper works along the Don produced a wide variety of containers for explosives and oils, and latterly fuel drop tanks for Mustang long range fighter aircraft and napalm tanks for Mosquito bombers. The engineering firm Henderson on King Street switched from cranes, cableways and handling equipment and produced howitzers, shells, ammunition hoists, mine sweeping equipment, tank parts and Bailey Bridges. McKinnon and Co, normally in the business of making machinery for coffee and sugar plantations, were soon turning out mortar bombs, howitzer and naval shrapnel shells, and aero engine parts. Crombie produced cloth and uniforms for British and US forces. The fishing fleet once again took up patrol and minesweeping tasks, with the shipyards doing the necessary conversions. The Hall Russell yard took a direct hit during a single aircraft raid and 32 employees were killed during their lunch break.

In Aberdeen's bars, cinemas and dance halls the normal question in conversation was not if someone was in the TA, but which unit they had joined. Aberdeen's TA at such sites as Fonthill, Hardgate, Ruby Lane, Great Southern Road, Skene St, and Woolmanhill offered a big choice of units: Gordon Highlanders, Scottish Horse, Royal Engineers, Royal Artillery of various types (medium, field and anti aircraft), searchlight units, a Royal Signals Divisional HQ Sqn, RAMC units, and RASC transport companies. Many AUOTC alumni were already in the TA or quickly joined it.

Bill Adam had been an officer cadet since 1938. In June 1939 he was commissioned in the 5th/7th Gordon Highlanders (TA). His war would be untypical. He was selected for service in the GHQ Liaison Regiment or 'Phantom Force' deploying on their special patrols in North Africa and Sicily. Montgomery introduced a system of having trusted small patrols with their own communications on or beyond the frontline. With his authority they reported on the actual positions and condition of friendly and enemy forces. Skipping the long formal chain of command with its inevitable time delays and distortions of fact, senior HQ's had their own 'eyes and ears' on the battlefield. The system, developed in North Africa and Sicily, was used by the British on and after the Normandy landings. General Eisenhower, the Supreme Commander of the Allied Expeditionary Forces, was amazed by the complete picture of operations available to an Army HQ back in Portsmouth. When told about the Phantom Patrols he wanted some for the US Army. Within 24 hours, a reserve Phantom Squadron, including Bill Adam, was brought down from Scotland. Men, vehicles and equipment crossed the Channel to join the US Army. The war in Europe would be won before the US could train its own Phantom Force and the contribution of the attached British 'Phantoms' was highly valued. Captain Bill Adam was awarded the US Bronze Star for his meritorious achievements in connection with military operations against the enemy in France, Germany and Austria.

In Orkney, former OTC cadet and officer Eric Linklater found himself mobilised in 1939 as 'Officer Commanding The Orkney Fortress'. '*A Stone in the Heather*' is a fascinating short film about Linklater's life and writings.

Made posthumously in 1976, it is available on the Scottish Screen Archive website and offers a pleasant half-hour's entertainment.

In 1939 all the OTC's unembodied TA officers were subject to swift mobilisation and deployment elsewhere. Within just a few days of the outbreak of war, the Medical Unit's officers were posted away. Major Fraser, the 'U' Company veteran, went to a RAMC Training Depot, Captains Logie and Gordon joined 15th (Scottish) General Hospital. With term starting in October 1939, the OTC had to be kept ticking over at Saturday morning parades for the infantry cadets and the many medics who still turned up despite having no instructors. The only Regular staff were the shared Adjutant Cottrell-Hill and Sgt Atkinson.

The Infantry Unit officers in line with an existing mobilisation scheme were tasked to initiate and operate Number 1 Reception Unit. This unit was to help a Joint Recruiting Board (JRB) assess and grade resident graduates and undergraduates wishing to join the Services, essential industries and Government Departments. Major Crichton was OC the unit, Capt Strathdee the Adjutant and Lt Henderson who had joined the unit at Aboyne, the Assistant Adjutant. The other OTC permanent staff would assist in documentation and shepherding candidates through the process. The JRB consisted of Principal Sir WH Fyfe and representatives of the Ministry of Labour, the Royal Navy, Army and Royal Air Force. In the eight or so weeks between the outbreak of war and 2 November 1939, 569 applicants were processed. The RN (including the Fleet Air Arm) and the RAF received roughly 60 men each. The Army figures were:

Men including some with Cert A attested for pre OCTU training:

Inf	66
RE, R Signals, RASC	37
RA	23
RA (Anti Aircraft)	<u>32</u>
	158

Medically Fit Holders of Cert B to Immediate Commissions:	30

Technical/Scientific duties	31
Under Age	12
Medically Unfit	29

No further action eg. not recommended for commissions	179

In addition to these men, the Reception Unit and Board dealt with 276 members of the Officer Cadet Reserve (OCR) which had been formed in 1932.

With its first task done Crichton and Henderson were formally posted from the Reception Unit to the OTC. The Reception Unit itself, assisted by the OTC, carried on for another 4 months processing 86 members of the Regular, TA, Indian Army and Army Officer Emergency Reserves of Officers. Job done, No 1 Reception Unit, closed on 18 Feb 1940.

In October 1939 all OTCs received a War Office letter stating that until a definite policy for senior divisions of the Officers' Training Corps had been settled, they should primarily concentrate on training students between the ages of 18 and 19½ up to Cert A standards. Written papers would be suspended in favour of a broader syllabus and practical exam until new wartime syllabi could be published. Cert A required the skills of a trained soldier and the ability to lead a section if need be, while Cert B required competence at unit NCO level.

It was stressed that such training would bring no special considerations for commissioning. The peacetime system of commissioning to fill vacancies was to cease. In a recognition of the shortage of doctors created by the call-up of medical students during World War 1, medical students who had already completed 5 terms at University were reserved from call-up. Also 'reserved' were some Divinity students. Call-up would be 'deferred' until course completion for science students particularly those studying radio physics, engineering (other than civil) and chemistry. On reaching military age these science and engineering students would be assessed by a technical committee of the JRB every 6 months. Acceptable academic progress would bring another 6 month period of deferment. On course completion such men would go to appropriate jobs in the Services or key industries. Men studying the Arts, Law, and Biological Sciences could anticipate the normal call-up.

In May 1940, a week before the evacuation at Dunkirk began, the Adjutant, Cottrell-Hill, was posted away to Staff College. There would be no replacement for him as Joint Adjutant for Aberdeen and St Andrews. Individual contingents were to make their own arrangements to cover the adjutant's training and administrative duties. Sgt Atkinson was now the only Regular left in AUOTC.

Around this time a former AUOTC Pipe Major was being evacuated via Le Havre and Cherbourg with 'Ark Force', the lucky part of the Highland Division which only just escaped the German encirclement and made it back to Britain. Patrick Charles Mitchell, from an Aberdeenshire medical family, had been commissioned into the 4th Gordons before transferring to the RAMC in 1939. He went with the BEF to France as MO to the Highland Division's Sappers. He later served in North Africa and Italy. He was mentioned in dispatches at Monte Cassino, and awarded the MC at San Apollinare in 1944 for evacuating over 900 wounded under enemy fire and in appalling weather. After the war he had a distinguished career in the RAMC and civilian medicine.

The AUOTC medical unit was now without officers or PSIs, and 30 first year medical students joined the Infantry Unit. The Dean of the Faculty of Medicine was asked to encourage more to do so. The absence of clear War Office guidance on the OTC's wartime future, the Medical Unit, and other issues required Lt Col Butchart, the University Secretary and Secretary of the MEC to go to London and discuss matters with Major Rennie who had visited the unit at Aboyne in the summer.

On the evening of 14 May 1940, the Secretary of State for War, Anthony Eden, made a radio broadcast inviting reasonably fit men of age 17-65 to form the Local Defence Volunteers (LDV). Within minutes of the speech being heard, across Britain, potential recruits started reporting. Exactly where and to whom they should report was often a matter of guesswork, trial and error. In Aberdeen City over 600 volunteers had enrolled by the afternoon of 16 May 1940. Students numbered among the crowds answering a call to arms reminiscent of those during Napoleonic invasion scares. With the Royal Navy and Royal Air Force still intact, a full German invasion was perhaps unlikely though still possible. Everyone had read what mayhem German parachute and glider raids caused during the Blitzkrieg, and there was the obvious risk of sabotage to key installations by agents.

The LDV, later renamed by Churchill as the Home Guard, rapidly organised itself across the nation. Initially those with previous military experience of whatever vintage took charge. North East Scotland had no shortage of retired generals and colonels. With time, as organisation, training and doctrine improved, the old and bold handed over to younger though less experienced men. Leaders were virtually elected on the basis of their current capabilities, character and energy rather than their military biographies. Even the fearsome University Secretary, Colonel Harry Butchart, now 58 years old, was said to have happily served under the command of a junior member of his University staff during his Home Guard duties.

The War Office did, in May 1940, issue guidance on the OTC/LDV relationship. OTC officers and cadets could serve with the LDV. They could, subject to their contingent commander's approval, use OTC uniform, equipment and weapons. The War Office guidance was 'permissive', letting individuals, headmasters and parents (in the case of Junior Division contingents of the OTC), and university authorities decide. In Aberdeen's case, the MEC supported Major Crichton in allowing students to serve in the LDV but not with OTC weapons

In June 1940, to avoid confusion with Officer Cadet Training Units (OCTUs), and in recognition of the fact that commissions would now be only available through the ranks, the universities' Senior Division of the Officers Training Corps was renamed the 'Senior Training Corps' (STC). It would be known as such throughout the war. The school contingents of the Junior Division OTC became the Junior Training Corps.

Harold Bowie, was in his second year of medical training at Foresterhill and reported to Ashley Road School to join the LDV. The first two parades were conducted by Professors Lockhart and Young in a gentlemanly and quietly spoken fashion. Thereafter parades were conducted in a more robust manner by a more voluble sergeant. Bowie had not heard of the STC and thus was not a member. His Home Guard duties suited him fine, less 'regimented' than the STC in his view and he continued with the 1st Aberdeen Battalion Home Guard until he graduated and was called-up in 1942. He normally paraded one evening per week. Initial guard duties were at the Gas Works armed with a 'pike', a steel rod with bayonet welded on top. Later with a rifle he would do sentry duty at the Electricity Works. A night's duty earned him a useful 4 shillings and sixpence. He was a dependable attendee for sentry duty even at Hogmanay and thus was excused some of the weekend exercises. Bowie's unit was eventually armed with Ross .303 rifles which had been in store in Canada since WW1. Training with these rifles was enlivened by frequent dangerous backfires. Bowie's company competed with other companies at the Union Grove small bore shooting club for a prize 'kitty'.

During the summer, students would do war work on farms, harvesting or helping erect anti-glider poles and wires in the fields. Some including Bowie stayed in Aberdeen to help dig out the very big holes required for bomb shelters. One day while having a lunch break from digging at Berryden

Road, they heard, then saw a German bomber dropping a stick of bombs close to King's, some falling into the sports field. Spitfires attacked the bomber which wheeled away, dropping more bombs to devastating effect on Hall Russell shipyard, before plunging into the Anderson Drive ice rink. Bowie later examined the shrapnel scars on the granite *cassies* (cobblestones) down near the damaged Neptune Bar at the harbour. Unlike the absorbent effects of French mud he would see later in his war service, Aberdeen's road surfaces sent blast and shrapnel lethally out sideways. A slightly more positive side of being 'the Granite City' was that generally only one house would be demolished by a bomb unlike elsewhere where whole red-brick or sandstone terraces would be flattened. On night duty, Bowie would sometimes see bombers caught in searchlights and 'ack-ack' fire . Bowie went on to serve as a Regimental Medical Officer in France and Germany He finishing the war with the Ox and Bucks Light Infantry as early Allied occupants of Spandau, long before onetime Deputy Fuhrer Rudolph Hess arrived after the Nuremberg Trials.

In June 1940, Crichton resigned his command and Roy Strathdee took over the contingent. The unit now had only two unembodied TA officers, Strathdee himself and Lt Henderson. They needed to find officers from the University staff and the LDV/Home Guard. The medics built up with Major Young, Professor of Pathology in command, supported by four Captains drawn from the University medical faculty. The Infantry would get Forestry Lecturer William McNeill, supported by a professor of French, a professor of Greek, and a Law lecturer. An HLI officer released for key scholastic duties at Robert Gordon College School and a Gunner subaltern released from active service on medical grounds, eventually joined the team.

Not surprisingly the scheduled Unit Inspection by Scottish Command was cancelled. The STC's officers and instructors assisted LDV/Home Guard training through the hectic summer of 1940. There was no Summer Camp that year, with training continuing in the environs of King's College.

On 20 July 1940, the Principal, Butchart, and a Major Caldwell from the War Office met in private. Caldwell had two big questions for the University. Firstly, he wanted to know if Aberdeen could accommodate an Officer Cadet Training Unit (OCTU) with a strength around 600 men. The OCTU would require about a dozen classrooms at least big enough for 50 men at a time. Rooms for sand tables and other permanent apparatus would be required. 24 hour access to all these facilities would be necessary. Additionally he would need a parade ground, preferably not on grass, offices and storerooms. After dismissing an inconvenient and time wasting option involving rooms at Marischal and a parade ground at Kings, the focus fell on King's. It could, the Principal and Butchart thought, cope. The nearby Beach Links could provide outside training space. Elphinstone Hall could act as a dining hall for 600 and space could be found for the erection of garaging for 50 trucks. As it turned out the option of establishing an OCTU at Aberdeen was never implemented, and probably just as well as it would have swamped the University facilities. However, Caldwell's second request was met.

The War Office wanted the University to run a Maths and Science Course for Royal Artillery Officer candidates. For this second discussion the small meeting was joined by the Professor of Natural Philosophy. Caldwell explained that the Army was suffering from a shortage of suitably qualified candidates for commissions in the Royal Artillery, Royal Engineers and Royal Signals. Many men who would in earlier times have wished to join the Army's technical corps were being recruited by the Royal Navy and the Royal Air Force. The normal Call-up and commissioning from the ranks would not, as had been hoped, satisfy the requirement..

It had been intended to set selection exams for boys aged 18 to 18½ in English, General Knowledge, Maths and Science. This had not been possible in the time available so certain 'approved' schools were asked to recommend boys, from which potential officers would be selected. Starting in October 1940, those selected would serve 3 months in the ranks then go to University for 6 months with a 10 day break in the middle. Royal Engineer and Royal Signals candidates would go to Oxford and Cambridge and Royal Artillery candidates to other Universities. These University Courses would thus run January to June and July to December starting in 1941. While at University these men would technically be civilians again but would be required to join the STC which would 'look after them' militarily and liaise with their parent units. With regard to this latter requirement it was pointed out to Major Caldwell that Aberdeen had never in its 28 year existence had its own Regular Adjutant. It would need one to take on the duties described. Caldwell said that one might be provided. It was also made clear that if daily pre-breakfast PT and foot drill was required, a PT Instructor would be needed too.

Discussions then moved on to the academic syllabus. Subjects covered would include maths, applied mechanics, sound, light, electricity, magnetism, theory of internal combustion engines and elementary survey. The University confirmed that it could cover the syllabus, set exams and provide the War Office with an order of merit. The best students would get the earliest places in Officer Cadet Training Units (OCTUs) and thus be commissioned ahead of those who had done less well during their short and far from normal stay at University. For the students, completion of the RA course would exempt them from their first science exams if they returned to complete degrees after the war.

The University told Caldwell that it would charge the War Office £80 per man for the whole 23 week course including board and lodging. Accommodation would need to be in local lodgings, typically costing between £1 and £2 per head per week. Part of the dependence on lodgings was due to the fact that more than 50% of the student population came from within 30 miles of the City, with many living at home. Aberdeen would be the last University to have no official student accommodation. The Crombie Hall of Residence eventually opened in 1960 as probably the first mixed hall, for male and female students, in Britain.

Aberdeen could cope with 100 RA students and 40 additional staff. Caldwell undertook to find and release anyone already called up who the University needed to teach the course.

Major Caldwell's visits to the Universities laid the groundwork for a big meeting of University Principals and Vice Chancellors in London on 31 July 1940. The country's academic leaders brought several issues of concern. Parliament had passed the Military Training Act in 1939 four months before war was declared. It applied to males aged 20 and 21 who would be required to undergo 6 months of full time military training before transfer to the Reserve. This, the UK's first peacetime conscription, would last for 3 years unless deemed no longer necessary. In the event, it was superseded by the National Service (Armed Forces) Act on the outbreak of war in September 1939. This called for the conscription of all males between the ages of 18 and 41 resident in the UK. Even the earlier Act of 1939 had caused concern in the schools and universities that their bright young men would not be put to best use in any war effort. Under the more sweeping National Service Act, conscript training would sit firmly between school and university.

Senior undergraduates including those in STCs were not entitled to any exemption from call up. Undergraduates were receiving conflicting and confusing messages as to their options. Were they, as initially instructed, to remain at their studies until called-up or were they to immediately join the Home Defence Battalions ? With all these concerns in mind the academics considered that the War Office was only just beginning to realise what an asset they had in the Universities and STCs. Indeed the War Office had been most impressed by the friendship and help experienced by the likes of Caldwell as they trawled around the universities with their 'shopping lists'.

The War Office was now in favour of the STCs conducting compulsory training for all male students. The Universities made the point that the War Office had made this more difficult than it needed to be by their policy of refusing or delaying STC officer appointments and withdrawing some equipment and funding. They pointed out that there were, and would continue to be, many undergraduates below 18 years of age. The university had no authority to force such students into military training. STCs in any case would always include people unsuitable for commissioning and the universities would have men unsuited or unwilling to serve.

A degree of 'elasticity' would be required of any scheme. The bottom line was that STCs would need skilled and up-to-date instructors, and places on courses for STC officers.

A small committee was formed to represent all the individual universities in dealings with the War Office. This committee operated at the highest level holding meetings with Churchill's Secretary for War, Anthony Eden. Eden had served as an infantry officer in WW1, had won an MC, and been the Army's youngest Brigade-Major (Chief of Staff). He had rejoined the Army as a Major in 1939 before returning to high level politics on the outbreak of war. An Oxford graduate in oriental languages he had a good understanding of University and the Army. He was joined at meetings with the University Committee by the Adjutant General, Director Military Training and appropriate Colonels from the War Office. It was agreed that the War Office would finance the University war effort. Time of course was of the essence and the universities had already agreed to start the Maths and Science Courses for RA, RE and R Signals, from January 1941. They could if needed start these in October 1940. The January 1941 date had been chosen to allow completion of the initial military training before the courses. In the interests of haste it was agreed that the first batch could start at University, then do the basic military training. Aberdeen's first course for the Royal Artillery started in October 1940 with 35 students. During the War ten such courses were held. Normal intakes consisted of between 30 and 40 students but Courses 6 and 7 had 80 and 69 students respectively. A total of 427 students went through the scheme at Aberdeen out of a national total of 4,970. In addition to their science and maths studies all the RA students did military and fitness training with the STC. The first course included soldiers released from their duties but from then on entrants were typically straight from school or short periods attached to a unit in the UK. Exams being found insufficient to select the correct people for the course, interview boards, with Strathdee as President, were set up. After the 9th course the War Office Selection Boards (WOSBs) took over. The last course was extended to cover a full academic year and allowed students to chose subjects outside maths and science. RAC and RASC candidates joined the RA students to enjoy fuller participation in University life than had been possible in the earlier crammer courses.

The men of the RA courses were welcomed into the social life of the small and still rather insular University. Most came from exotic and far off places such as the English Home Counties. It was deliberate policy for Scottish RA cadets to go to English Universities while their English counterparts came North. Although the Army paid the RA students and covered their food and accommodation costs, they were technically civilians while on the course. Uniform was not to be worn unless they were under official training with the STC. On at least one occasion several students were arrested at dance halls by Military Police (MP). The charges being wearing uniform against regulations and not having the correct ID papers. These establishments and other entertainment facilities offered entry free or at much reduced rates to servicemen in uniform. Although actually *bona fide* servicemen the RA students were disobeying standing orders for their course. After 'capture' by the Military Police they had to appear before Butchart who explained, most forcefully, but no doubt with some tongue in cheek, the error of their ways.

The First Royal Artillery Maths and Science Course 1940/41

As to existing undergraduates, as yet not called-up, guidance was still vague. Could Universities decide their own policy on compulsory part-time military training? The Universities thought a clear Government decision on this matter and the handling of Conscientious Objectors was required. Further, STCs, could simply not absorb the large increase in numbers without the provision of Regular officers, PSIs, new equipment and weapons. The War Office responded that such help would be forthcoming if the STCs became Home Defence units. As had been the case since their inception the OTC/STC had no operational role. When

172

asked whether or not Cert B holders would continue to be fast tracked to OCTUs, the reply was that this would cease in the face of such extended numbers. Training should concentrate on infantry skills at least for the first two years. A training requirement of 9 to 12 hours per week was considered bearable for first and second year full-time students but excessive for more senior students, particularly medics in their clinical years.

In the same medical year as Harold Bowie, who had joined the Home Guard rather than the STC, was Alexander Adam. He had joined the OTC from the start and had great fun and much appreciated the few shillings that could be earned. He had been one of the unfortunate 'bookless' Cert B failures in 1938/39. He had great admiration for Dr Strathdee both as a Chemistry lecturer and as the STC commander of 'Strathdee's Own'. He, like others, had to take his turn at fire watching in King's and Marischal and other Home Guard duties. For a time he was on night duty at the Railway Station as part of a decontamination squad trained to deal with the aftermath of any German gas attacks.

On holidays at home near Aberchirder, Adam was required to report to the local Home Guard unit. Once while at home he was called out to defend a crossroads during the big UK wide stand-to in September 1940. British intelligence had detected the build-up of transport shipping in the Low Countries and the concentration of Luftwaffe aircraft on coastal airfields. This information and the likely optimum moonlight and tidal conditions for invasion led to the release of Codeword 'CROMWELL' on the evening of Saturday 7 September 1940. All Home Forces including the Home Guard came to the highest state of readiness. If Alexander Adam sighted enemy parachutes he was to set off his younger brother on a sprint to HQ with the news. Adam meanwhile was on no account to load his 5 rounds of ammunition into his rifle. Imminent invasion or not, nervous and probably quite war hardened Home Guard commanders were all too aware of the hazards of friendly fire at night.

By midday on Sunday 8th September, the 'stand-down' order had been promulgated. The 'CROMWELL' incident revealed just how difficult communications, command and control were over large areas when most houses had no telephone and operator manned exchanges were far from robust. Home Guard units began to improvise their own Signals assets with landlines, field telephones, buzzers, flags and Aldis lamps. Home Guardsmen with their own motorbikes became despatch riders.

In October 1940 it seemed that another organisation might share the burden of war training with the STC. Aberdeen had researched how many students would consider joining a University Air Squadron (UAS) if one existed. The survey results from the University's 579 male students were as follows:

Faculty	Total	Willing to transfer to a UAS.
Arts	126	33
Science	136	49
Law	15	1
Medicine	302	66
Totals	579	149 (39%)

The MEC approved the formation of a UAS at Aberdeen and a senior member of staff with air experience, Professor of

Mathematics, Edward Wright, offered his services. Wright, an outstanding pure mathematician, had been appointed to his Chair in 1935, when only 29 years old.

Harold Watt, who had shared a tent with John Reid at Aboyne in 1939, was one of those who opted to move across to the UAS. Strathdee did not hide his displeasure. Watt enjoyed the training in air navigation, meteorology and the principles of flight conducted by Flying Officer Wright. He also continued his term time fire watching and summer holiday harvesting until joining the RAF.

The question of non-British members of the STC was again discussed. The OTC Regulations of 1933 still stood and called for British subjects of pure European descent. After discussion, Aberdeen's OTC policy would now accept British students without British parents, and those of non-European descent. On the question of 'alien' non British, Strathdee and Butchart argued against the more lenient view of some of the professors. A compromise would allow individually 'vetted' and approved 'aliens' to join.

In the autumn of 1940 the STC's cadet strength stood at 285, 49% of the male undergraduate total. Early war years and expansion saw the arrival of some Regular officers. Capt Strathdee had Lt Myers from the Gordons as his acting Adjutant until Oct 41 when the latter was replaced by a Cameronian Lt Kemsley. Kemsley, whom Strathdee thought an excellent man with an eye for detail and flair for admin, would be Adjutant then Training officer, serving with the contingent until Jan 45 when illness ended his duties. Sgt Atkinson Scots Guards, with the contingent since 1937, was promoted WO1. Atkinson had to take care of Quartermaster duties too.

It had been agreed with the CO of Aberdeen's Home

Guard Battalion that all students who had already joined the Home Guard could transfer to the University's own Home Guard Company. This company would be designated 'U' Company and would be officered by the STC. Students could opt to stay with their present companies if they wished but anyone in 'U' Company would be exempt from the Battalion duty roster.

In addition to those in Home Guard units, about 70 fourth and fifth year medical students were doing Air Raid Precaution (ARP) duties. Some other senior medics were members of on-call surgical teams.

Normal peacetime regulations for the OTC required a minimum of 30 drills per year for recruits and 15 drills per year for trained cadets. Strathdee hoped that students would willingly do more during wartime. The University arranged with teaching departments that Saturday mornings would be left clear for 'Senior Training Corps' training. All faculties were asked to stress the importance of joining and attending the STC. To inform the enlarged membership, arrangements were made to fix a refurbished Notice Board at the King's STC HQ. To protect sensitive information and any petty cash, the Contingent HQ acquired an old safe from the Students' Union.

In the Winter Term of 1940, the STC put its kilts in store and cadets were issued with Battle Dress (BD) which would be worn without collars or ties. 1938 pattern webbing, tin helmet and gas mask became the standard accoutrements for operational duties.

Central authority had hoped to impose the standard 'fore and aft' field service cap on the Home Guard and others. This was met with considerable hostility in Scotland where the TA Associations pressed the War Office on the matter. Most units wished to wear the headdress and cap badges of their local infantry regiments. The Director General of the Home Guard noted that '*..history shows that sooner or later we generally have to defer to Scottish feeling in the matter of dress....*' Permission for Scottish headgear was duly given on the understanding that uniformity at least within battalions was required and any differential in cost would be met by those units. Thus when stiffer head protection was deemed unnecessary the Bonnet Tam O'Shanter (TOS) or Glengarry was worn with, in Aberdeen's STC case, the Boar's Head cap badge.

As 1941 commenced, Strathdee's de facto position as Contingent Commander was confirmed and backdated His command now included 3 rifle companies, which would expand by another 2 platoons in November. Sgt Adams from the Infantry Training Centre at Gordon Barracks had been posted in as a third Sgt Instructor. As at February 1941 the STC Regular permanent staff establishment was:

HQ/Inf = 1 Maj, 1 Capt, 1 Adjt
Inf Unit = 1 x WO1, 3 x Sgts
Med Unit = 1xWO2, 1 x Sgt

The STC was now officially open to non-pure European Brits but the difference between 'eligibility' and 'suitability' was heavily stressed. 'Aliens' suitably cleared by the War Office could join but subsequent access to 'Secrets' would not be overlooked. Any coloured students from the colonies would be admitted if deemed to have potential as officers in their home Colonial Forces. The Colonial Office would process any such requests.

The new Home Guard 'U' Company under its own STC officers and staff had been declared available for emergency deployment. The Medical Unit had received Dr MacDonald to fill the second of the three establishment officer posts. STC strength now stood at 320 and additional armoury space had been acquired.

As the war progressed weapon allocation became increasingly generous. With his command being both an STC and a Home Guard unit, Strathdee now made the best of the two channels open to him to acquire weapons, stores and training pamphlets. By Sep 1941 all STC cadets had to enrol in the Home Guard. This entitled them to issues of uniforms, boots, and some allowances. They also became eligible for compensation if injured on duty. Strathdee's training routine now involved 5 hours per week, 3 hours on Saturday morning and the balance at some other time in the week. Medics who had clinical commitments on Saturdays trained on Sunday afternoons.

The primary role remained that of training potential officers for the Services. However 'Strathdee's Own' had also to be an efficient component of Aberdeen Garrison's defence arrangements. Because the STC cadets paraded each Saturday a sympathetic 4th City of Aberdeen Home Guard Battalion Commander excused them from Sunday Sub-District and Garrison exercises.

A census of the University's male student population as at 8 Dec 1941 reported as follows:

University male students	652
STC (OTC)	494
UAS	49
Exempt	27
Balance	82

The Balance of 82 was broken down as follows:

> 17 medically discharged
> 8 in other Home Guard Companies
> 4 Conscientious Objectors
> 16 under the age of 18 years
> 2 who had left University
> 7 students from 'abroad'
> 1 'foreign' student
> 12 various reasons
> 1 who had refused to join
> 8 who had not replied
> 6 who had joined since

Strathdee informed the MEC that it had been the practice to excuse anyone who failed the entry medical twice. He would now encourage men in this category to join anyway and make themselves efficient, doing themselves no harm, and indeed some good, in the meantime.

The 1941 Summer Camp took the form of a 'trek' between Deeside and Donside. Each infantry company with a detachment of medics was transported out to 18th Century Monaltrie House near the eastern end of the Pass of Ballater. Summer camps during the war were more austere affairs than in peacetime. No contract caterers with waitresses and tablecloths. The cadets did all the necessary duties and

179

fatigues themselves. After a night billeted at Monaltrie, the cadets made an early start off through the Pass, along Glen Gairn, up and over Morvern and down the Deskry Water to the River Don. The last mile or so of slogging brought them to the Lonach Hall where Mrs Smith provided a hearty meal after the 20 mile trek. The next day the company columns returned to Ballater via Corgarff Castle and the old Wade military road knotching up another 20 miles and doubtless many more blisters.

Proposals to increase the Infantry Unit by two Platoons and the Medical Unit by a second company, were approved in November 1941. A contingent of three infantry companies and two medical companies now had a total establishment of 600. Strathdee, still a member of the University Staff, and not paid by the War Office, proposed not to ask for another Captain, but to try instead for another RAMC Sgt.

By the end of December 1941, the Senatus had allocated a week before the start of each term to military training in the STC and the UAS. The notion of applying to the War Office for a grant to cover any additional student lodging costs for these weeks was dismissed by Strathdee. He pointed out that Aberdeen would be on its own if it did so, since the other Scottish Universities allocated some of their own 'teaching time' to military training.

A project to construct a parade ground and two huts for the Medics, on a site at Foresterhill, was costed at £602. The year closed with 416 cadets in the Infantry Unit and 118 in the Medical Unit. Despite the War Office's coolness on the matter, 1941 had seen the award of 99 Cert As and 61 Cert Bs, very good results in comparison to other universities.

In March 1942 the MEC heard that the Principal

himself had severely reprimanded three STC cadets who had missed one Saturday parade in February. Strathdee reported that the pre-term training weeks were very successful despite the poor weather. Only one cadet had incurred financial difficulty with additional lodging rent and he was being assisted with a grant.

With effect from April 1942 Strathdee and Major (Professor) Young became Local Lt Cols. Belated noises came from the Senior Service regarding the possibility of Sea Cadet Corps contingents in the universities. The negative response to this proposal was qualified by doubt over the number of applicants, and the unlikely success of attempting this at present with everything else that was happening

The Ministry of Labour issued an instruction that all students of military age and 'reserved' or deferred' from call-up by a Joint Recruiting Board (JRB), were to give some form of part time national service. In May 1942 Aberdeen's Senatus Academicus decided to impose this uniform obligation on all male students by insisting that only service in the STC or UAS would satisfy the requirement. It would be a condition of matriculation that all medically fit men should join the STC or UAS. Membership of the University's service contingents would remain compulsory for the next two and a half years. The regime for Aberdeen's undergraduates was pretty tough given the conflicting demands of their academic studies and compulsory part-time military training. Every student was made aware that he would not be allowed to enter for his degree exams without possessing 'Efficiency' certificates from the STC or UAS, or an exemption chit from the University Secretary, Lt Col Butchart. Strict discipline was imposed by the University authorities for those who did not meet all their STC or UAS

181

commitments.

May 1942 also brought a letter from the War Office regarding physical training standards in the STCs. The MEC considered the proposals in a joint meeting with the University's Physical Training Committee. Strathdee would need an extra compulsory parade to meet the new requirement. This could only be done on Saturday mornings and during the pre-term week. He asked if the swimming pool could be re-opened.

In early 1942 the £3 clothing grant per cadet ceased with all clothing now to be issued by Ordnance. Cadet strength now stood at 424 Infantry and 148 Medical. In May 1942 the second Medical Company was formed.

In the Spring Cert exams the following passes were attained.

Cert A Inf	152
Cert B Inf	54
Cert B Med	20

Two cadets, one of them a South African, were deemed 'unsatisfactory' and the Senatus would consider their cases before degree exams were started.

When students left the University STCs, successful commissioning candidates progressed through 'Other Rank' Training Units to OCTUs according to gradings received while in the STC. Those cadets holding Cert Bs would be graded as follows:

Grade A Outstanding - should spend little or no time in other rank training.

Grade B Well Up to Average - should spend 6 weeks in other rank training
Grade C Below Average - should spend period as necessary in other rank training

The continuous training period for 1942 was set for the period 28 Jun to 18 Jul. As in the previous year this included taking to the hills. Cadets took the train out the Deeside line to Dinnet Station from where road transport took them across to Donside and camps established in Glenbuchat and at the Lonach Hall.

In early Summer something provoked the University Senate to seek confirmation that the STC training rendered students fit for Home Guard duties in the event of an invasion. Strathdee, probably with some justifiable irritation, confirmed that 'U' Company of Aberdeen's Home Guard was more than ready to help see off any 'Gerry' who arrived uninvited by sea or air. The Junior Training Corps in schools were considered fit to be included in Home Guard orders of battle (ORBATS) and initially young JTC schoolboys had even instructed World War I veterans in musketry. The STC training mirrored that of the JTCs and indeed went further. All students joining the STC were required to sign the Home Guard's own enrolment paperwork. As all male students over 18 years old were bound to join the STC, and all those under 18 were encouraged so to do, the University was clearly fulfilling its duty to the Home Guard.

Lt Col Strathdee was considering the formation of another sub-unit. At present students other than medics could on completion of Cert A Infantry only progress to Cert B

Infantry. The addition of a Signals Unit would provide an option to students, and real benefits to the Army. Such an option would be particularly attractive to Engineering and Science students who were increasing in numbers. For example, within a Natural Philosophy (physics) class of 100, 30 to 40 students were studying radio physics as part of their degrees. Officers for such a unit could perhaps be found within the relevant departments. Any volunteers need not have Royal Signals experience as they could be sent on Army courses. The MEC submitted a formal request to the War Office for approval of a Royal Signals unit.

Unlike their fellow cadets who had to go through the OCTU procedures, the medics received automatic commissions into the RAMC on graduation. This placed great importance on the training they received in the STC. Col Young, Capt Philip and the PSIs ensured the Cert B Medical syllabus was relevant and current. Col Young developed an excellent syllabus for post Cert B (Med) training which was later adopted by the War Office and promulgated across the country.

The intensive and varied commitments of the STC continued through 1942 with the very few students found to be 'unsatisfactory' continuing to appear before the University Authorities for reprimands and dire warnings as to their future in the institution.

In Summer 1942, one man key to the maintenance of standards, Atkinson, handed over to fellow Scots Guardsman, RSM McCready, and the long line of Scots Guards RSMs began.

In September 1942 the War Office summoned all STC contingent commanders to a conference to address concerns even about 'satisfactory' products of the system. Unfortunate comparisons were being drawn at pre-OCTU assessments between STC men and other candidates. Many lacked arm and chest strength and lacked the required depth of battledrill knowledge. The STC reps pointed out that battledrills to the level apparently required were not in the STC war syllabus as approved by the War Office. They also pointed out that upper body strength in university students was unlikely in general to match those of older men coming up from the ranks or from civilian jobs reliant on physical labour. It was decided to try and introduce a 'hardening' process to STC training to better prepare university men for pre-OCTU.

The Contingent itself underwent a reorganisation of training to differentiate between the two types of cadet in the Infantry Unit. Those who would soon be definite candidates for Army commissions would now undergo 200 hours of training during drill nights and Saturday mornings and have a 3 week period of continuous training. Reserved Students whose call-up was being deferred for a lengthy period would only be required to complete 108 hours and a 2 week continuous period. Staff and other resources could therefore be concentrated upon those most likely to be seeing active service first.

STC real estate continued to expand with the use of History classrooms as unlit and unheated store rooms, and the use of a garage behind the 'groundsman's old house'.

Detailed management of a student's available time was constantly required to satisfy the competing needs of teaching faculties, the STC and the UAS. For example the Natural Philosophy Department, the STC and the UAS were involved in sorting out double bookings for BSc Agriculture and Forestry students on Wednesday afternoons. Cancellation of practicals suited UAS cadets but not the remaining STC cadets who couldn't do them at any other time. Another example arose in the announcement by the Medical Faculty that there would be a relaxation in the compulsory training required of final year medics. Strathdee described this action in an angry note to the Dean of the Medical Faculty as 'premature, irregular and discourteous'. It was for the STC to promulgate such decisions.

In December the MEC considered the case of another 'unsatisfactory' cadet. Despite warnings a geology student had absented himself from one set of Friday and Saturday parades to prepare for exams. Strathdee was unimpressed, saying the man had had all summer to prepare. The student's defence was that he could only access the geology specimens collection during the day and having a home in distant Wick had complicated matters further. The MEC wished him to be sent down from University but this was later relaxed to a £5 fine by the Senatus.

January 1943 saw the Ministry of Labour and National Service conduct medical examinations of all those liable to call-up. Of 671 Aberdeen cadets, 590 received the top grading.

Although no official War Office sanction for a Signals Unit had been received by October 1942, the Chief Signals Officer at Scottish Command was already informally arranging the loan of suitable personnel, equipment and vehicles. JD Stewart, an engineering lecturer from Robert Gordon Technical College had been recommended as an officer for the Signals Unit. A Sgt Instructor and a Cpl Instructor had arrived with some signals kit and about 40 existing cadets were eligible to join the new unit. The War

Office eventually authorised a signals unit with an established strength of 53 cadets if the required resources were in place. To compensate the infantry unit reduced to 3 companies. Requirements all met, the new signals sub-unit, which was already up and running, started officially in the 1943 Spring Term. Later Strathdee, noting that most of those who achieved Cert B in the Signals Unit actually went on to commissions in the Royal Electrical and Mechanical Engineers (REME), pondered whether or not a REME unit might have been a better choice. The early years of the Second World War had brought the realisation that the existing repair system was not able to support the massive scale of equipment being deployed in every theatre. In 1941 the War Cabinet directed an enquiry into the employment of technical manpower in the Services. As a result of the recommendations of this enquiry, the REME was formed on 1st October 1942. However having his own signals capability was vital for Strathdee's Home Guard role which, in 1943, was significantly upgraded.

On 10 February 1943 the University's Home Guard 'U' Company of the 4th (City of Aberdeen) Battalion was subsumed by a whole University battalion designated the 9th City of Aberdeen (University) Battalion. The new Signal Unit had arrived in time to provide wireless and cable communications for the much expanded organisation. The new Battalion had a total permitted establishment of 700, consisting of an HQ, 3 Rifle Companies and a Medical Company. Final year medical students however, on any stand-to of the Home Guard, came under District Medical Staff. They would be deployed to assist Medical Officers in Casualty Reception Stations.

The change of status had many advantages and some

disadvantages. The STC staff had to take on the orderly room work formerly done by HQ 4th Battalion. The STC's training had tended to focus at platoon level. Now competence in procedures, drills and tactics at battalion level was required. Many extra Sunday parades were needed for battalion level exercises. Across the Don, around Scotstown Moor, Shielhill, Leuchlands, Corby Loch and Perwinnes Moss cadets learned how to fight as a whole battalion. Defensive tactics concentrated on those required to channel any enemy forces into killing areas for destruction or capture. Offensive exercises included the successful surprise 'capture' of Dyce Airfield.

The University Battalion's weapons included the Army standard Short Magazine Lee Enfield (SMLE) .303 rifle, Bren Guns, 2" Mortars, Boys 0.55 inch anti-tank rifles, 0.45 Thompson Sub Machine Guns, and later 9mm Sten Guns. Beyond the official weapon inventory the Home Guard prided itself in an array of improvised grenades, Molotov Cocktails, mines, flamethrowers and booby traps. For urban fighting the Home Guard weapon of choice was the shotgun loaded with solid shot. Participation in the Home Guard role gave students wider opportunities in weapon handling and battle training facilities set-up across Scotland by static and mobile training teams. Derelict properties at Footdee (Fittie) were put to use by the Aberdeen Town Fighting School.

On the night of 21 April 1943, nearly thirty Dornier bombers left their temporary forward base at Stavanger in Norway and crossed the North Sea reaching the coast just north of Aberdeen around dusk. The city, a relatively soft target, had been chosen to demonstrate improvements in the Luftwaffe's lethality after a serious of air war setbacks had attracted Hitler's displeasure. After three quarters of an hour the Germans departed unscathed having dropped high explosive, phosphorous and oil bombs and terrorised the streets with machine gun and cannon strafing runs. A total of 125 people were killed in this single raid. The north of the city bore the brunt of attacks. The dead included 27 soldiers at Gordon Barracks, and 19 killed by a single bomb on Bedford Road. In the aftermath of Aberdeen's worst raid, the Home Guard provided escorts and route lining detachments for funeral corteges.

Not all Luftwaffe crews were convinced by the Nazi cause. In April 1943 the Air Squadron and the University Maths Department lost Edward Wright to war work of considerably greater consequence. He had been invited by RV Jones to join the scientific intelligence war against the Germans. Only a month after leaving Aberdeen, Wright was accompanying Jones on the night sleeper back north on an urgent visit to Dyce aerodrome. The previous day a German Junkers 88 night fighter had landed at Dyce. The Junkers crew had decided to defect and been lucky enough to encounter two Canadian Spitfire pilots prepared to risk escorting them over Aberdeen and into Dyce. Fate smiled on them again when Dyce's anti-aircraft fire was not as accurate as it might have been. For Jones and Wright, the chance to examine the radar and other capabilities of the aircraft hurriedly wheeled into a hangar, was a real coup in the intelligence war.

Wright later helped Jones prepare Bomber Command for the first use of the 'Window' chaff radar counter-measure. Wright and others lectured at two or three Bomber stations every day for a fortnight. For a full account of Window; countering German bombing navigation devices in the 'Battle of the Beams'; uncovering Hitler's 'V' weapons; and other projects read RV Jones's *'Most Secret War'* the details of which appear in the Sources section. Jones would take the Chair of Natural Philosophy at Aberdeen after the war, assisted by his wartime colleagues and no doubt the recommendations of Churchill. Practical assistance came from old OTC stalwart Colonel Harry Butchart, when, as Secretary, he somehow managed to tell Jones between the interview room door and the chair, to speak up at the interview. The selection panel had been concerned that the quietly spoken Jones would not be up to controlling first year classes. RV Jones's overly enthusiastic response to the covert advice apparently quite shocked some of the professors. Wright and Jones would be strong supporters of the service units during their post war tenures.

Summer Camp 1943, again in the hills, was based in Glenbuchat. In glorious weather, training focussed on those cadets who soon would be called-up to the Army. The new scheme, discussed the previous autumn, had been introduced to bring added incentive to dedicated membership of the STCs. The War Office undertook to accelerate progress through the pre-OCTU process for candidates who attended more parades and a 'hardening-up' course at summer camps prior to them reaching call-up age. About 50 Aberdeen cadets accepted the War Office 'contract', worked hard during term and at camp, ending up in great physical shape. Having upheld their side of the deal the men waited through the summer of '43 for the expected call-up to much reduced pre-OCTU training and the chance to go for commissions. Weeks passed without news until the reason for delay became apparent.

The Summer and Autumn of 1943 had seen frantic

negotiations between the Services and the Ministry of Labour. In 1940 Winston Churchill had made Ernest Bevin, then General Secretary of the Transport and General Workers Union, his Minister of Labour and National Service. The Emergency Powers Act gave Bevin authority over everyone, male and female, between 14 and 64 years of age. With the backing of the unions he had deployed the nation's human resources to address the desperate situation in the munitions and other industries, in transport and in food supply. The manning and output of the coal mines had been a concern from the outset. Many miners had left the pits when called up under their Reserve and TA commitments or had volunteered for the Forces. Others had been allowed to transfer their labour into better paying factories. The result was that Bevin was obliged to use the call-up as a means of getting more young men underground and extracting precious coal. Thus, in December 1943, when the long awaited call-up envelopes were delivered, four of Aberdeen's 50 'hardened' STC Army candidates received the news that they were to be coal miners.

They had been selected by draw using their National Service Registration Certificate numbers. Each draw selected one in ten men. On this first occasion and sometimes later, two draws were made thereby selecting for the mines one in five of all those called-up. This was the first use of a ballot since the militia ballots of the late 18th Century which had enhanced recruitment to the exempted Volunteers. There was no exemption from 'Bevin's Tombola'. It selected men from all classes, and with all aspirations for war service. Even men already provisionally accepted for critical trades in the Services were grabbed for the mines. There was an appeal process where parents, schoolmasters, JTC, STC, and ATC

191

officers could present evidence, but appellants were very rarely successful. Two of Aberdeen's men won their appeals and went on to the perils of war service above ground. The other two became Bevin Boys for the duration of the war and beyond. Strathdee was furious about this treatment of his cadets and regretted that the affair harmed any perceived prestige and benefit associated with dedicated STC membership.

From the start of the University's battalion level training it was clear that more junior officers were required to lead the platoons. During the life of the OTC to date, the commissioning of cadets from inside the contingent had often been considered as a way to fill vacancies. Other OTC's had adopted this strategy but Aberdeen had never been keen on the idea of placing student officers over other students. It was considered that morale, discipline and fun would suffer. However in the absence of any hope of filling platoon commander vacancies by any other means, seven selected members of the third year medical class with Cert B (Inf) qualifications were gazetted as Home Guard 2Lts. Subsequently 3 cadets from each of the two succeeding medical years received Home Guard commissions. The new 2Lts learned the necessary tactical and administrative skills on various courses, for example on the Battle Training Course at Moncrieff House, Bridge of Earn.

*Aberdeen's new 2Lts Gardiner and Copland enjoy a break
with older Home Guard officers from Glasgow.
Battle Training Course, Bridge of Earn, 1944.*

Because of its relative youth and fitness, the University
Battalion was given the role of mobile reserve for Aberdeen
Garrison and the wider Aberdeen Sub-District. The latter
responsibility had them exercising rapid deployment to
defensive positions on the Ythan Estuary. For two years the
STC had unsuccessfully attempted to get more transport. The
Home Guard role entitled them to personnel transport
vehicles, a Utility vehicle and a 15 Cwt Truck. The increase
in the vehicle establishment made routine, exercise and camp
administration much easier. The unit could now organise its

own lift of rations from the RASC depot. More vehicles meant more drivers and two women students Julian Dodds and May Johnson volunteered as drivers. Two other women students reinforced the Battalion clerical team.

The Home Guard role had brought the STC into closer contact with the HQ staffs of Highland District, Aberdeen Sub-District and Aberdeen Garrison. Visits to his students' duty and exercise locations, and frequent liaison trips to other HQs meant Captain McNeill was heavily reliant upon his own motor car. Indeed he only kept the car to fulfil his STC and Home Guard duties. He was finding it all a bit costly. The MEC agreed to recompense him with £15, representing half of his total annual motoring costs.

For other running costs the War Office paid the University for some but not all of its outlay on heating, lighting, electricity and cleaning.

The University had also made available land it had acquired from the old Powis Estate west of Kings College. Here a 30 yard weapon range and an assault course had been constructed. Later in 1944 a STC parade ground was prepared at a cost of £275. Prior to that, drill had been conducted along University Road or on the King's playing fields. The latter location saw cadets being deliberately heavy footed within sight of the groundsman who was glad when they moved their turf destroying activities beyond the Powis Gates.

Fitness and competition featured highly in training and the inter-unit swimming gala was held in the Robert Gordons swimming pond. All STC cadets underwent regular medicals. Men deemed 'not fit' attracted no grants from the War Office but Strathdee undertook to train them anyway and do them some good in the process

Powis Gate in 2012
An impressive entrance to the Senior Training Corps
range and assault course during World War II.

The Contingent's expansion during the war is evident in the strengths table produced in November 1943:

Year	Inf	Med	Signals	STC Total	RA Course
39/40	120	50		170	
40/41	245	98		343	72
41/42	425	151		576	74
42/43	373	163	53	589	118
43/44	328	158	49	535	75

Training output as measured by Certificates awarded was as follows:

	Certificates				
	A	B	B	B	
	(Inf)	(Inf)	(Med)	(Sigs)	Totals
Year					
39/40	38	21			59
40/41	99	42	19		160
41/42	268	123	24		415
42/43	151	97	59	42	349
Totals	556	283	102	42	983

Disciplinary action against cadets for failure to attend a parade or persistent lateness was still not delegated to the Contingent Commander. Discipline remained a University function using the established system of Senatus decisions and the right of appeal to the University Court. The Principal continued to issue severe reprimands for missed parades. Transgressors were left in no doubt that any further indiscipline would cause their expulsion from the STC and the University.

In the Autumn of 1943, six specially selected cadets went to the Seaforth & Cameron Highlanders Infantry Training Depot at Fort George for three weeks of weapon training. The results from this detachment were very satisfactory and two further detachments were sent, in 1944 and 1945, to the Infantry Training Centre's new location in Elgin.

In March 1944 Albert Regensburger a medical student, and Hans Meyer, an engineering student, joined the unit as officially approved 'aliens'.

The training programme for the summer term was lightened for students preparing for end of year exams. Saturday morning parades were cancelled and replaced by two Saturday range days and three Sundays devoted to Home Guard exercises. The Physical Training hour could now include Highland Dancing.

Among those graduating MBChB in 1944 was STC Pipe Band drummer Andrew Shivas. Shivas was also a leading light in the University Dance Orchestra. After service with the Merchant Navy as Ship's Surgeon, 'rounding the Horn' twice under steam, he returned to Aberdeen joining the Rowett Institute staff. He helped revitalise the University's Pipes and Drums in the post war years, continuing to play an active role in Pipe Bands, and judging at drumming competitions. He would command a TA General Hospital and Edinburgh UOTC.

Summer camp 1944 was again held in Donside, this time on land belonging to the Colquhonnie Hotel, with messing being provided at the Lonach Hall. They listened to the news of the successful Allied Landings in Normandy. After stiff resistance around the beachheads the Germans started to withdraw back through France. After fierce breakout battles the 51st Highland Division was tasked to take Le Havre. That allowed them the satisfaction, on 1 September 1944, of retaking the town of St Valery the scene of the first 51st's surrender four years earlier. The Divisional HQ and brigades were deployed in their predecessors' positions and a few days later the Divisional massed pipes and drums conducted a ceremonial Beat Retreat.

Although there was still a great deal of fighting to do, the River Rhine to be crossed, and a German surrender forced, things back in the UK began to relax. In October 1944 the Ministry of Labour and National Service no longer required male students to undergo compulsory part time service in the Home Guard or STC as a condition for reserved status. Accordingly the University Senate confirmed that the STC and UAS were to revert to a voluntary basis. Unsurprisingly numbers began to drop but unit life continued with Strathdee's command tour extended for two years. Mr MacPhail Massie presented a fine snuff horn as a trophy for open range shooting. On 25 October 1944 the Senatus formally recorded its appreciation of the services of the contingent's officers.

In most other contingents Permanent Staff Officers conducted the training. In Aberdeen, unembodied TA officers and their NCOs had trained their own companies. In recognition of their efforts Sgts Henderson and Hendry received certificates for good service. Major Jimmy Henderson had been Assistant Adjutant for the Reception Unit, Infantry Company Commander, and 2IC of the Home Guard Battalion. He too, in December 1944 received a Certificate of Good Service. Major McNeill, who led most of the infantry training during the war, was rewarded with an MBE.

The 9th City of Aberdeen (University) Battalion Home Guard stood down. To fund celebrations for the Stand Down Strathdee sought grants to compensate for the STC's lack of funds in comparison to other battalions. At a Guest Night marking the Stand Down, a pipe major's pipe banner, presented in 1939 by Sir George Adam Smith, was flown for the first time. Smith, the OTC's founding father, chaplain and loyal supporter, had died at home in Balerno, in 1942, at the age of 85.

On 14 December 1944 the War Office, in an attempt to encourage recruitment and retention in the now voluntary STC, reduced the training commitments. A capitation grant would be issued for every cadet who was physically fit, attended not less than thirty 45 minute training periods, and underwent a weapon training course. Medics in their clinical years would be exempt the latter. All cadets would be required to attend at least 10 days of continuous training up to a maximum 14 days. Not so positive, and typically British, was the later announcement that since the STC no longer had operational commitments, there would be no free issue of boots. Strathdee's reaction can be imagined and it was swiftly pointed out through COMEC that the continued issue of proper clothing and equipment was essential to maintain morale and numbers.

On 8 May 1945 the Allies accepted the unconditional surrender of German Forces. Celebrating the good news and with wartime tensions swiftly abating, the Contingent went to Fochabers for its Summer Camp, where Italian POWs did the necessary camp fatigues. The Japanese, finally convinced of the hopelessness of their situation by atomic bomb detonations at Hiroshima and Nagasaki, surrendered in August.

The University and its Training Corps had played a full and diverse role in national survival and eventual victory. Staff with useful skills had again been seconded to the Services, Government Departments and Industry. Examples include the already described secondment of Professor Wright to join future Professor of Natural Philosophy, RV

Jones in the 'Most Secret' War. A predecessor of Jones, Professor of 'Nat Phil' and astronomer John Carroll was seconded to the Admiralty Department of Science and Research in 1942 to work on early computing and numerical analysis.

In addition to the 427 RA students who attended the Maths and Science Courses, 367 cadets passed straight from the STC into the Services and around 250 medical graduates were commissioned directly into the RAMC. As in the First War, University staff, students and alumni served all over the world. Some died in the cause.

In Memoriam

The University Roll of Honour records 182 men who gave their lives in World War Two. 85 of these served with the RAF. The RAF like the Royal Artillery ran special cadet courses at the University. Unlike the listings for World War One, no photographs of those listed were collected. Instead a picture of the King's Chapel Memorial Window is included with each entry in the Roll. As for World War One, time spent browsing the University's online Roll of Remembrance for World War Two will be time well spent for those interested in the backgrounds and war service of all those who died.

The following two entries, include specific mention of the OTC. Let them represent all those who, while undertaking their degree courses before or during the war, passed through the OTC/STC and gave their lives in World War Two.

Mackenzie, Alistair Campbell,
Lieutenant, The Argyll and Sutherland Highlanders.
Son of Donald William and Margaret Mackenzie, Ashley Gardens, Aberdeen ; born Aberdeen, 1918 ; educated at Aberdeen Grammar School. He entered the University to take Economics, and became an enthusiastic member of the OTC., distinguishing himself in shooting. In 1939 he was commissioned in the Argyll and Sutherland Highlanders, but later volunteered for Commando duties and took part in the raid on the Lofoten Islands. He lost his life in an accident at Troon, Ayrshire, on 20 August 1941.

Robertson, John Kennedy,
Sergeant, Royal Air Force.
Son of John and Jessie Langlands Kennedy Robertson, 10 Linksfield Road, Aberdeen ; educated at Robert Gordon's College. In 1940 he entered the University as a student in the Faculty of Arts and joined the OTC. Volunteering for the Royal Air Force he became a Bomb-aimer, and later was trained to intercept German messages during flying operations. He lost his life when the bomber in which he was flying was shot down over Germany on 26 November 1943. He was buried in St. Trond Cemetery, Belgium, and later removed to the British Cemetery at Louvain, Belgium.

The following entries record the sacrifice of those who came to Aberdeen for the Royal Artillery, Maths and Science Courses and who, while there, were very much considered to be members of 'Strathdee's Own'.

Banks, Joseph Eric,
Second Lieutenant, Royal Artillery.

Home address Linden Lawn, Linden Road, Halifax; on joining the Army he attended a R.A. Cadets' course at the University in 1941. He lost his life in this country as the result of an accident in March 1942. Buried at Horsforth Cemetery.

Barlow, Rollo Alexander,
Captain, Royal Artillery.

Son of John Miles Staveley Barlow and Margaret Barlow, Bexhill-on-Sea ; born Kandy, Ceylon, 1922 ; educated at Sutton Valence School, Maidstone. After joining up he attended the R.A. Cadets' course at the University in 1940. He served with the Eighth Army from Alamein to Italy, being awarded the Military Cross, and later took part in the operations on the continent. At the close of the war he joined the British Borneo Defence Unit and died as the result of a car accident in Sarawak on 1 January 1946. Buried at Labuan War Cemetery.

Bingham, George Hexter,
Lieutenant, Royal Artillery.

Son of Ernest George Bingham, Major, Indian Army and Annie Adeline Bingham, of Beckenham, Kent; born Wellington, South India, 1922 ; educated at St. Dunstan's College, Catford. He joined the Army in 1941 and attended the R.A. Cadets' course at the University. He then volunteered for service in the Far East, and was killed by a mine in Burma on 21 January 1945. Buried at Taukkyan War Cemetery.

202

Boileau, Brandram Francis Etienne,
Gunner, Royal Artillery

Son of Brandram Francis Shirwill Boileau and Ness MacKenzie Boileau, of Cranleigh, Surrey.; born Darjeeling, 1 February 1925 ; educated at Cranleigh School. Joining the Army in 1942 he attended the R.A. Cadets' course at the University in 1943. In the following year he served with his regiment in Western Europe, and on the 22 November 1944 died of wounds as a result of driving over a mine. He is buried at the Mierlo British Cemetery in Holland.

Blincow, Joseph Sydney,
Lieutenant, Royal Artillery.

Son of Joseph Wallace Blincow and Constance May Blincow, of Bedford; born Bedford, 2 March 1924; educated at Bedford School. He joined the Army in 1942, and in the same year attended the R.A. course at the University. Later on he served in Western Europe, and was killed in action on 10 July 1944. Buried at Banneville-la-Campagne War Cemetery.

Brimmell, Edmund Stuart Byron,
Officer Cadet,
Royal Artillery.

Son of Edmund Richard James Brimmell and Violet Byron Brimmell, of North Harrow, Middlesex.; born Altrincham, Cheshire, 24 January 1926; educated at Watford Grammar School and the Regent Street Polytechnic. He entered the Army in 1943 and in the same year attended the R.A. Cadets' course at the University. Later he went to India, and was taking a course for Officer Cadets at Deolali when he fell ill and died on 1 August 1945. He is buried in the Military Cemetery at Deolali.

Firth, John Robert Colleton,
Lieutenant, Royal Artillery.

Son of Major Firth, Royal Artillery; On joining the Army he attended a course for R.A. Cadets at the University. In the course of the fighting in Western Europe he was severely wounded and died on 24 September 1944. Buried at Valkenswaard War Cemetery.

Fisher, Allan,
Lieutenant, Royal Artillery.

Son of Robert Noel and Nellie May Fisher, Elibank Road, Eltham ; born Stockwell, 2 January 1922 ; educated at Woolwich County School. He entered the Territorial Army in 1939 and served for a time in Anti-Aircraft Defence Units, after which he attended the R.A. Cadets' course at the University. He was then sent to the Middle East where he served until his death from typhoid fever on 23 June 1943. Buried at Suez War Memorial Cemetery

Macdonald, Ian Lester,
Lieutenant, Royal Artillery.

Son of Alexander Macdonald, C.B.E., Santiago de Chile ; born 6 April 1923; He joined the Army and attended the R.A. Cadets' course at the University in 1941. He later transferred to the Black Watch and was killed in action on the Western Front on 25 February 1945. Buried at Rheinberg War Cemetery.

Milne, Robert,
Lieutenant, Royal Artillery.

Son of Col. Robert and Lilian Cecile Milne, Old Alresford, Kent ; born 5 January 1924; he attended the R.A. Cadets' course at the University and was gazetted to the 151st Field Regiment, Royal Artillery. After a long spell of service he died of wounds received in action in North-West Europe on 1 March 1945. Buried at Groesbeek Canadian War Cemetery.

Power, Michael Edward,
Officer Cadet, Royal Artillery.

Son of E. J. Power, Welwyn Garden City ; born Slough, 1925; educated at Bishop's Stortford School. He joined the Royal Artillery in 1943 and attended the R.A. course at the University. On 13 June 1945 he died at Deolali in India where he was undergoing a training course for Officer Cadets. Buried at Kirkee War Cemetery.

Primhak, Leonard,
Lieutenant, Indian Mountain Regiment.

Son of Jack and Phyllis Primhak, London ; born Greenwich, 1923 ; educated at City of London School. He joined the Royal Artillery in 1942 and took the Cadets' course at the University. In December 1945 he arrived with his battery at Surabaya and was killed on 17 January 1946 while leading a reconnaissance patrol. He is buried at Kembang Koening Cemetery, Surabaya.

Silly, James Lovitt,
Lieutenant, Special Air Service Regiment.

Son of Air Commodore Benjamin James Silly and Frances Fanny Silly, Berkhamsted ; born Berkhamsted, 1924 ; educated at Berkhamsted School. In October 1942 he joined the Royal Artillery and attended a Cadets' course at the University. Later he took part in several operations, and in his last one in September 1944 was dropped by parachute on the Vosges Mountains. He was captured by the Germans and kept a prisoner till 22 October, when he was shot. Buried at Moyenmoutier Communal Cemetery.

Smith, Sydney Robertson,
Lieutenant, Glider Pilot Regiment.

Son of Sydney Smith, Sheffield ; born Dundee, 19 October 1922 ; educated at Aberdeen and Manchester Grammar Schools. He entered the Army in 1941 and attended a course for R.A. Cadets at the University. He was commissioned in the Royal Artillery but was afterwards transferred to the Glider Pilot Regiment. On D-Day he took part in airborne landings in Normandy and on 18 September 1944 at Arnhem. Two days later he was killed by a sniper.

Thorpe, Douglas Sidney,
Lance Bombardier,
Royal Horse Artillery.

Son of Charles Edward and Grace Florence Thorpe, of Felixstowe, Suffolk. Chartered Accountant.; born Felixstowe, 3 January 1922 ; educated at Ipswich School and then articled to a Chartered Accountant. He joined the Army in 1939, and later attended the R.A. Cadets' course at the University. He was killed in action in North Africa on 15 January 1943 while serving with a battery. Buried at Tripoli War Cemetery.

Chapter 6

NATIONAL SERVICE, WINTER WARFARE
AND WOMEN
1946-1961

Once more Britain emerged from war with battered finances, industries, and transport systems. Rationing in one form or another would continue until 1954. The notion of Empire was clearly at an end but Britain still had considerable global interests and responsibilities. Meeting European and Overseas aspirations, as in former times, would demand lots of people in deployed and reserve forces.

Immediately after the cessation of hostilities women conscripts were released. Men were demobilised between 1945 and 1949 depending on their age, length of war service and possession of any key skills needed to rebuild damaged cities. National Service continued after the war with a new Act taking effect in 1948. The last National Serviceman would join in 1960 and leave in 1963. National Servicemen would be involved in protracted active service in the Korean War, the Malayan and Cyprus Emergencies, Kenya, and Palestine. Some would be involved in the short Suez Crisis of 1957 which removed any doubt about Britain's place in the new world order.

While the Western and Russian armies watched each other across the line they had reached when Germany surrendered, the Cold War was taking shape in the Greek Civil War, 1946-49. Britain poured sorely needed cash into training and other support before handing the expensive mission over to the USA. Bitter struggles ended with Greece in the Western sphere of influence rather than the Communist one. Confronting and containing Communism would be the purpose of most military activity for the next four decades. The North Atlantic Treaty Organisation (NATO) formed in 1949. The first NATO Secretary General stated that the goal was *'to keep the Russians out, the Americans in, and the Germans down'.*

The University Senior Training Corps across the country faced considerable new challenges to which they would need to adapt. The fundamental purpose of the STCs was under discussion and any clarity on future plans from Whitehall officialdom was absent. There was, as after World War One, the inevitable reaction against military life as men concentrated on restarting their education, careers and family lives. With ongoing National Service, Contingents would need to simultaneously provide worthwhile training for different categories of student. Some would have completed their full time National Service and have a part time commitment to complete. Others would be too young to start National Service. Some would have their National Service deferred until they completed their studies. A few would still welcome preparation for Regular Army careers.

Whatever the future held, Contingents faced immediate shortages of permanent staff and accommodation. To start addressing all the challenges of the post war world, a conference of Scottish STC COs and Adjutants was held at Perth in November 1945. The main conclusion from the Conference was that the training emphasis should be on 'Leadership' rather than technical 'special to arm' skills. 'Cap Badge' training could and would be done after cadets left University for the Army. With cadet numbers low in all the Contingents, the conference delegates decided to collectively lobby Scottish Command for a 1946 Summer

Camp location. Castle Park Barracks, a wartime Officer Cadet Training Unit (OCTU) in Dunbar, was allocated for 1946 and 1947. Aberdeen sent 5 officers and only about 20 cadets in 1946, but nearly 80 cadets in 1947. Students were apparently dismayed at first not to be camping but soon saw the domestic advantages. From here on, Annual Camps would be in hutted rather than canvas accommodation. At Dunbar, local military history was brought into the programme with the study and spirited re-enactment of Cromwell's 1650 victory.

Back in the 1890s, WO Duncan of U Company had thought the involvement of the 'professors' undesirable. However, since 1912, the Contingent had relied on unembodied TA officers from the academic staff to keep things going and Dunbar proved the point. The very small sub units were commanded as follows. Capt Stewart, a Maths and Natural Philosophy Lecturer, led the Signals. Capt Dr Morgan led the Medics. McNeill, Forestry Lecturer, led the Infantry and the overall Contingent. A fortnight's tactical training was conducted with the assistance of Professor of French, Capt Roe and Lecturer in History, Maj Henderson. They were assisted by Regulars Maj Macarthur HLI, and the RSM WO1 McReady SG.

Aberdeen's MEC convened frequently to discuss the future including financial aspects. Capitation grants to the unit were being set at £3 per cadet with an additional £1 per Cert A pass and another £2-00 per Cert B pass. The MEC concluded that merely 'certificate hunting' to acquire funds did not boost the overall attractiveness or efficiency of the contingent. It was also agreed that the STC should resist calls to work closely with the younger members of the Army Cadet Force and the Air Training Corps. This was considered inappropriate given the difference in ages, educational standards and entrance requirements. Any proposals to pool STC instructors with those of the ACF and the ATC were to be refused. Combined duties of this sort would commit instructors to extended day and night duties and would give them at least two 'bosses' with conflicting priorities.

The STC now occupied accommodation at King's, Marischal and Foresterhill. During the War the University had given the STC the use of Powis Gardens for training. This strip of land, originally part of the Powis Estate, ran from the imposing minaret towers of Powis Gate opposite King's College, through to Bedford Road. By the end of the war Powis Gardens boasted a 30 yard open firing range, an assault course, and a levelled parade ground. The University Air Squadron had also established itself there. Indeed inter-Service friction was created by the UAS setting up their Link Trainer dynamic cockpit simulator next to the Firing Range. Strathdee was not amused. More buildings were needed and Strathdee and his staff scoured Banchory Lodge and other locations in the North East for any still serviceable and yet moveable huts, now lying abandoned by their wartime occupants. Nothing suitable being found, a letter on the topic was sent off to the War Office. Another missive to Whitehall sought reassurance on the situation regarding liability for any injuries incurred during training.

The RAF was in post war turmoil too. In April 1946 the Principal was moved to protest against the proposed mothballing of the University Air Squadron especially since Aberdeen UAS had the highest membership in Scotland.

The Universities, desperate for clarity and firm commitments about the future, continued a heated dialogue with the War Office. Edinburgh University made it clear that unless any new scheme included benefits for those students gaining 'Efficiency' status, it would discontinue its STC. Aberdeen chose to follow Edinburgh's lead and sought the support of its University MP (and first Infantry Unit commander) Sir John Boyd Orr. Butchart and Strathdee would take the fight to a special COMEC meeting in Sep 1947.

In preparation for COMEC, Aberdeen's committee deliberated on the future organisation and function of the Corps. Was it advisable for students to do National Service before or after University given that men matured at different rates? The STC's would need to cater for both instances and concentrate on training those likely to become officers. The 1947 COMEC made it very clear that the existence of individual contingents and the Corps as a whole depended on definite explicit statements regarding the benefits of voluntary military training at Universities within the whole framework of National Service and defence policy.

In 1947 the Labour Government's new Secretary of State for War, 'Manny' Shinwell, was pressing for the recruitment of 100,000 men to bring the TA up to 150,000. As incentives a 50% increase in tax free bounty levels was announced, as was payment for weekend training. It remained to be seen how the authorities would countenance students serving out their TA commitment in University contingents rather than in local TA units.

Shinwell's call to arms reflected the fact that the TA, having lost all its 2nd line divisions and some 1st line divisions after Victory over Japan (VJ) Day in August 1945, was restructuring and trying to expand once more. Some 1st line divisions, only very recently disbanded, were hurriedly reinstated. The TA would keep its original role of supplying complete divisions until 1967. The TA would for a while consist of six infantry divisions, two armoured divisions and an airborne division. In 1955 all the TA divisions became infantry and the parachute division reduced to an independent parachute brigade group. The TA would also provide most of the country's air defence until the coming of the Thunderbird missiles in 1959. The Thunderbird would be the Army's first British designed and built missile.

Late in 1947 the University still awaited responses from the War Office and Boyd Orr MP regarding the STC's future. The UAS however had been reprieved after Principal Fyffe's direct intervention with the Air Ministry. It was set up with new rules regarding commitment to flying hours, ground training and emergency call-up liability. A clear path from University to RAF Commissions was also set out, with apparently far fewer hurdles and conditions than appeared to be the case for Army candidates. All this made the STC's uncertain future even more galling and frustrating to those keeping the Contingent going.

At last in March 1948 a letter came out from the War Office, Horse Guards, Whitehall setting out the future of the Senior Training Corps. Indicative of the post war spread of the Army was the distribution of the new policy to British Army HQs scattered across the globe including those of occupation forces still in Japan and Austria, and the HQ British Troops France. Senior Division Contingents would now belong to the University Training Corps (Territorial Army). Students in the UTC(TA) would be paid and receive tax free training bounties if they satisfied the rules regarding attendance and progress.

From 1 April 1948 the Junior Division of the Officers Training Corps was amalgamated with the school sea and air

214

cadets into the Combined Cadet Force (CCF). One factor in the reorganisation is said to have been the Labour Government's opinion that having 'Officer' in the full title of such contingents was 'elitist'. It is probable that this view also led to the dropping of 'Officer' from the title of University contingents formerly of the Senior Division OTC. Elitist or not the CCF school contingents would continue to be major feeders of pipers, drummers and the purely military minded to the University Contingent. A large proportion of Aberdeen's Student Soldiers had always come from the Aberdeen Grammar and Robert Gordons. These two schools and the University each had their own sub-units within the pre-World War I, 4th Gordons. During the Second World War the three pipe bands had cooperated when numbers were low. This was helped by two of the three Pipe Majors being MacTaggart brothers. The two local CCF contingents, would, with other CCFs from further afield, supply Aberdeen's UTC(TA) with experienced recruits. For a short post-war period in Aberdeen a third school, the Central School (later the 'Academy' which moved to Hazlehead), had a CCF with a similar relationship to the University Corps.

The new policy recognised that some undergraduates and deferred students would not have completed National Service. Some would have done their full time service and have no compulsory TA liability. They should receive advanced training either as officers or in technical subjects allied to the available University faculty expertise From 1950 undergrads would arrive at University having served one year with the Colours but still being required to serve out some part-time commitment with the TA. It was recognised that for the ex-National Serviceman, basic military training with a UTC would not be a great attraction. Any cadets who had not yet done National Service should be trained with a view, if they were suitable material, to getting commissioned early in their service. Bizarrely, given this stated need to assess 'suitability', the War Office was considering dropping the Cert A and Cert B system given that under the new scheme they would have no value. Commanding Officers would be asked to devise their own exams in order to maintain standards.

With the future structure and organisation of the Contingent now set out, if not completely settled in all its detail, Roy Strathdee submitted his letter of resignation to the MEC. His command tenure had been extended twice and it was time to go. 'Strath' would be hard to replace. The Contingent, 'Strathdee's Own', owed him much. A World War One Gordon Highlander, he had been a cadet and an officer with the Infantry Unit. He had led the STC through all the turmoil of World War Two and the uncertainty in its immediate aftermath. A farewell ceremony was held in the Staff Room at King's where he had presided over many training conferences and 'O' Groups. His efforts would be officially recognised with an OBE in the 1949 New Years Honours List and thirty years on, the Contingent's new HQ Building would be named for him. He would serve with the MEC and be Honorary Colonel 1957-64.

Lt Col McNeill MBE took over command as the hard work of bedding in the new structure began in earnest. The next two years were difficult and heartbreaking for McNeill and his staff, who in McNeill's words 'perceived an incredible lack of help from without and difficulties from within'. Anyway, all male student's matriculating in October 1948 received a leaflet from the new CO UTC(TA). It contained the usual mix of inspiring erudite quotations and real detail in the hope that something would stir potential recruits to get in touch.

The cause of freedom and resistance to tyranny in all its forms, whatever livery it wears, or whatever slogans it mouths, is a world cause, and to uphold it is a duty which every man and woman owes to the human race.
- Winston Churchill

'*The strength of an Army depends on the quality of its leaders, the officers. I hope that the students of Aberdeen university will take the opportunity of training themselves as leaders while at the University.*'
- Field Marshal The Right Honourable The Earl Wavell, Chancellor.

'*We do well to remember that the secret of happiness is freedom and the secret of freedom is courage; but courage by itself is of little avail without the skill and training to make it effectual.*'
- TM Taylor, Principal

'*Socrates served in the Infantry and you too will discover the benefit of military training if you undertake it briskly and willingly, in the spirit of a Volunteer.*'
- Eric Linklater, Rector.

These stirring words were set against a nationwide drive for more patriotism and commitment. In the same month as the recruiting leaflet went out to Aberdeen's new students, the YMCA Hall on Union Street was the venue for an event under the auspices of the National Rally 'Britain

Needs You'. The local press relished the opportunity to report that the meeting for 'the general public, ex-servicemen and their wives' had been disrupted by 'fifth column hooligans' from Aberdeen's Communist Party.

The UTC leaflet listed the benefits promised by the War Office:

'The deferred student, or student who comes to University before completing his year of whole time National Service, may now enlist in the UTC(TA). This will bring the following advantages:

1. He may complete his 10 weeks of Army Basic Training during one, two or three vacation periods while still at University.

2. If he is recommended by his UTC(TA) contingent commander as a suitable candidate he will appear before WOSB for selection as a potential officer.

3. If the cadet has completed Basic Training and is accepted by the Selection Board before or after graduation, he will be posted to an OCTU and will serve the rest of his National Service as an officer.

4. Efficient UTC(TA) service prior to call-up entitles the cadet to exemption from TA Service up to a maximum of two years on completion of one year's service with the Colours.

5. Parades, attachments etc will be arranged at times which do not interfere with academic studies.

6. The cadet will benefit financially. He will receive:

    a. Training allowances - 9d per hour for periods over 2 hours with increases according to rank.

    b. Pay at Camp etc of 4 Shillings per day, with rank increments.

    c. TA Bounty - up to a maximum of £12 per year.

The leaflet closed by emphasising that ex servicemen with their valuable experience would be made most welcome. Volunteers were asked to apply through UTC(TA) HQ, Marischal College, Monday to Friday 9am-5pm, or UTC(TA) HQ, King's College, Saturdays, 0930-1200.

The relationship between the Regular Army and the Universities was also in flux. The War Office was questioning the apparently more 'general' content of Scottish degrees. The heavy liability for a student cadet keen to progress to a Regular Commission included normal training, 6 weeks at a primary training centre, attachments to Regular units, OCTU courses, appearance before the RCB and medical boards. By contrast students destined for RAF commissions merely had to be aged between 21 and 24, have a satisfactory degree, 2 years in the UAS and the nomination of their CO and a University Board.

The university contingents would now enjoy the same rights, material and financial benefits as other TA units. MECs would continue to be responsible for training and administration within War Office policy delegated to Commands and Districts. Administrative matters would be managed within the TA framework. UTC representatives would be members of their local Territorial and Auxiliary Associations. Some War Office funds passed to the TA Associations would be ring-fenced for UTC use only. As an alternative to ABTU, undergraduates with a strong preference for service in a technical corps could, with faculty assistance, study for those arms and services. Nor would medics need to go to an ABTU. They could chose to use the UTC to gain basic military training before training at the RAMC Depot. The War Office even hoped for some 'staff college' level activity at Universities, geared to prepare suitable officers for staff appointments in the event of a general mobilisation. It was recognised that such training would be beyond the scope of the UTCs but might be achieved by attendance at courses and vacation attachments to formation headquarters.

One of the more heated topics between the Universities and the War Office was that of the liability for part time TA service included in National Service. The UTCs would welcome students who had completed their full time National Service. However the scheme required such men to be allocated to local TA units. This flow of manpower would in theory be managed in order to keep TA units up to strength with the outflow from National Service. It was deemed neither desirable nor practical to strip TA units of their 'cream' for 3 or more years by letting students serve out their time in the UTC. It was finally agreed that, with the permission of their TA COs, students could train with their UTC during term time but would be required to attend Annual Camp with their 'home' TA units. The other TA aspect for debate was just how much service in an UTC(TA), before full time National Service, would count against the overall TA liability. These and other complicated manning issues were debated and remained annoyingly fluid for several years.

McNeill faced serious challenges. He had to train a disparate body of students for a disparate number of purposes within a framework that was still not entirely settled. Issues of finance, accommodation, HQ staff, and even continued University enthusiasm for the Contingent pressed hard upon him. Above all he hated official vacillation which was already leading to the sad demise of some University Contingents across the country.

Despite the problems, out of 21 UTCs, Aberdeen was one of six with sufficient ambition and confidence to apply for the maximum of six sub-units. To its existing Infantry, Medics, and Signallers would be added Royal Engineers, Royal Electrical and Mechanical Engineers (REME), and Intelligence Corps sub-units. These would be supported by an HQ and enhanced by the Pipe Band. The REME had been formed in 1942 during the war in order to rationalise the maintenance of an increasingly large and complex equipment inventory. An Intelligence Corps had been formed for World War One but disbanded later. The current Intelligence Corps was formed in 1940.

Activation and equipping of each sub-unit depended on sufficient numbers of students wishing to join and the availability of unembodied TA officers with the necessary 'cap-badge' experience. In a somewhat 'chicken and egg' situation, Regular Warrant Officer Permanent Staff Instructors (PSIs), specialist equipment and vehicles would be provided once minimum student numbers were reached. The theoretical establishments were lavish in permitted student, TA and Regular staff numbers. Full strength sub-units were, in theory, entitled to copious quantities of equipment, jeeps, motorcycles and trucks. Reality was of course different.

The 1949/50 parade state for students at Aberdeen UTC(TA) was as follows:

Subunit	Cadets 2nd year and above	New Recruits	Totals
Infantry	8	6	14
Signals	13	-	13
Medical	2	2	4
RE	5	1	6
REME	6	2	8
Intelligence	8	2	10
Totals	42	13	55

Under the 1948 UTC policy, Annual Contingent camps would cease in favour of periods of continuous training at ABTUs, Army Schools of Instruction, and individual or group attachments to units and establishments. This ruling did not apply to Queen's Belfast since Northern Ireland's citizens had no National Service obligations.

All four Scottish Universities opposed the abandonment of Contingent Camps. The removal of annual camp from the unit calendar would, they thought, impact upon team spirit, fun and the opportunity to conduct leadership training. However, if a contingent considered that holding an annual camp would be beneficial, they could apply

222

for permission to their Command HQ.

The new instructions arrived too late to cancel plans for the 1948 camp at Berwick. A diminished contingent deployed to Magdalene Fields with its officers billeted in the town's KOSB Depot. The camp was happy and successful. It did mark the end of an era and a last gathering of the 'old family' of permanent staff. Major Macarthur, as in previous years, acted as Adjutant and Training Officer, working with his usual zeal and conscientiousness. In 1949 there was no camp but several Aberdeen cadets attended a leadership course run by Edinburgh at Tain.

In October 1948 the Contingent had no Training Officer, no QM, no QMS, no Orderly Room Sgt and no PSIs for the new sub-units. The unit had lost the stalwart James Grant who was found dead in his storeroom at Marischal College. He had been the backbone of the 'Q' side of unit life for many years, ensuring cooks were up in the morning, the officers were looked after, and that all the essential minutiae of 'behind the scenes' admin happened at the right time and at the right place. Major Macarthur who had been with the unit since 1944 was released from service in November 1948 despite requests and pleas for an extension of his tour in the hard pressed appointment of Adjutant. Macarthur was succeeded by Captain, later Major, Close of the Gordons who himself was posted out in Apr 1950, having already been away on a course for 4 months during 1949. Only eighteen months after Strathdee's departure, McNeill reported that there had been no fewer than five changes of Adjutant during the period, and the Training Major post remained gapped. He wondered whether the War Office actually cared about the UTCs at all. Great credit was due to the unembodied TA officers who kept things going; Major

Rennie took over the RAMC; Capt Reid ran the Intelligence Section and Lts Eastwood and Jones the RE subunit.

The question of unit accommodation also came to a head in late 1948. The University had been as helpful as possible to the Contingent since 1912. The unit still had its HQ and a store at Marischal, and King's hosted a cadets' room, office, armoury and miniature range. The unit still had use of Powis Gardens. The Medical Unit huts at Foresterhill were still occupied. With expanding staff and student populations, the University now wanted McNeill to move his unit out of Marischal College and the Foresterhill site. McNeill told the Faculty of Medicine that if they wanted the Foresterhill site they should pay for it. Harry Butchart consulted the TA Association who advised that it would be inappropriate for the Government to make any claim against the University. After successfully resisting any immediate takeover at Foresterhill, McNeill moved his HQ out of Marischal and up to his Foresterhill huts. The HQ would operate from there until June 1950 before finally surrendering the position to the Faculty of Medicine. The University Court, no doubt heavily influenced by Harry Butchart, gave the MEC £400 to match the value of the Foresterhill site.

While based at Foresterhill the HQ conducted some long overdue housekeeping with a full stores audit. Deficiencies in items purchased over a long period with MEC funds were as follows: 26 kilts, 31 sporrans, 76 Tam O' Shanter cap badges, 498 Tam O' Shanters, 12 Glengarries diced, 67 tunics beige, 3 bagpipes, 5 practice chanters, a silver dirk, drumsticks, a sand table, a desk, a cabinet, a set of playing cards, 3 sets of darts, and sports kit including a leather rugby ball cover. Write-offs were approved but it was optimistically noted some stuff might still turn up. An apparent lack of direct responsibility for such items would be corrected and annual inventories undertaken.

As regards current uniform, the Contingent retained the Boars Head cap badge and wore UTC shoulder badges common to all contingents. Silver UTC lapel badges were available for proud cadets to display when wearing 'civvies'.

As the UAS already occupied the Powis Gardens/Bedford Road site the University Court agreed that it made sense to develop the site further as the permanent base for the whole reorganised UTC contingent. In any case the University intended to significantly expand the whole King's College campus over the coming decades. By early 1949 plans were drawn up by the local TA Association's official architects for a central admin block and hutted accommodation for all the sub-units. For the first time proper Messes for officers and cadets would be built. The plans were dependent on the acquisition of surplus War Office buildings and this, competitive tendering procedures, and the satisfaction of a plethora of regulations, led to frustrating delays in implementation. McNeill and the MEC were very disapproving of these delays and the consequent serious effect on UTC business. In July 1949 a delegation even made the journey to the Adjutant General's staff at the War Office in an attempt to speed things up.

Finally, in Spring 1950, sections of huts and vehicle sheds arrived and construction began. By the Summer the buildings were up and every effort was being made to make them habitable before the start of the University session in October. The unit's 'Powis Gardens' or 'Bedford Road' home was now established and would be at the centre of work and play for the next quarter century. A period of two years from original idea to occupation would nowadays seem notably fast. Having become used to how fast things could be done in wartime, and being under many other administrative pressures which threatened the unit's viability, McNeill and his team can perhaps be excused their evident impatience.

Unit finance was in a tight spot. The original, now venerable system, of direct capitation grants from the War Office for qualified cadets would be discontinued under the new scheme although promised training grants would replace them. Administrative funding would now come down through the TA hierarchy and be, it was assured, ring-fenced. The contingent funds accumulated over the decades from capitation grants and careful management had been frozen by the Treasury. Only in 1950 were matters partially resolved leaving the unit with only a fraction of its original savings. McNeil thought the grants coming from the TA Association were insufficient for a UTC. He noted that Edinburgh UTC was still receiving an annual grant from its University and secured an annual grant of £100 from his. Despite hard times £84 was found for equipping and furnishing the Cadets Mess and another £85 to buy ski equipment. The latter purchase set in train what would be a favourite part of the training calendar for decades to come. Grants were also sought towards the £400 necessary to bring the Band's ceremonial uniforms and equipment, all University property, up to standard.

On top of everything else McNeill was somewhat dismayed that the Principal was considering breaking long tradition by not officially encouraging UTC and UAS membership over and above other University clubs and societies.

There having been no Camp in 1949, Summer 1950 was marked with a return to the tried and tested Annual Camp

226

system. Aberdeen went to Cultybraggan near Comrie with St Andrews and Edinburgh. The Nissan huts had been built only nine years earlier, in 1941, to house 4000 German POWs assessed as the toughest and most fanatical Nazis. Separate compounds were set up for Army (including many Afrika Corps soldiers), Navy, Air Force, SS and Officers. After the war it became a heavily used training camp. It would become a frequent haunt of school and University cadets. This recapture of the fun and spirit of bygone days was highly successful. Also Aberdeen rejoiced in at last receiving a Training Officer.

The new base more or less established at Bedford Road and ready to receive the HQ evicted from Foresterhill, McNeill announced he wished to relinquish his command in June 1950 at the end of the session. During his two year tenure he had achieved much under very difficult circumstances. He kept the Contingent alive, with depleted numbers, but with a strong kernel of 'volunteer spirit'. He was hearing early talk of women University contingents being established. He supported this concept but felt that he and his HQ would have trouble running two new platoons of women. Further, many students would from October 1950, be returning from National Service to serve out their TA commitment. McNeill recognised that in addition to his University teaching commitments he could not carry on against a background of continuing accommodation issues and staff shortages particularly of young officers. Nor in his view would any other member of University staff or someone from within the UTC be found to take over. He suggested that the MEC should apply for a Regular Army CO. The MEC considered this would be a most regrettable break with a 38 year old tradition and should be avoided if possible. It was avoided; the first Regular CO would only be appointed 36 years later.

McNeill's mood was not lifted when it was heard that two former cadets who had dutifully completed their 10 weeks of basic training during their University vacations had, on being called-up, been made to do it all over again. Expressions of displeasure again winged their way from the Granite City to Whitehall.

After McNeill announced his retirement plans, Professor TB Smith, a renowned authority in Scots Law and occupier of Aberdeen's Chair of Law, had indicated a willingness to be considered for the post. His impressive military record included: Under Officer in his school Junior Training Corps; Oxford UOTC with 2 years in a RA Horse Battery and 1 year in a machine gun company; and TA service in the ranks of the London Scottish (Gordon Highlanders). His war experience included a Mention in Dispatches, commissioned war service in the field artillery with the BEF before Dunkirk, and in the Middle East. He had later served on the intelligence staffs of infantry and armoured divisions, been an instructor in German tactics at the War Office School of Infantry, and had served in post war political intelligence with the Foreign Office, rising to the rank of Lt Col. He pointed out to the MEC that he was still subject to emergency recall to commitments that, intriguingly, were not detailed in his Army dossier, nor, it was agreed, would they need further mention. Butchart asked if Smith would take command on 30 June 1950.

Smith recognised in his first report to the MEC that, despite the problems and uncertainty, McNeill's efficiency, perseverance and enthusiasm had handed him a unit in healthy condition. There was a nucleus of capable staff with

228

recent battle experience. The lessons these men had learned in 'the hardest school' were being passed on to the cadets. The staff themselves allocated Tuesday evenings to share their extensive and varied military knowledge with each other.

Aberdeen though was not keeping up with the other universities in terms of recruiting. Those who had joined however were good quality and were quickly on parade alongside the UAS for Remembrance Parade. Colonel Lachlan Mackinnon DSO, OC of 'U' Company at the start of World War One but who had handed over before Hooge, took the salute. He returned with the others to a great reunion in the new Bedford Road HQ. Smith welcomed the fact that the new site allowed the Contingent to concentrate and bond together. Of further value was the sharing of the site with the UAS.

With his wartime experience of Allied and German tactics he emphasised in his training directives the importance of close land/air cooperation. Joint exercises to this effect were conducted with the UAS de Havilland Tiger Moth biplanes searching areas for camouflaged UTC positions. A typical land/air exercise saw the Adjutant join RAF Dyce as the Air Liaison Officer, and aircraft being tasked to find and 'destroy' a disabled lorry and the rescue team dispatched to recover it. With the incentive of inter-unit pride, the UTC's camouflage standards steadily improved.

The UAS was flying over 1500 training hours per year. Sadly during this period a flying accident killed the UAS CO and a Cadet Pilot. In 1952 the UAS extended their all weather capacity with the receipt of monoplane Chipmunks to replace the ageing Tiger Moths.

As TA units, UTCs could, with Her Majesty's

approval, nominate candidates for appointment as Honorary Colonels. In 1951 Harry Butchart became Aberdeen's first Honorary Colonel. An inter war CO and constant supporter of the unit from his long-held and influential position within the University's senior management, he was an obvious choice.

This history describes, as it should, the management challenges and frustrations faced by the Contingent through the decades. Of course for most of the time, and quite rightly, student cadets were oblivious to the headaches and heartaches of the senior management. Cadets continued to join, work hard and play hard. Despite the upheaval of reorganisation and relocation, unit life and laughs continued with lectures, range work, field training and ceremonial duties. The rare combination of Army and student humour could overcome the gloom of most situations.

The 1951 Camp was at Dallachy near the mouth of the Spey. Dallachy airfield had been home to a wartime Strike Wing of Beaufighters and latterly of the Royal Navy's aged Swordfish biplanes. After the war the TA adopted the installation as a training camp. Weather was poor, testing endurance and morale especially during hill marches at Spean Bridge and Ben Rinnes. With the proximity of the Spey the Sapper sub-unit had excellent opportunities to practice watermanship and river crossing techniques. Despite some nervous moments, the visiting GOC's staff car was successfully rafted across the river to everyone's relief.

In preparation for the Installation of Tom Johnston as University Chancellor, 30 men of the UTC were billeted at Gordon Barracks for intensive drilling under RSM Howitt SG. The local press reported how a squad with only a few ex-servicemen in the ranks met the challenge of a Full

Ceremonial Dress Parade. The UTC detachment, under Lt Jones RE(TA) added élan and colour to the occasion. They and their ladies were invited to the Reception in Mitchell Hall.

Administering the new training regime was a heavy burden. The intention of the new scheme was good in that cadets could get their basic training done before call-up to National Service and, if they wished, get two attempts at a Commissioning Board. If successful, they would then serve the bulk of their National Service as officers. Training for TA commissions would involve attendance at District Selection Boards where successful cadets would be recommended for direct commissions to the TA. Such men would then follow a War Office specified training syllabus. Cadets, at different stages and from a variety of sub-units, had to be placed for varying periods at a number of different ABTUs and other units all over the country. The necessary constant liaison with ABTUs, Corps Depots, TA Units, Commissioning Boards, Commands and Districts required detailed time-consuming staff work customised for each student. This had to be done despite the inevitability of gapped posts and frequent changes in appointment holders.

Aberdeen was especially favoured by its proximity to the Grampians and the Cairngorms. Aberdeen's Cairngorm Club was established in 1887 making it Scotland's oldest and largest hill walking and climbing club. Individual students and groups of friends had taken to the hills for hard healthy recreation for many years. Part of Sniper Sergeant JK Forbes pre-World War One renown rested on his 'prodigious tramps' through the hills in all weathers. Former CO Harry Butchart had been one of the pioneers of Scottish Skiing. The STC had deployed as a unit to the hills during the World War II toughening-up exercises in Deeside and Donside.

The Scottish Highlands had become a training area of choice for wartime Commandos and the Special Operations Executive. Post World War II, 'adventurous training' quickly gained ground as a legitimate military activity. Walking, climbing and skiing were increasingly popular civilian recreational pursuits.

In 1951, the unit took receipt of 12 sets of skis and, with many zealous volunteers, the unit was ready to conduct winter and mountain warfare training as part of the training cycle. TB Smith pointed out to the University that during the war Scottish troops had prepared for this specialist role. The small degree of irony involved in this statement would not have been lost on ex-soldiers. It was the 52nd Lowland Division which had trained in this 'highland' role. Having done so, their sternest actions were actually fought below sea level in the flooded polders around the Scheldt Estuary during operations to open up the port of Antwerp for Allied use.

A couple of screws placed in the heel of the issue 'ammo' boots accommodated the cable bindings, and, with a pair of bamboo cane ski poles, winter warriors were ready for the slopes. Weekend trips were made to wherever there was sufficient snow, Aviemore and Abergeldie being the most frequently visited. Increasingly long and fast downhill runs were of course interspersed by tiring ascents. The unit possessed some specialist touring 'skins' which allowed uphill movement on skis. For the majority, muscle building side stepping and 'herring bone' techniques prevailed. Others chose to remove their skis and carry them uphill for another all too brief descent. An enterprising local at Abergeldie would on occasion install a tractor powered rope tow.

For many years Aberdeen's mountain training would

232

centre on Rothiemurchus. In 1948 Colonel Grant of Rothiemurchus suggested to the Army that they should build a hut on the NW slopes of Castle Hill overlooking Loch Morlich. This would enable soldiers to conduct challenging character building outdoor pursuits in the neighbouring mountains. A basic timber hut with accommodation for 40 and really only accessible by foot, opened in December 1950.

In 1951 professors and lecturers were helping to encourage students to join and supported those who already had. It was important that UTC membership was favourably regarded. Many of the staff had distinguished military and academic careers discrediting the notion that they could not be combined successfully.

Autumn 1951 would see the start of the biggest and longest lasting change to Contingent life recorded in this history. With effects far deeper and longer lasting than anything Kaiser Bill or Fuhrer Adolph had caused, women would, from October 1951, at long last join the ranks of Aberdeen's Student Soldiers.

Suaviter in Modo, Fortiter in Re
(Gentle in manner, resolute in deed).

The Women's Royal Army Corps (WRAC) with the above Motto, had replaced the wartime Auxiliary Territorial Service (ATS) on 1 February 1949. All women in the Army other than doctors, dentists, vets, chaplains, and nurses belonged to the WRAC until 1992. The WRAC cap badge was a lioness rampant within a laurel wreath surmounted by a crown.

Only nine months after the birth of the WRAC, Aberdeen's MEC was considering a War Office letter about the possible formation of WRAC University Companies. They would develop the capacity for leadership in women who were considering commissions in the WRAC or the other corps open to them. The companies would help women undergraduates reach the required standards for selection to WRAC commissions. They would further the military education of ex-servicewomen undergraduates who had reached commissioned rank.

The companies would be integral to the nearest local WRAC battalion. They would receive the same training and be under the same obligations as the WRAC (TA) but would not fire a weapon course. Companies would form only at Universities with more than 500 women and sufficient interest. They would get a regular junior commander and WRAC Coy Permanent Staff. They would receive Grants through the TA Association.

Butchart stated that Aberdeen had 536 women students of whom 492 were fulltime. The then CO, McNeill, thought the MEC should support the initiative but he was worried about the additional administrative and logistic burden. The Principal thought the Students Representative Council (SRC) should be advised of the scheme and asked to assess the likely response from the student body. A few months later the SRC Women's Committee reported that they had investigated thoroughly the question of a WRAC Company and found no woman willing to join. Indeed the general attitude had been one of antipathy. The MEC concluded that they would inform the War Office that, as yet, the University of Aberdeen would be unable to raise a WRAC company. This was of course not the end of the story.

Once in command TB Smith reported that a number of enthusiastic lady students of 'personality and charm' had approached him regarding the formation of a WRAC unit. Clearly the SRC Women's Committee had not investigated matters thoroughly enough or were the wrong people to ask in the first place. Aberdeen applied for and, on 24 September 1951, was granted a WRAC University Company of its own with Captain Mary McLeod appointed as the first commander. Recruiting started in October 1951. Reflecting the WRAC's duties in the Army, the WRAC cadets' training focussed on general duties, motor transport, signals (mainly wireless) and some knowledge of other arms responsibilities.

Female recruiting did not depend upon the University alone. The 'Dumf' was the Dunfermline College of Physical Education for aspiring female PE teachers. It had first moved from Dunfermline to Aberdeen during the war when the Royal Navy commandeered their buildings. After the war it returned briefly to Dunfermline but overcrowding led to a return to Aberdeen in 1950.

The 'Doe' (or perhaps 'Dough') School trained Domestic Science teachers and was another steady source of women recruits. In addition to the Dumph and the Doe School were the Teacher Training College, Robert Gordon Institute of Technology, Grays School of Art, Agriculture, Nutrition and soil science courses, the Nursing Colleges, and courses for speech therapists, physiotherapists and other professions. Students from all higher education institutions were eligible for UTC or WRAC membership. Further, although Aberdeen did not generally do so, regulations allowed anyone undergoing professional training to take advantage of the courses and qualifications a Contingent could offer.

The TA Association approved funding for a WRAC Hut at Bedford Road and the University awarded them a £200 grant towards set-up costs. Obviously feeling especially benevolent towards the Contingent, the University granted another £100 to allow all male cadets to wear the Balmoral Headdress.

Not every citizen had the unit's best interests at heart and in October 1951 the Cadet's Mess was burgled and the losses, all fortunately insured, consisted in the main of cigarettes. This breach in security led to urgent action to properly secure mess silver, unit trophies and other valuables.

Summer Camp 1952 was once more at Cultybraggan with military lessons covering the spectrum from Commando style raids on 'vital installations' to the treatment of very sore feet.

In November 1952 TB Smith instituted the annual Remembrance Sunday Parade at King's. The names of those who had died in World War 2 had been added to the Memorial. The chapel service and impressive parade and inspection was followed by a party back at Bedford Road, allowing Contingent members old and new to socialise and thank invited supporters for their continued efforts to the benefit of the unit..

Discussion of who should replace Butchart as Honorary Colonel in 1953 included mention of Field Marshall Lord Auchinleck as a possible candidate. The logic behind this notion is not minuted in the MEC proceedings but TB Smith argued the case that somebody far less distinguished and with closer connections to the unit would be more appropriate. In the event Colonel The Lord Strathcona would fill the appointment from 1953 to 1957.

In 1953 the Contingent became properly affiliated with the Gordon Highlanders. WRAC first year students went to the WRAC Depot at Guildford visiting the Army

School of Cookery, Aldershot and a 'mixed sex' Anti Aircraft Regiment at Lingfield. Second year students went to the WRAC School at Liphook and among other things took part in a Battle of Britain parade, particularly proud of their new distinctive Gordon tartan skirts.

The UTC's men went to Garelochhead for camp. Constructed in 1940 the site formed part of the complex of defences around the Clyde and was used by American forces prior to D-Day. Like many 'temporary' wartime camps it would remain in use by TA and Regular units for decades. This year West Coast weather held up well, far better than that experienced by the units of the 51st Highland Division (TA) exercising down on Salisbury Plain. The Highland Midge more than made up for the lack of heavy rain as the main enemy during unit training. The Reserve Fleet concentrated in the Gare Loch provided some distraction. A visit was arranged to the battleship *HMS George V* and her 14 inch guns which had helped sink the German battleship *Bismarck* 12 years earlier.

In October 1953 the WRAC students became officially part of the UTC Contingent rather than a distinct Company reporting through the WRAC chain of command. The latter of course maintained a close watch on progress and made frequent inspections. Often senior WRAC visitors would be displeased by the level of integration and shared training even when this had been diluted especially for those visits. University contingent practice remained resolutely ahead of WRAC official, and somewhat conservative, dogma.

1953 - With the WRAC in place at Bedford Road the Contingent's extended family could now begin to add daughters, mothers, sisters and wives to its set of possible relationships.
Capt Mary Hendry (McLeod), seated fourth from left.

The unit maintained links with its past steadily acquiring trophies and mementoes. TB Smith encouraged the interest of those whom he called the 'great uncles', many of whom had served with U Company. The University Librarian, Dr

W Douglas Simpson presented a dirk and claymore to the unit. They had belonged to his late brother who had served with the 4th Gordons and the Machine Gun Corps before being killed in action in 1918. The claymore had been given to his brother by no less than WO Duncan of the original University detachment and U Company. Duncan had carried the claymore during the Boer War. Unit property thus now included a direct link to the infantry sub-unit's famous predecessor. The claymore would be employed as the unit's own Sword of Honour.

On relinquishing the post of Honorary Colonel, Harry Butchart presented a splendid Pipe Banner. He also presented a blue uniform helmet that had once belonged to the University's pre-OTC medical unit. It remains to this day, with many other artefacts, in the Officers Mess.

During TB Smith's tenure the University's student population was still below 2,500 and Corps membership would soon equate to roughly 10% of all male undergraduates, most of whom came from the North of Scotland. Good contingent recruiting was being achieved despite understandable resentment in the University by those who saw National Service only as a serious barrier and impediment to their careers.

The MEC noted that, although the University staff was increasing, there was no corresponding increase in those coming forward to help the UTC meet the challenges of National Service. More officers were needed especially from the science faculties since many science students were joining the Contingent's specialist sub-units. The MEC were most grateful to Capt Lucas a French Lecturer, when he brought his wartime infantry and Commando experience to the unit despite a war disability. The Principal again circulated information to University staff , in the hope of alleviating the shortage of TA officers with University connections, who were living in the local area, and were willing to devote time to the UTC.

Ceremonial duties were particularly frequent during 1952 and 1953 with participation in Aberdeen's ceremonies marking the death of George VI, the Proclamation of the Accession of Queen Elizabeth and in June 1953, the Coronation itself. After a well attended Easter camp at Cultybraggan, hectic preparations began. In May, three weekends of ceremonial practice were held at Gordon Barracks and Barry Buddon. The Contingent sent off a detachment of three to the London Parade. In Aberdeen, on 2 June 1953, 8 officers and 114 cadets formed one of the largest parts of the City's own Coronation Parade. RSM Howitt was particularly striking in full Guards ceremonial dress. He later received the Coronation Medal. Harry Butchart, Deputy Lieutenant of Aberdeen since 1948, planned and oversaw the whole City celebration with his usual zeal and energy. Later in June a detachment of 29 cadets went south to Edinburgh to help line the streets for the new Queen's State Visit to the Scottish Capital.

In 1954 the WRAC's first leader Mary McLeod, now Mary Hendry having married the Training Officer, handed over to Jenny Macbeth at a parade saluted by a fly past courtesy of the UAS.

Since 1947 the Scottish contingents had been expressing the view that War Office policy was having the effect of splitting contingents into virtually self contained specialist sub-units. COMEC was also urging a return to full Officers Training Corps status. Despite these protestations the War Office emphasis on detachments to Army Basic Training Units and other units prevailed for a while and Aberdeen had no summer contingent camps in 1955 and 1956. However the long awaited War Office announcement arrived on 25 Jan 1955. The UTC(TA) would revert to its old title of OTC with the prime role of training undergraduates for commissioned service. The OTC would remain part of the TA albeit with different terms of service.

TB Smith was convinced the OTCs would help the Army and individuals by making the best use of graduates. He had observed that, during general mobilisation for a World War, suitable niches were found for gifted men who lacked strong leadership ability. In National Service this was not the case and the full potential of clever men was often wasted. The OTCs would give such men the chance to develop their full leadership potential to their own benefit and that of the Army. With this in mind the MEC backed TB Smith's recommendation to the War Office that all cadets should follow a common syllabus of basic training before joining the specialist sub-units.

Aberdeen solicitor Stuart Aitken's experiences illustrate the intended progression from University to National Service. In 1954, Stuart Aitken sat down with fellow first year law LLB students at 0800 hrs for the first introductory talk by Professor TB Smith. Many of the law, accounting and medical lecturers at that time had 'day jobs' so lessons had to start early. Aitken had previously completed an MA in English but had decided that teaching was not for him. Although he had served in Aberdeen Central School's cadets, he had not joined the UTC during his first degree. Prof Smith wasted no time in stressing that his course demanded high pass marks and had high attrition rates. Smith mentioned what a good thing the UTC was and that his new students should seriously consider joining. Reasoning that joining Smith's unit could only help their academic survival, Aitken and a few others went along to an introductory dinner night at Bedford Road. One of the party was Denys Henderson, a future Chairman of ICI. The dinner was held with full formality and military ceremony, with a piper for each officer of major's rank and above. Suitably impressed Aitken joined and was soon participating in drill nights. He particularly enjoyed shooting, attending extra range sessions at Bedford Road and Black Dog,. As well as the possibility of increasing his academic chances with Prof Smith, service with the UTC had the real advantage of gaining swift access to the War Office Selection Board (WOSB) for commissioning once called up for National Service. Without this route, aspiring officers could spend most of their National Service in the ranks, going through various selection procedures and training before WOSB. To qualify for the fast track to commissioning Aitken attended two periods at the Bridge of Don barracks being treated exactly like the infantry recruits for the Gordon Highlanders and London Scottish. He enjoyed these sessions and on call-up he and two other cadets went to WOSB. Two of the three were successful. Aitken went to his second choice, the Royal Army Service Corps (RASC). He trained as a potential officer cadet at the RASC Training Battalion, Buller Barracks, Aldershot before attending OCTU at Mons. Special to arm training followed back at Buller. While awaiting posting in the Summer of 1956, Aitken was involved in the sudden move of parachute gunners to Southampton Docks. This was part of preparations for the Suez deployment after Egypt's President Nasser took over control of the vital Suez Canal. Aitken spent his National Service with the RASC's own substantial water transport fleet some of which was based at Cairnryan. Although his ship the Marquis of Hartington started its long journey to Egypt, mechanical troubles meant that it only got as far as Portsmouth before the UK/French/Israeli Suez operation ground to a halt under USA pressure. The remainder of Aitken's Army maritime service was in Scottish and Ulster waters, towing targets for coastal artillery practice, towing oil barges through the Caledonian Canal and most notably dumping tons of WW2 munitions at sea.

At the end of the war the UK was host to 500,000 tons of RAF bombs and 2 million tons of land munitions including that taken off captured enemy ships and U Boats. Since the 1990s, it is also now public knowledge that in the final months of the war, the Allies had seized German chemical warfare facilities and munitions. Hitler had never authorised their use, in the mistaken belief that the Allies had the capability of massive chemical retaliation if he did. In 1945, 14,000 tons of Tabun nerve agent loaded in 71,000 bombs were taken by sea, train and truck via Newport and Llanberis to RAF Llandrog where they were stored in the open on the hard standing. The inevitable deterioration of the bomb casings led to the decision to dispose of the hazard at sea. Over three years the bombs were transferred by sea from Llandrog to Cairnryan where, under Operation Sandcastle 1956/57, they were transferred into merchant ship hulks which were then scuttled in at least 6000 feet of water.

At the end of his full time National Service Aitken served with a TA Beach Brigade, including a detachment to the 8th Argylls at Lochgilpead. Returning to Aberdeen he had long service with the local TA including command of transport units.

In January 1955 the University Training Corps became once again the Officers Training Corps. The training regime continued to emphasise pre-National Service ABTU training, attachments and external courses. There were no Contingent Camps in 1955 and 1956. For the 1956 camp, the Pipe Band and those who had done their National Service went with 5/6 Gordons to Stobs just south of Hawick. This camp had a long history as a 'Volunteer' Camp stretching back to 1903 and was served for a while by its own branch railway. German POWs had enjoyed its charms during both World Wars and it served as a TA and National Service training facility until 1959. The Medics went with 152(H) Field Ambulance on their annual camp.

TB Smith handed over to Lt Col Frank Burnett Gordon Highlanders (TA) in May 1955. Burnett had served as a Private in the Black Watch before being commissioned in the Border Regiment. He served in North Africa before participating in special operations including time as a Liaison Officer with Tito's partisans in Yugoslavia. After the war he qualified as a chartered land surveyor and managed land for the Admiralty before joining Aberdeen University as its Land Manager.

Burnett would only command the unit for 18 months before taking up a civilian appointment in Salisbury, Southern Rhodesia (now Zimbabwe). Former RSM and now Adjutant/ Quartermaster Howitt would soon follow Burnett to those warmer climes.

Burnett was replaced by the unit's unofficial second in command, John Reid, who would command for nine years. The early years of his tour had the continued pressures of meeting the different requirements of those who had completed National Service, those still waiting to go, and the RAMC cadets earmarked for National Service duty as Medical Officers. Despite these strains Reid fostered a strong unit spirit and was keen for example to re-establish the OTC's presence at the annual Wapinschaw Shooting Competition. He thought that the local 'officer producing' unit must be represented in the Rifle and Light Machine Gun (LMG or Bren Gun) events. He strived, in his quiet but effective manner, to build the unit up towards full strength, a significant challenge as National Service began to waste out. For some time the Pipe Band was his largest sub unit.

Steady improvements to the unit accommodation at Bedford Road continued. In February 1956 Harry Butchart opened a refurbished Cadets Mess noting its new smart coats of paint, inside and out, and the civilising effect of curtains and better heating arrangements.

Aberdeen's WRAC Contingent was now bigger than any of its equivalents and approaching equal size with the male contingent. The 1955/56 unit strength was:

	Officers	Other Ranks
Male	4	52
Female	3	41

As National Service drew to a close, Reid's principal challenge became nourishing student interest in joining and staying in the Contingent once the recruiting incentives related to National Service ended. From the Autumn 1957 intake onwards matriculating students would have no National Service commitments.

Winter training continued as a very popular part of the annual programme with 25 cadets mountaineering and skiing from their base at the Rothiemurchus Lodge over the 1957 Easter break. Skiing skills were painfully developed in the Coire Cas and mountain patrols became acquainted with the rapidly changing Arctic conditions on the Cairngorm Plateau and on Britain's third highest peak, Braeriach. This gem in the training calendar was heavily oversubscribed and it was hoped to double the vacancies in 1958.

Reid's first Annual Camp as CO was held at Milton Bridge, Glencorse, in the company of Sheffield and Durham OTCs. This 1957 camp was of historical significance in that it was the first time the whole Contingent, men and women, shared a common camp. Some of the older men were still obliged to do ABTU training in preparation for call-up. The sub-units conducted separate training weekends of their own. The Medics could take the opportunity of attending the local 152(Highland) Field Ambulance's Camp. University WRAC contingents organised their own 'cap badge' weekends as did the signallers who often joined other signals sub-units for training.

1957 saw the Pipe Band win the Inter OTC Competition for the third time in succession and the WRAC won the Scottish Country Dancing. Capt Shivas RAMC of the Pathology Department, who had done much to revamp the band, won the Solo Drumming but left in September 1957. His drive and musicianship were matched by his tact when he would gently encourage former band members to maintain an

246

interest in the band and return any items of uniform they no longer had use for.   Shivas went on to command a TA General Hospital and Edinburgh UOTC.

The expanded 1958 Rothiemurchus party took two days to establish themselves at the Hut due to thick and drifting snow.   Even in Summer the mountains provided challenges requiring cool heads, self confidence and basic skills.   Good compass and map skills were required if embarrassment or worse was to be avoided while patrolling Lochnagar.

Summer Camp 1958 was held at Barry Buddon with Glasgow, Durham and Sheffield OTCs. Aberdeen sent a very smart and well drilled Ceremonial Detachment to Edinburgh. They formed part of the TA 50th Jubilee Parade in Holyrood Park where they were inspected by Her Majesty, The Queen. The Barry Buddon Camp was also memorable for the chance for all to fly in two visiting helicopters.

Helicopter Drills 1958 style - Barry Buddon

During the second week of camp the Combined Pipe Bands of Aberdeen and Glasgow played at a Beat Retreat on the Edinburgh Castle Esplanade. Back in Aberdeen the Band performed in a very crowded and hot Beach Ballroom for the TA Jubilee Ball.

Full Officer Cadet status was conferred on students in 1958. With the new status came the hope that on detachments to Regular units and courses students would be treated and accommodated as officers. Despite this welcome official confirmation of status there remained widespread confusion in the Army regarding University officer cadets and schoolboy CCF and ACF cadets. Confusion about OTCs extended to the War Office itself. Aberdeen OTC was asked to explain why attendance figures dropped between July and October, the Summer Vacation.

AUOTC's first parachute course, Abingdon 1958

World War Two had seen the development and large scale employment of parachute forces. In 1959 several Aberdeen cadets attended the Parachute Course at Abingdon and received their Parachute Badge. One of them JH Glennie was later accepted for a Regular Commission in the Parachute Regiment, no mean feat in a highly competitive field from which the Paras could take their pick. One of the party, Jamaican medical student Karmody, unfortunately broke his leg during the course.

The unit often provided communications support for local events. One such event was the Aberdeen Motor Club Meeting at Edzell. This allowed cadets to practice extensive cable laying for field telephones and radio voice procedure on a real task.

1959 was noteworthy for the production of a Unit Newspaper , *Non Confundar,* by WRAC LCpl Anne Murchie. Cadets at this time earned NCO's stripes and the extra pay that went with them. The paper, price 3 old pence, included a tribute to Barry Buddon by Alan Lamont:

BUDDON
(A Lament by A Lamont)

If you ever take a train to Barry Station,
Then, looking out towards the distant sea,
You will see a vast expanse of barren country,
That's Buddon, where they sent the OTC.

For last summer we all travelled down to Buddon
As primitive a camp as there can be -
Cold water was the only thing for shaving
Unless you used a mug of NAAFI tea.

Oh to sit beside the juke box in the NAAFI
And sing once more a soldierly refrain
Or to crawl upon my belly through the marshes
Oh! Thank the Lord we're not going back again!

The town nearby the camp was called Carnoustie
The pubs are very fine, was what they said.
We had some merry drinking in the evenings
But Reveille brought a blooming awful head.

We wanted ammunition for the shooting,
A simple thing you'd think but what a game!
The officers had lost the keys between them
And the PSI got all the blooming blame.

And at nights we had exciting exercises
We had to steal a flag the Captain said
But all that I could do was get my feet soaked
Why couldn't they have left me in my bed?

But this summer we are going across to Ireland
The emerald of beauty, so they say
At least it should be livelier than Buddon
We can always go and shoot the IRA.

And if there are going to be such camps hereafter
And the War Office will ensure that there will be
They may send me off to John O' Groats or Land's End
But please not back to Buddon by the sea!

The 1959 Summer Camp was overseas at Magilligan, Northern Ireland. A request for a first air deployment to Camp courtesy of the RAF was rejected and the unit moved by train to Glasgow for embarkation on a cattle boat to Belfast. However once settled at Camp some cadets got into the air on a Shackleton maritime patrol aircraft based at Ballykelly.

Range practices were held with familiar weapons: No 4 Lee-Enfield .303 inch rifle; 9mm Sten Gun; and .38 service revolver. In addition, cadets fired the 3.5 inch rocket launcher, and each threw three standard No 36 grenades. There was also the opportunity to fire the relatively new Energa anti-tank grenade. This was propelled from an attachment to the Lee Enfield .303 rifle. It was eventually replaced in the British Army by shoulder launched rocket based systems.

The ammunition for live firing had to be collected from, and returned to Ballykinler, involving road party escorts armed with live rounds. The ammo bunker and armouries at Magilligan were kept under armed guard throughout the camp. Considerable excitement was caused at one Guard Mount when the 'negligent discharge' of a live round projected gravel 'chuckies' up a young officer's kilt.

Pay parades involved hard cash, so trips to the bank required more cadets to be 'armed and dangerous'.

Two main exercises were held. The first, Exercise 'WARE SKIRTS involved the men attempting to become invisible by skilled map reading and use of ground. The women set up observation posts and used their wireless sets to coordinate the capture of half the men. The result was deemed a draw.

251

The other main scheme Exercise DIG THIS was a 36 hour tactical exercise commencing with an assault landing from two RN patrol vessels. The invaders embarked at Londonderry and made the 20 mile approach down Loch Foyle to Magilligan. The Infantry landed, secured the beach and dug in. The RAMC established a Beach Dressing Station then a forward Regimental Aid Post. The WRAC operated two skeleton platoon HQs and provided wireless operators for Company HQ. They also turned their hand to cooking and serving food to the troops. The second phase of the exercise involved a tactical withdrawal and a road move to face a series of challenges set to decide the winner of the Initiative Cup.

1959 was a memorable year for the Pipe Band when it acquired its own World Champion. Olly Urquhart received the Charles Hepburn Mace as winner of the Drum Major Competition at the World Pipe Band Championships held at Kirkcaldy.

October 1959 brought rather disappointing recruiting figures despite the star attraction at the Contingent stand. The unit had received, on loan from the Gordon's Depot at Bridge of Don, a 7.62mm Self Loading Rifle (SLR). This represented a significant technological step from the bolt action .303 inch Lee Enfield Rifle which had been in use, more or less unchanged, since World War One. It would be a while before the OTC converted to the new weapon but unit shooting received a boost in the next couple of years with the opening of the new Drill Hall/Indoor Range built next to the Cadets Mess at Bedford Road. When not in use as a range, the target area and bullet catcher doors were closed and the firing platforms stacked. A sizeable lit and heated hall was then available for unit training and recreation protected from the elements during dark winter evenings or thoroughly dreich weekends. The recreational use was aided by only the need for a quick dash of a few paces from the Cadets Mess door to the Hall entrance. The hall provided enough space for the Band to conduct full rehearsals, the acoustics providing full amplification, needed or not. Unit dances and other parties could now be held on site with enough room for several eightsomes to reel energetically.

Cultybraggan was the Camp venue for 1960, shared with Edinburgh, Bristol and Glasgow. The War Office again approved a full 15 day paid camp (before it was 14 days pay maximum). The Infantry and Medics underwent the normal activities and the Sappers had the opportunity to lay a minefield. 2Lt Peter Clark a 2nd year forestry student had completed his National Service with the Royal Engineers and undertook to re-vitalise the Contingent's Sapper troop. It needed to grow from its current 12 members to a minimum of 30 students to get War Office recognition including the allocation of a PSI. The sub-unit benefited from PSIs from 1952 to 1957 but then, due to inadequate numbers, suffered a gapped post for six years until 1963.

The WRAC dealt with exercise 'casualties' suffering from gruesome 'wounds' realistically and enthusiastically simulated by creative RAMC cadets.

For the first time since the War sub-units competed for the George Adam Smith Trophy. Past concerns that too much concentration on sub-unit training would have an adverse effect on Contingent life have been documented. However now, with the right balance achieved between contingent and sub-unit programmes, the intense competitive spirit between sub-units delivered high morale, higher standards and real enjoyment.

Camp included a three day exercise conducted while hiking from Bridge of Orchy to Kentallen on the Loch Linnhe coast. Night bivouacs were made at the head of Loch Etive and in Glen Creran. The worst (or best?) enemy on this exercise was declared, not for the first or last time, to be the Highland Midge. After camp the Training Major, Oxley of the Camerons, left the Army to take up a career at a prep school in the Malverns. In his four years the unit produced 3 Regular and 5 TA officers. Oxley had particularly encouraged mountain warfare and ski training and had brought them up to high standards. His last Rothiemurchus session was spoiled somewhat by a late March hut booking and wet and limited snow cover. As usual, learner skiers had to show grit and determination even before they started on the slopes. OCdt Mike Hewitt and others had on the first day to carry their skis 5 kilometres from their Rothiemurchus base up to Jean's Hut, then in Coire Cas. (With the development of the Cairngorm ski area the hut was later dismantled and moved to Coire an Lochain on the backs of Gurkhas). The skis would be left cached there during the week until being carried back to Rothiemurchus on the last day. Students provided their own safety straps but despite these, after falls and collisions skis would often disappear down the hill into the far distance. This was particularly dispiriting given that every descent required a long slog back-up. Coire Cas often had a rope tow in place but most of the students couldn't afford the ticket and ascended by carrying their skis up over the heather or side-stepping and herring boning up the narrow strip of wet snow which masqueraded as a piste. Once the basic skills had been mastered, largely by trial and error, Aberdeen's winter warriors would climb and descend Coire

Cas or White Lady up to six times a day before starting the slog back to Rothiemurchus.

In addition to ski training, mountain patrols took full advantage of the local wilderness often with overnight expeditions. For example, in 1961, with much more snow around than in the previous year, a winter patrol task, set students off into the Lairig Ghru and up the Lurcher's Crag path bound for Ben Macdui. As is often the case the weather once up on the plateau was very bad and forced a route change. The party descended to the Shelter Stone then up to Loch Etchachan before arriving at the haven of Etchachan Hut for an overnight stop. Everyone was freezing and resorted to pulling up heather to boost the fire. The following day the patrol descended Glen Etchachan, crossed to Loch Avon, went over the Saddle, down Strath Nethy, up over another ridge and finally got back to Jean's Hut. A hard couple of days by anybody's standards but leaving a lasting satisfaction and respect for the Scottish mountains especially in winter. Young Hewitt would continue in the Contingent, get commissioned and would introduce many young cadets to the joys and pains of travel in the Scottish mountains.

Autumn 1960's recruiting, in contrast to the previous year, was a success and unit strength sat at 80 male and over 50 female cadets. The OTC recruiters at Freshers' Day even succeeded in recruiting all those manning the adjacent Forestry Department stand.

The WRAC unit was now the second biggest in the whole UK and included some excellent shots, capable of winning individual prizes at Scottish Command level. The new indoor range did indeed help improve small bore shooting and the Contingent became the first non-Regular unit to win the Highland District Young Soldiers' Trophy.

Garelochhead played host to the 1961 Camp. The camp was marred by the death of a cadet when a medical truck, loaded with tentage and other stores, left the road and overturned.

The unit's sappers spent 5 days at Cultybraggan on demolitions, bridging and mine warfare then rejoined the contingent at Garelochhead to support everyone's watermanship training.

The Ramshorn Trophy was competed for on the Auchencarroch Range with the winners receiving the prize from Honorary Colonel Roy Strathdee. CSM Grant of the SG initiated the Wooden Spoon award before his handover to RSM Whyte SG. The main two day exercise conducted around the Tighnabruaich perimeter in Argyllshire, was abandoned late in the first day after everyone was soaked by torrential rain. The worst storm for years developed overnight and the prudent decision to retreat back to Camp was appreciated by all. The WRAC took a tour of the Four Lochs and 20 cadets visited the Royal Navy submarine depot ship HMS ADAMANT and were shown over one of the latest submarines.

By 1961 the unit structure, composition and training calendar had settled into a stable form that would more or less persist for the next fifty years. With initial planning underway to celebrate its 50th birthday in 1962, the Contingent could look back over its first half century. It had survived and adapted through two World Wars, major economic depression, and compulsory National Service. In its fifth decade it had welcomed the long overdue participation of women in unit life. With its old title back, AUOTC, would continue to have its ups and downs in recruiting but its overall stability would generally stand in contrast to the big changes in Aberdeen, the discovery of oil, and especially the rapid growth of tertiary education hosted by the City. The continued Cold War, intensified by the building of the Berlin Wall in August 1961, brought much of that stability. Facing the Russians demanded the continued presence of a large British Army on the Continent, supported by the TA and in their own small way the OTCs. Domestic and international politics would however continue to provide sufficiently 'hot' experiences for some of the OTC's alumni and staff.

Chapter 7

THE COLD WAR FROM BEDFORD ROAD
1962-1977

Through the winter of 1961/62 frequent weekend outings during term time allowed many cadets to acquire the rudiments of skiing before the annual expedition to Rothiemurchus. At last, Royal Engineers had built a road all the way up to the Hut. Sherpa-like portering of stores, even before the real mountain training could start, was now replaced with the convenience of a ride by 'three tonner'. Shovels and sweat might still be required when snow conditions were good for skiing but not for trucks. Evening 'runs ashore' to Aviemore also became possible. The development of the Cairngorm Ski Area itself was now well underway with a good access road and the first chairlift and permanent tows in place. A day's skiing no longer involved walking up to the corries, and five out of the eight days at 'Rothie' were spent skiing hard. Everyone undertook at least one 24 hour patrol up on the plateau.

At the end of March, Jennie Macbeth handed over command of the WRAC after 7 years. Having initially producing a fair crop of TA officers, WRAC commissioning figures had declined. Most women were attracted more by the notion of being paid to ski and hill walk, than by any fascination with the niceties of Military Law and Army organisational charts. Such subjects seemed to form a significant part of the WRAC lecture syllabus and perhaps contributed to a lack of interest in taking soldiering further beyond university or college. The chain of command was

259

monitoring commissioning figures against the perennial problem of funding and this would soon threaten the existence of the WRAC detachment only ten or so years after it had been created.

Meanwhile, unit life went on with the build up to the 1962 Camp at Monmouth. The unit entrained for a trip reaching further south than any camp since the Medical Unit visited Salisbury Plain in 1914. It was perhaps the excitement of reaching such a balmy latitude that led many to declare this camp the best for years. Monmouth Camp was primarily, although not exclusively, for Royal Engineers training. Therefore the RE sub-unit had a great time as did everyone else during the watermanship training and competitions. Some of the male cadets took watermanship a stage further by competing in the Monmouth Rowing Regatta, at which the Band gave a stirring performance. Other band engagements included the Army Apprentices College, Chepstow and Beating Retreat at Monmouth Castle. The Castle was, and remains, the RHQ of the Royal Monmouthshire Royal Engineers (Militia). As well as being doubly 'royal' the unit survives to this day (2012) as the last remaining 'militia' unit and thus the oldest regiment in the Reserve Forces.

Tactical training concluded with strenuous manoeuvres during the final exercise on the Black Mountains. Stanley McGrath joined the unit as Adjutant/QM at this time and would serve in this capacity until 1976 seeing both his daughters serve in AUOTC.

For those who had the time and inclination a variety of summer attachments were available. Having a Seaforths Training Officer, Major Wood, it was probably easier than usual to secure an attachment for three officer cadets to the

WRAC Passive, 1962, Monmouth

WRAC Active, 1962, Monmouth

11th Seaforths (TA) camp at Folkestone. Here they were treated as members of the Officers Mess and had the very worthwhile experience of commanding full strength platoons.

Eight RAMC officer cadets got a chance to sample London's life while on attachment to the Millbank Military Hospital situated on the Thames next to the Tate Gallery. A few cadets again went off to test their luck on the parachute course.

Recruiting began as usual in the Autumn. Each sub-unit suffered peaks and troughs in strength as people came and went. The Band was no different, at this time going through a slump with only 5 pipers on the books compared to 15 at St Andrews.

From 1958 to mid 1962, AUOTC produced 3 Regular and 22 Reserve Officers. These statistics and those from the other UOTCS were being scrutinised by the Treasury. In preparation for the inevitable debate, Defence Minister Peter Thorneycroft prepared a Cabinet Memo on the future of UOTCs. Thorneycroft had been a gunner officer in the 1930s and in WW2 he served for a brief spell with the Royal Artillery on the south coast before serving on the General Staff's Joint Planning Committee. His memo re-asserted that the UOTCS had three functions of <u>equal</u> importance:

1. Pre-service training for undergraduates considering joining the Regular Army. The Army, like all major employers, badly needed recruits from the Universities so as to have suitable material for filling their highest posts. The supply was inadequate but in 1960 the importance of OTCs had been emphasized to Universities and improvement was expected, at least over the 3 year duration of a degree course.

2. Pre-service training for candidates for commissions in the Army Emergency Reserve, the Territorial Army and the Combined Cadet Force. The end of National Service meant that no more young officers were joining the Reserve and Cadet Forces with previous full time experience. This fact increased the value of OTC training.

3. Providing a practical link between Service thought and the Universities. Abolishing the OTCs would sever a link valued by both institutions. The ending of National Service again made the OTC's role in this respect more important than ever.

In common with most departmental dealings with the Treasury a potential sacrifice was prepared. The fourteen WRAC university detachments could be disbanded to save some money while preserving the remainder of the OTC.

Probably unaware of the looming threat, 120 past and present members of AUOTC celebrated its 50th Jubilee with a ball in Elphinstone Hall on 6 Nov 1962. The following evening the MEC marked the 50th by entertaining 40 serving and ex-officers. At that year's rather special Remembrance Parade, the Sword of Honour was carried by Mike Hewitt.

On Thursday 29 Nov 1962, a Cabinet Meeting got underway in Admiralty House. Of the 22 men sitting at the table, 14 had direct experience of wartime commissioned service in the Army, one had served in the RAF, and one at the Bletchley Park code breaking centre. Future Cabinets of any political hue were unlikely to include such corporate experience and understanding of the TA, the Regular Army and the demands of commissioned service.

The Cabinet worked its way through the agenda: agreeing to send Winston Churchill an 88th Birthday Card; discussing compensation for victims of crime; broadcasting policy; and the pros and cons of increased office block development in London. The final item concerned the future of the sixteen University OTCs. The Chief Secretary to the Treasury recommended they should be abolished. They were producing too few officers for the Regular Army, cost £460,000 per year, and now needed an additional £150,000 for new equipment. The Minister for Defence replied that provision of Regular Officers had never been the sole or main purpose of the OTCs. Their real value lay in their contribution to the Reserves where quality officers were at a premium. They also maintained a link between the Universities and the Army. This link was now more than ever necessary following the end of National Service. Half the running costs were for the regular staff who would be re-employed elsewhere thus only about £230,000 would actually be saved annually.

The First Secretary of State, Rab Butler, supported the view that the links between Universities and the Army were of great and increasing importance at a time when pacifist organisations were flourishing and the steadying influence of National Service had disappeared. All too little was being done to instil patriotism and a sense of public service into the young. He pointed out that the University authorities themselves would strongly resent the disappearance of their OTCs. Further discussion brought the conclusions that it was total OTC membership that counted, not just those going on to commissioning. Morale especially among the instructors had been affected by policy uncertainties over the past few years. Absence of policy was also affecting the supply of up to date equipment which would in turn not help recruitment. Prime Minister Harold Macmillan concluded that there were two options. Firstly, the OTCs could be allowed to continue under the present unsatisfactory uncertainty for a year or so longer and then be closed. The second option however was to give them firm support now and encourage the Universities to make more of them. The Cabinet seemed to favour the second option. The PM undertook to consult further. Saving the £30,000 annual running costs of the WRAC detachments would be included in his deliberations.

Back in Aberdeen, cadets eagerly awaited the first snowfall so that winter warfare training could recommence on Sundays. The end of term was celebrated by a Christmas Dance in the drill hall at Bedford Road with over 200 participants. It was becoming clear however that the WRAC detachment was to be disbanded at the end of the session.

The unit pressed on with its usual programme of training and competitions. Success was achieved in small bore shooting, pipe band and country dancing competitions. In 1963 the unit would once more go overseas for Camp. AUOTC would, at Benbecula, conduct the first ever TA annual camp in the Outer Hebrides. The infrequent steamer ferry timetable meant that the first two days of 'camp' were actually spent in Aberdeen. Black Dog Ranges were used for the Ramshorn Competition shoot and familiarisation training with the 3.5 inch rocket launcher, the 2inch mortar and the Energa Grenade. Range work complete, the Contingent set off by coach for Kyle of Lochalsh and the MacBrayne's steamer to Lochboisdale. On arrival everyone was made welcome by the Advance Party and the staff of the Royal

Artillery Guided Weapons Range. Ten days of training included a 36 hour patrol exercise covering 20 miles and many tasks including ambushes, night navigation, recce boats, casualty handling, and improvised rafts. The WRAC completed a shorter 24 hour exercise.

Former WRAC leader Jennie MacBeth came 'over the sea from Skye' to visit her old unit which she had been dismayed to hear, was about to vanish. The sad departure of the WRAC from Contingent life was marked by a special farewell parade at the end of Camp.

The rest of the summer was spent with the usual attachments and courses including five Officer Cadets assisting at ACF Camps. In the hope and expectation that disbandment would soon be reversed, HQ staff took steps to preserve the WRAC detachment under the administrative care of the WRAC within the local TA Royal Signals unit. Happily these camouflage arrangements were not required for too long and the WRAC Detachment was restored to its rightful place in 1964. Hindsight indicates that any notion of ending WRAC student soldiering was misguided. The role and integration of women in the Army, Regular and Territorial, steadily increased over the following decades. On 1 April 1998, the Army increased the ratio of posts and trades open to women from 47% to 70%.

In 1964 the separate War Office, Admiralty and Air Ministry centralised under the Ministry of Defence. At the other end of the military scale, AUOTC was pleased to have appointed to it, a Non Regular Permanent Staff (NRPS) RQMS.

For all of Aberdeen's citizens, 1964 was notable for the famous Typhoid Epidemic. Typhoid spread from a can of corned beef that had been processed in an Argentinean factory using untreated river water. Schools were closed early, giving pupils a memorably long summer holiday. Travel restrictions were put in place and over 500 people were hospitalised and placed in isolation. National and world media had a great time at Aberdeen's expense, the City losing millions of pounds from tourism alone. Once the all clear was sounded the Queen was welcomed by 40,000 people lining the streets when she made a morale boosting visit to thank medical staffs, and signal to the world that Aberdeen was a safe place to visit. Needless to say the AUOTC Camp planned for Cultybraggan had to be held at home in Bedford Road but was nevertheless deemed reasonably successful and enjoyable.

Two members of the Contingent did however manage to get well beyond Bedford Road during the Christmas vacation. Ian Proud and Chris Harrison were attached to 14/20 Kings Hussars in Benghazi, Libya. They became familiar with Ferret, Saracen, and Saladin vehicles. During their second week, an Army Air Corps Auster gave them a flight over Benghazi to view World War II bomb and shell craters, and Rommel's old Afrika Korps HQ. They took part in night exercises, escape and evasion, desert recce and navigation by sun compass. In a *Gaudie* newspaper article titled 'Sand in Their Sporrans', it was explained that this was the first time AUOTC had sent officer cadets overseas on detachment. It was hoped to repeat such trips to regiments in the Middle East and Germany. Five years later Colonel Gadaffi would take control of Libya removing it from the list of British Army training destinations. The need for wide expanses of land to conduct large scale manoeuvre, and live firing with increasingly powerful weapons, led planners to start considering the Canadian prairie as an option. In due course Aberdeen's Student Soldiers would get there too.

'Sand In Their Sporrans', Libya, 1964

In February 1965 the MEC thanked Reid formally for his 8 years as CO and his previous service to the Contingent particularly running the Intelligence sub-unit. The MEC noted TB Smith's support of the nomination of Major PEG Mitchell RAMC(TA) as the next CO. Smith believed that having a CO drawn from the University staff was highly desirable. His recommendation was based on his own experience of OTC command and his membership of two University MECs. Mitchell as CO AUOTC became an ex-officio member of the County Territorial and Auxiliary Forces Association.

In 1965, the unit escaped the bounds of Aberdeen and even Scotland, by holding Summer Camp at Leek in Staffordshire. The usual exercises and activities were supplemented with visits to local places of interest such as the Rolls Royce factory at Crewe. Former CO and now the

Honorary Colonel, Professor TB Smith, visited the Camp at Leek.

Rothiemurchus Hut 1966 - Now Accessible by Vehicles

In November Reid's long and valuable service was marked by a Dinner at the Northern Hotel. He was presented with a silver tobacco box.. As usual for departing COs he would continue his involvement as a member of the MEC. All too soon there was concern that the unit would suffer another short tenure CO. OTC CO standard tour lengths were now accepted as 5 years with options for extensions. In October 1966 Mitchell left the University's Department of Clinical Chemistry for a Consultant post in Dundee. Mitchell did feel that he could continue in command given that the distance was manageable and the fact that he was in Aberdeen on most weekends in any case. The University Court agreed to the arrangement and undertook to pay

Mitchell's travel costs if the Army wouldn't.

As Mitchell settled into his new command, Lieutenant Commander Murray RN arrived to set up Britain's first University Royal Naval Unit. Formally established in 1967, Aberdeen URNU was the pioneer for fourteen others across the country. Aberdeen harbour was soon the home port for HMS THORNHAM.

While new things were afoot, the past was saluted by naming the University's first student house at 7/8 Rubislaw Terrace, 'Forbes House', after U Company's Sniper Sergeant JK Forbes.

Major and controversial changes were about to happen in the TA. Under the Labour Government's Reserve Forces Act of 1966, the TA lost its, almost sixty year old, structure of formed reserve divisions. The Territorial Army and Volunteer Reserve (TAVR) would consist of individual units in 4 categories:

TAVR 1 - 'Volunteer' Units for all purposes.

TAVR 2 - 'Volunteer' Units with a NATO role particularly with the British Army of the Rhine (BAOR).

TAVR 3 - 'Territorial' units for Home Defence (these would be disbanded or cadre-ised in 1969).

TAVR 4 - University OTCs and Bands

The TA had already been drastically reduced in 1961 as the supply of manpower from conscription and National Service ended. The TA reduced from 266 fighting units to 195. Forty-six regiments of the Royal Artillery, 18 battalions of infantry, 12 regiments of Royal Engineers and 2 regiments of the Royal Corps of Signals disappeared, mainly by amalgamation of under strength units. The 1967 change to the TA involved further cuts and many thought the heart was being ripped out of the institution. Military Historian Correlli Barnett at the time summarised the case against the reorganisation as follows:

'Indeed after the Labour Government's re-organisations the reserves were weaker than they had been for a hundred years, far weaker than in 1914 or 1939, when at least there had stood behind the regulars the fourteen divisions of the Territorials. Even at the cost of totally denuding the United Kingdom of troops......BAOR could only be brought up to war establishment not enlarged. That army was therefore capable of fighting for no more than a week or so before wasting away from want of sleep and reinforcements.'

The Government case was based on the conclusion that in the nuclear age there would not be a protracted war on the Continent which required the large scale formed reserves of 'Volunteers' which the country had relied upon in the past. If nuclear deterrence failed NATO conventional forces would fight as a tripwire and short fuse while politicians attempted to avoid Armageddon. Everyone trained for intensive operations including the early use by one side or the other of tactical nuclear, chemical and perhaps even biological weapons. If all that failed then the ultimate solution lay in the firepower of the Royal Navy's new submarine launched ballistic missile system, POLARIS. The RAF, the Royal Artillery and the Royal Engineers had their own atomic munitions. Nuclear, Biological and Chemical (NBC)

Training was an important part of everyone's schedule of lectures and tests. During senior TA staff map exercises or study days, participating US officers would usually be the first, when things started to look desperate for the Allies, to call for someone to 'bring on the nukes'. For decades, unless an unlikely victory had been achieved against the Warsaw Pact hordes, Armageddon brought a neat if depressing end to exercises. Maps were then folded, vehicles washed down and everyone retired to barracks for a well earned drink comforted to know that, in the real world, deterrence based upon mutually assured destruction seemed to be working.

North East Scotland played its full part in the Cold War acting as the base for maritime reconnaissance and fighter aircraft. Russian long range bombers continually tested the UK's air defences, and were routinely intercepted by the RAF.

Some members of the old TA, especially those with war service, growing families and stable careers, had often questioned their own continued commitment. Scares like Korea, Suez and the Cuban Missile Crisis were unsettling to the more mature. The new role of the TAVR especially in the higher liability categories caused many to leave. Turning out, as in the past, in whole divisions under a general mobilisation to fight for national survival was one thing. Mobilising as units to reinforce lesser but no less deadly military adventures tipped the balance for some against the positives of TA lifestyle, pay, and annual bounties. Of course the TAVR retained many people and attracted many new ones. There remained a need for young officers, for which the OTCs were a key source.

Between Camps OTC training carried on in the local area. In November 1967 an intrepid reporter from the *Gaudie* reported his visit to a night exercise on Black Dog. On a Saturday evening the OTC mounted a deliberate attack on positions held by the young Highland Brigade recruits from Gordon Barracks. The reporter was suitably impressed by the para-flares, Very Lights, Thunderflashes and expenditure of blank ammunition. In the pre-dawn darkness of Sunday morning, roles were reversed with the young Jocks on the attack. Defensive fire opened prematurely to assist them in direction finding, their axis of advance being initially somewhat askew. Of course much of the point behind field exercises was that at least as much was learned from mistakes as from things that went right.

After Summer Camps at Cultybraggan and another two across in Benbecula, for 1969 the Contingent headed once more for the far south and Longmoor, Hampshire. After that Camp Mitchell handed over command to Dr John Mann. Mann had served in Epsom College Junior Division OTC and served as an Air Raid Warden in Camberwell during the War, earning him his Defence Medal. He had served as a Regimental Medical Officer (RMO) during his National Service 1950-52, mostly with the Gurkhas during anti-communist guerrilla operations in Malaya where he had been Mentioned in Despatches.

On returning from full time National Service he started his long TA career with RMO and staff appointments in London. Once a member of the University's teaching staff he became 2IC and Training Officer with Aberdeen's 152(H) Field Ambulance (TA) and later commanded that unit for 6 years including its redesignation after TA restructuring, to 252(H) Field Ambulance (V). In 1968 he was the senior medical officer and advisor to Commander Highland Area and also chaired the Executive Committee for Aberdeen's

Wapinschaw. He would command AUOTC for six years.

Olly Urquhart, former World Champion Drum Major, was one of several former cadets who after graduation, became commissioned and joined the staff. Urquhart passed a Commissioning Board at Stirling Castle, and took command of the RE sub-unit. The sub-unit members came from all faculties and colleges but included many budding architects from the Scott Sutherland School.

Scotstown Moor provided a local opportunity for trying out the TAVR Plant Troop's machines and blowing limited size demolition charges. Training with improvised and equipment bridges and rafts was available at Sapper weekends at Drip Camp outside Stirling. Usually only Summer Camp, visits and detachments gave the opportunity for bigger and better demolition bangs. Finding a task near Aberdeen that would involve steel cutting charges and the collapse of concrete walls was a very welcome event.

The World War II RAF at Dyce had built a shooting range on Brimmond Hill. In latter years, this range had been heavily used by the TA as a handy alternative to the Black Dog or Gordon Barracks ranges. The range however had fallen into disuse and in particular the butts were filling with water and presented a hazard to children. To the delight of the AUOTC sappers, the removal of the target frames and the collapsing of retaining walls into the flooded trenches would require explosives. Olly Urquhart visited all the neighbours to warn them of the forthcoming explosion. A chicken farmer was not thrilled to hear the news. His chickens and their egg production were only just recovering from the shock of a recent air display at Dyce. An RAF Lightning interceptor fighter had graced the display by roaring vertically and loudly into the skies.

However preparations proceeded and when everything was ready and tested the button was pressed. Nothing happened and, after the required pause, Olly and the PSI made the long walk out to see what had gone wrong. Eventually it was found the electrical cable had been damaged during previous use by the Signals sub-unit. Fault fixed, the demolition was successfully completed. Brimmond Hill later became a communications site supporting the Forties and other central North Sea oilfields.

By the late 1960s the unit was equipped with the 7.62mm Self Loading Rifle, the old Bren LMG adapted to the new calibre, the Sub Machine Gun and 9mm pistols. Field uniform had also stepped forward with the inevitable lag behind the Regular Army. The old Battle Dress, leather soled ammunition or 'ammo' boots and gaiters had given way to olive green combat suits, Boots DMS (Directly Moulded Sole), short ankle putties and heavy pullovers. Personal load carrying webbing for exercises and range work remained of the 1937 pattern for most with the lucky or really keen with spare pocket money, acquiring 1958 pattern. By the end of the decade the unit's distinctive blue/yellow/blue stable belt had been designed, approved and introduced.

The WRAC in the field remained distinctive with gaiters and brown leather boots. The WRAC continued to wear battle dress tunics and WRAC berets for parades for a while but would in the early 1970s soon acquire the Lovat Green jackets and peaked WRAC caps for ceremonial occasions. They were intrigued when issued with dress shirts with 'granddad style' detachable collars.

The men's Balmoral's were replaced by khaki Tam O Shanters for the field and Glengarries for parades. Ceremonial parade dress for Remembrance Parade or other smart occasion involved the time consuming application of ironing, boot polish, whitener, and Brasso to the appropriate bits of Brogues Highland, white spats with black buttons, diced hose tops, properly 'belled' red garter flashes, hair sporrans, kilts, white belts and No2 Dress Kilt Jackets.

The 'Swinging Sixties' appeared to end with many significant events. One of the more inspiring projects of the Cold War triumphed with the successful landing of Apollo 11 on the Moon. British politics would now benefit from more undergraduate participation as the minimum voting age was reduced from 21 to 18.

For the British Army 1969 saw the first deployment of units to Internal Security operations in Northern Ireland under OPERATION BANNER. Units normally based in Germany and the UK started to rotate through six month 'roulement' tours and some occupied barracks as 'resident' battalions for 2½ year tours. OP BANNER would run for nearly forty years only ending formally in 2007. At its peak the Army would have 27,000 soldiers in Ulster. The fight against the IRA would kill 763 members of the British Armed Forces and wound another 6,100. Nearly all of the OTC's Regular Army alumni from that period, of whatever cap-badge, would serve in Northern Ireland.

Northern Ireland operations brought changes in tactics, equipment and doctrine. The Royal Engineers were once again required to be innovative in 'fortress' construction. Army observation posts, patrol bases, barracks and police stations required protection against car bomb, mortar, rocket and sniper attack. Any movement by the Army ran the constant risk of attack by Improvised Explosive Devices (IEDs). Building and route searches led to the steady development of tactics and equipment for specialist search and bomb disposal teams. Infantry tactics for urban and rural patrolling, cordon and searches, and Vehicle Check Points (VCPs) constantly evolved to match terrorist inventiveness. In mainland UK, Germany, and elsewhere in the world, barracks and personal security grew in emphasis. Checking under cars before the drive to work, in civilian clothes, became the norm. Coaches taking soldiers anywhere were subjected to close inspection before anyone boarded. The Army became more acquainted with helicopters than it had ever done before. Some places in 'bandit country' could only be reached safely by air.

With an Army actively involved in training for the highest level of military operations on the North German Plain, and simultaneously conducting low intensity security operations in Ulster, PSIs posted to AUOTC soon brought a wealth of varied training and experience to enliven the programme.

For a time the Infantry sub-unit benefited from the influence of an SAS(V) officer. In addition to acquiring an enthusiasm for heavy load carrying, speed marching and blindfolds, the young infanteers learned a few tricks which were definitely not included in the Marquess of Queensberry's boxing code. It is unrecorded if such techniques were employed in a brief and fortunately unique punch-up on Aberdeen's quayside. After the merriment of a shared social occasion a few OTC cadets found themselves invited onboard HMS THORNHAM. It is alleged Naval hospitality included the tramping of Army fingers on companionway steps by Navy boots just once too often. The ensuing mêlée celebrated an age old pastime between Her Majesty's Armed Services. Friendly relations were soon re-established, although occasionally a nocturnal attempt would be made to move THORNHAM from her allocated berth. A Tug o' War on heavy warps never got very far. THORNHAM provided many a cruise for AUOTC cadets, whether on sea days up to Fraserburgh or on amphibious operations off Black Dog.

A typical OTC year in the 1970s would start as ever with recruiting. Stalls would be set up at the Freshers' Days in Mitchell Hall and as many as could be 'hooked' were transferred by minibus out to Bedford Road for more information and a chat with the staff and chosen cadets. Many joined having heard from flat mates what the unit offered. Some had already decided that the OTC would be part of their University experience, having acquired a taste for such things in their school cadet contingents. The opportunity to continue in piping and drumming brought many in who otherwise would not have been that keen.

The Winter term involved the frantic effort to drill and clothe cadets in time for Remembrance Sunday. Near the day itself, local residents would be treated to the Pipes and Drums leading the OTC, URNU and UAS out for practice parades along Bedford Road, around the roundabout, and up Tillydrone Avenue. Final rehearsals would include the proper route out on to Bedford Road and down Meston Walk, behind the Chemistry Building, to King's College. The day itself would normally go without hitch, a credit to the hard work of the cadets and the OTC staff. A piper would play *Flowers of the Forest* and someone with the necessary aptitude played the bugle for the *Last Post* and *Reveille*. After inspection by a senior visiting officer the whole parade marched back to Bedford Road where uniforms would be retrieved and everyone would enjoy various grades of sherry

An AFV 432 armoured personnel carrier visits Bedford Road in 1973. MT Garage visible behind left and Signals and Band Hut behind right.

in the Cadets Mess and Drill Hall. Members of the MEC and other senior friends of the Contingent from the University and Colleges would be entertained along with former cadets and staff members. The party would normally continue for the rest of the day including refuelling stops at Indian Restaurants and visits to the UAS HQ which by now was in Fairfield House, Fonthill.

During winter term new cadets would conduct short exercises by day and night out on Black Dog to learn the

279

basics of living in the field. Weapon training would commence with naming of parts, frequent stripping, cleaning and assembling. Safe handling of weapons was continually emphasised in expectation of the first days of live firing. The Drill Hall and Cadets Mess offered enough space for formal and impromptu celebrations. After training on a Thursday evening students would relax with a few drinks and be joined by more senior and studious colleagues coming in from sessions in the library or labs. Saturday evenings were normally heavier affairs with often long bouts of folk singing and general banter interlaced with Eightsome Reels and Strip the Willows in the hall. Some of the WRAC would be involved in more technical and precise Scottish Country Dancing in preparation for the Northern Lights Inter University Competition due in the Spring. The band would be working up its competition March, Strathspey and Reel set and other renditions of Slow Marches, Quick Marches, Hornpipes and Jigs. The band usually included accomplished solo pipers who would take advantage of the band hut or Drill Hall for their own practice.

After Christmas, the next big social event was Burns Night. With the Cadet's mess laid out for Dinner, characters such as Gabby Galbraith would give highly theatrical renditions of *Tam O Shanter* accompanied by flashing room lights and banged metal drinks trays for storm effects. The full set of speeches would be programmed, forcing 'volunteers' to gain confidence in public speaking if not in Burns-era Scots. Excesses of haggis, cranachan and whisky would be worked off later during wild dancing in the Drill Hall.. In retrospect it is amazing how these events were catered for so well given the small and rather basic facilities. The likes of QM Sgt Dod Rennie and Cadets Mess Sgt Bill

Lowson certainly earned their pay on those long evenings.

For cadets who had completed their basic training the sub-units offered deeper insights into life in the Infantry, Royal Signals and Royal Engineers. The REME and Intelligence Corps subunits had not lasted long and wasted away for want of qualified staff and sufficient volunteers.

AUOTC's originals, the Medics, around since 1912, survived as a distinct sub-unit until the end of the 1960s. One factor in the demise was a significant reduction of the University medical course's length. Fewer medical students were prepared to allocate precious study time to the OTC. With smaller numbers the Army could no longer justify the allocation of an RAMC PSI, the last being WO2 Cross. Medical students of course would continue to join the unit. They featured particularly at this time among the Band's ranks. The still relatively long course meant much prized continuity and constantly improving ability for the Pipe Sergeants and Pipe Majors of the future.

Of the three remaining sub-units, women cadets chose between the mixed Signals and Sappers, the Infantry remaining a male-only pursuit as did the Band until the arrival of Elaine Marnoch who went on to achieve many firsts for women Army pipers.

Signallers would learn all about their radios and how to keep them working. The Larkspur range of radios included the A40's (carried at section level), A41's and A42's (carried at platoon level). All were VHF manpacks and very heavy, even without spare batteries. The A41 weighed 18lb 8oz and the spare battery a further 8lb 8oz. At camp the signallers would also use the B70, a man portable SHF radio-relay, and the C11 vehicle mounted HF transceiver. The latter was very susceptible to changes in atmospherics and many a night was spent huddled in the back of a Land Rover on watch, listening to the awful white noise of interference. The British Army's Larkspur radios would be replaced by Clansman and then in the 2000s by Bowman.

Voice procedure and other aspects of correct radio net discipline were practiced along with the more physical aspects of setting up, camouflaging and operating command posts. In the days before secure voice radios, manual code systems were used. SLIDEX, which had been introduced before D Day in 1943/44, continued as the basic low level code through the Cold War into the early 1980s at least. It consisted of different cards for different topics, each with a grid with commonly used words and short phrases. Two plastic slides, with daily changing code letters written on in chinagraph pencil, completed the system. GRIDDLE and MAPCO were used for coding grid references. These encryption systems were replaced in the mid 1980s by BATCO.

In the early 1970s Morse Code was still being taught in the Bedford Road Signals Hut , with speed and accuracy at sending and receiving being slowly built up. Some basic Signals intelligence techniques were practiced during attempts between operators in separate rooms to identify each other by their Morse 'fist'. Individuals could indeed be identified by their own unique speeds; and the durations of their 'dahs', 'dits' and gaps.

At the weekends, lessons from classroom lectures, pamphlets and training films could be practiced in the field. For the Sappers this might involve a pleasant tour of Deeside involving recce for bridge demolition. The Sapper role in Germany was centred on creating large obstacle belts of minefields, demolitions, wire and booby traps to stop and channel any Warsaw Pact land attack. Most major bridges in Germany had inbuilt chambers ready to receive pre-calculated demolition charges. Every major bridge and tunnel had its own demolition target folder setting out exactly how much explosive and other stores were required and where they should be placed to guarantee destruction. Deeside offered a range of different bridge types and sizes. Having measured up a few bridges, consulted pamphlet tables and done the arithmetic, the various demolition proformae were completed in the comfort of a local hostelry.

In any defence plan some bridge demolitions would be 'reserved'. 'Reserved Demolitions' and their defence were given great emphasis in Army training. Strict protocols were set for stages of readiness and who could order the blowing of the bridge. As World War II had demonstrated, getting all this wrong could either prematurely strand significant friendly forces on the wrong side of a river, or allow the enemy to sweep across unhindered with tragic results.

Choosing Aberdeen for a post graduate Ecology Course, Australian forester and officer, Rob Youl joined the RE Sub-Unit. Weekends were spent on minor MACC tasks, such as building footbridges and blowing up tree stumps. Youl loved the mountains and joined Hewitt, Ewen and others on a trip to Glencoe. On the way, a deer was hit and lay badly injured on the road. Youl's otherwise deep knowledge of hand tools did not extend to the veterinary use of the ice axe. Under instruction by Hewitt, Youl dispatched the deer, thus guaranteeing a venison diet for the climbers.

In addition to the technical sub-unit and contingent training, the WRAC occasionally went off for their own cap-badge weekend. For example, in the 1970s Captain Di

Henderson took her girls off to the comforts of Letham Grange near Arbroath.

For the WRAC the road to equality was not without its painful experiences. At one summer camp it was decided to issue Boots DMS to the women as replacements for the old but comfortable WRAC brown leather boots. This was done immediately before a night exercise involving many miles of walking. The resulting damage to feet meant only a few WOCdts could wear their parade shoes and participate in the CO's end of camp inspection.. Even the oldest military lessons, such as wearing-in new footwear gradually, appear to need frequent re-affirmation.

The presence of the WRAC caused occasional alarms in the night. At one Summer Camp a young soldier from another unit, only transiting through the camp, returned worse for drink from the local town. Later, returning from the loo, he became lost and stumbled naked into the WRAC billets. The ever alert WRAC raised the alarm in magnificent style. Inebriation was probably all that saved the young man from a coronary event. The Band, ever gallant and living in a nearby hut, came to the rescue. All was quickly put right.

At Easter the unit's traditions at Rothiemurchus were preserved on Exercise COLD COMFORT. On arrival everyone was allocated to walking groups based on hill fitness. With the summit just over 900 feet above the Hut, timed ascents of Castle Hill's heather and snow clad flanks, sorted out the 'half hour per thousand feet' mountain men from the rest. For the skiers, equipment had progressed considerably from ammo boots and screws. The standard boot was now a double laced affair made for the purpose. Cable bindings were still the norm although the more experienced or better off skier might now display the latest in clip boots and step-in bindings. Despite the road access and some further building and improvements, the old Hut retained much of the remote log cabin atmosphere of its early days with the deer visiting the cook's window for scraps. Further improvements were at a planning stage when sadly in 1974 the Hut burnt down. Timber built and festooned inside with unit badges carved from firewood, its complete destruction was inevitable once fire took hold. Many of the firewood plaques had gone up in flames well before the big fire. Some occupants were too lazy to go outside in the cold for firewood. In order that the AUOTC's record might survive such vandalism Dr Colin McIntosh had painted the unit capbadge and dates of occupation on the metal plate above the fireplace. That too was destroyed in the blaze.

AUOTC's Engineer subunit helped break up the scorched concrete foundations in the Summer of 1976. The more modern facilities were extended and due to funding arrangements and a move more towards service family R&R, paid winter training days were no longer possible. The OTC's long and regular association with 'Rothie' ended in the 1980s.

Formal examined OTC training at this time centred on the Certificate of Military Training (CMT). Although all graduates commissioned into the Regular Army received antedated seniority, a CMT Pass gained attendance at a shorter Sandhurst Course beside University Cadetship Officers. Training would take place during term time and a crammer/revision session would be held immediately before the written and practical tests. Aberdeen allocated a full year to preparation for CMT while some other OTCs rushed it through in less time. OTCs took it in turn to host the CMT weekends in the Spring and Autumn sometimes at a training camp but if possible at halls of residence, a conference centre or some other location with more style and individual study bedrooms. Middleton Hall, a Grade A listed classic country house in Midlothian, south of Dalkeith, provided very comfortable surroundings for cadets mugging up on unit organisation diagrams, weapon ranges and other military matters. Nearby Soutra Hill, where the A68 climbs up from the Forth Valley, provided the required extensive view for map reading tests and sufficient rough pasture for presenting novel ideas on platoon defensive positions and avenues of attack.

Before exams loomed too large on the horizon two big events took place. The Students' Charities Week had evolved from the earlier Gala Weeks set up to fund Aberdeen's new hospitals. The week, including the Student Show in His Majesty's Theatre, brought in huge amounts of money for charity. During the lead up to the big weekend, Council buses took parties of students out to city and county schools. Schoolchildren would sit in their classes while the noise of rattling donation tins approached up the corridor then burst into the room. All manner of fancy dress and make-up was in evidence as loose change was handed over by teacher and class after the traditional initial refusal to do so. As quickly as they arrived the students got back on their buses and set off for the next school on their list. During the week various stunts would be executed. For example, one morning the City woke to the news that students had climbed out on the Rubislaw Quarry cables, bivouacked for the night and unfurled a big charity banner. In Marischal Quad lorries from the local road haulage industry would be converted to all manner of themed floats. The stars of the fleet were the fire breathing 'monsters'. The OTC would usually have its own float and most cadets, including the band, would be out during the Saturday with collecting tins to do their bit. All pubs, offices and shops were generally fair game as were pedestrians, buses and cars on Union Street. Indeed people went especially into town to see the fancy dress and be accosted in a good cause. Unit pipers busked for cash. The climax of the campaign came in the evening when the Marischal Gates opened to the sound of hundreds of cans being shaken in unison in the Quad. Barely able to hear their instruments, the OTC Band would lead the Procession out under the arch and down Schoolhill bound for distant Queens Cross. Dozens of floats, vintage cars, old fire engines, traction engines and hundreds of students in fancy dress gathered at Queens Cross just before dusk. As darkness set in, tar rope torches were lit and the parade set off down St Swithin Street and along Union Grove. The pavements would be thronged with folk and coins would be thrown out from the surrounding houses and flats. By the time the procession got down Union Street and the Band re-entered Marischal Quad to *'The Black Bear'* everyone was tired. The bass drummer had certainly had enough exercise for the evening. There would be relief that no drum skins or feather bonnets had been damaged by tar rope embers or flying coins. Refreshed by a few drinks and sandwiches in the Mitchell Hall, cadets would get on the trucks for the next phase of merriment back at Bedford Road.

Exercise Northern Lights involved all the Scottish University OTCs and that of Queens Belfast. For the latter, the weekend in Scotland would be a welcome relief from the tensions back home. There would be shooting, orienteering, dancing, piping and drumming competitions. Venues varied with OTCs taking it in turns to administer the weekend.

Normally one of the usual TA training camps would host the affair but in the mid 1970s Aberdeen made the event special by taking over most of Aviemore's hotel complex. Fort George and the local forests hosted the shooting and orienteering events.

The OTC would go quiet for a spell as nearly everyone swotted for their end of year exams. At that time there was much less continuous assessment than now and nearly everything rested on the end of year sprint. Robert Gordon courses tended to end earlier to get their people out on the graduate market early. Different exam and graduation timetables meant some cadets were sometimes unable to attend camps and other activities.

As exams were completed preparations could start for deployment to Summer Camp. Throughout the Seventies all the Camps were held in England, the nearest at Ripon, North Yorkshire and most further off in the balmy south.

In the 1970s, moving an OTC to Camp in the south of England by rail was still an economical option. Cadets would form up at Aberdeen's Joint Station and after roll call load on to the allocated corridor carriages. A few days before the Main Party arrived at a railhead as close to camp as Beeching's Axe had made possible, an Advance Party would set off by road. Driver training including Heavy Good Vehicles (HGV) was available for a few. So cadets would join permanent staff in driving the unit Bedford trucks and Landrovers, some with trailers. Additional vehicles could be picked up from depots such as Stirling. For camps in the south of England an overnight stop would be made at Halton Camp, Lancaster. On one such stop the unit's Scots Guards RSM found it necessary to inform, as only a Guards RSM can inform, the unfortunate transit camp cook that his officer cadets did not carry knives, forks and spoons with them when not in the field. Buckled and bent cutlery of the Uri Geller mould, was duly found just before very hungry student soldiers reverted to using their fingers on the gravy.

IRA intervention on any aspect of military activity on the mainland UK was certainly possible if not probable. Before leaving Bedford Road, RSM WO1 Danny Macmillan emphasised to one Advance Party that they should be ready to 'shoot to kill' to protect themselves and the weapons, ammunition and detonators being carried. This was no controversial statement of secret Government policy but merely a recognition that in real life shooting anyone would probably kill them. Thus it was best to aim for the centre of any target rather than harbour notions of winging people as in the cowboy films. Fortunately there appears to be no record of any gunfights involving AUOTC in any of England's delightful motorway service stations of the period.

Advance parties arrived hot and sweaty to take over camp accommodation and set things up before the main party arrived. The building allocated as cadets mess would soon have its beer barrels on tap and strips of Gordon Tartan would be covering tables (6 foot folding flat) and most of the walls. McEwan's Export ('Heavy') and Tennent's Lager formed the staple diet with Newcastle Brown Ale in bottles for the more discerning. The mess record player and the stack of favourite LP records (33 1/3 RPM) were soon in action. A set of flashy lights and suspended camouflage netting would complete the atmosphere of sophisticated nightlife.

For those inured throughout the training year to the poorer meteorological aspects of Black Dog, Cultybraggan or Barry Buddon, Salisbury Plain on a good day had something of the African savannah about it. Heat, blue skies, waving grasses, and larks singing far overhead helped melt away the tensions of exams if not the fear of re-sits. Range work and grenade throwing would be conducted with the usual scares for the staff. The new Electric Target Ranges (ETRs) were novelties at this time. The enemy popped up and fell down at the command of the range officer in a console. No need for butts parties, glue pots, brushes and paper patches. The scores for each firer could be read out immediately after weapons were 'cleared' to cheers or derision from earlier firing details now scrubbing fiercely at blackened SLR gas plugs, assorted springs and pistons. Even the band members, when encouraged to lay aside practice chanters and drum sticks, could put these 'moving parts' together again in a form closely resembling a working weapon. The Infantry sub-unit was always eager to demonstrate natural superiority by re-assembling things blindfolded, standing on their heads or chewing gum at the same time. They could be surprised however. Once, one newly arrived member of the RE Sub-unit out-performed them all in blind weapon maintenance. This was a mystery until they divined that before his appearance as a post graduate at Aberdeen, he had served briefly with the Australian Army in Vietnam, where the weapons were the same but the incentive for dexterity at night much greater.

Everyone would take their turn at Guard and Fire Piquet Duty and have fun with the far from impressive fire fighting cart and its standpipes and hoses. Any minor disciplinary infringements were rewarded with more exposure to the fire pump and amateur astronomy at the main gate.

Camp days would include sub-unit training on the camp or away at suitable host units. The Infantry would get the chance to fire something bigger and noisier than usual or become 'heavy metal' mechanised infantry for a while. The Signallers would handle unusual radio sets and even bigger antennae than normal. The Sappers might get to plough in Barmines or scatter hundreds of dummy Ranger anti-personnel mines at the press of a button. More hands on effort would be required for the Mark VII mine with its options of single impulse, double impulse or tilt mast.

This and the chance to fire big demolitions involving shaped charges, such as Beehives and Hayricks, gave a good feel for what would be the Sapper's bread and butter work in Germany if the Soviet Third Shock Army ever decided to visit the English Channel. Bridge building without finger loss, and the construction of water supply points might also keep Aberdeen's sappers busy between visits from the range NAAFI wagon.

Some training areas included Fighting in Built Up Area (FIBUA) villages where the infantry and sappers could learn techniques for clearing and holding buildings.

Training done, dinner consumed and no duties to do, groups of cadets could then wonder down a lane, perhaps for some miles, to experience country pubs, thatched roofs and exotic ales. The latter liquids, especially when mixed with too much strong cloudy scrumpy, made next morning's reveille more unpleasant than necessary.

A duty piper, or if unusually motivated to get up, the whole band, would ensure that everyone was awake early each morning ready for more fun. Masochistic pursuits included early morning PT, assault courses, night orienteering, and lying interminably in ambush for an enemy who never came.

Once Dave Smith formerly of 15 Para(V) arrived as 2IC in his run up to command, night manoeuvres would often start with everyone jumping out of the back of a moving Bedford to simulate an attack from the sky. Those whose ankles remained intact and who had not impaled themselves on their SLR Blank Firing Attachment (BFA), reorganised and moved off to contact. Smith assumed command in 1974. He was the Technical Education Advisor with the Aberdeen's Education Authority. His TA service was with Scotland own volunteer parachute battalion, 15 Para, which had its B Company in Aberdeen.

Band engagements would be arranged at local fetes, in pub car parks, town centres and even on one occasion inside Stonehenge. The show often included the women and sometimes the men of the Scottish Country Dancing Team. The Band would Beat Retreat for the camp cocktail party and play for the COs Formal Inspection of the whole Contingent. Sub-units held their own annual dinners at local hotels and restaurants before everything had to be packed up for the long slog back to Aberdeen and other home destinations. The rear party drove back north, sunburnt and ever wary for IRA ambush and spare cutlery.

For those with nothing better or more financially rewarding to do, the Summer vacation after Camp could involve more OTC fun. There could be a Sapper MACC task somewhere for a few days. One such cleared the remains of the old Hut at Rothiemurchus and constructed the bin compound down by the Bailey Bridge at the main Glenmore road.

At the Summer (and Easter) breaks a piper or two might join the AURNU crew of HMS THORNHAM for a cruise across the North Sea or over to the Hebrides. The whole Band sometimes gathered for participation in the Braemar Highland Gathering, or to play for University visitors in Elphinstone Hall. In Summer 1976, unit dancers performed in the USA.

Qualified drivers often assisted the University by driving foreign visitors around or supporting major events such as the International Festival of Youth Orchestras. At one of these the Band competed with jet engines at Dyce to welcome Thor Heyerdahl, the Norwegian adventurer famous for his Kon-Tiki crossing of the Pacific. Norway played a significant part in the OTC summer programme for several years.

Throughout the Cold War Norway played an important role on NATO's northern flank. In the Sixties one or two OTC people had taken part in exercises across the North Sea. VIKING SHIP was a Highland District exchange exercise with the Royal Norwegian Army involving patrolling skills. One year everyone travelled from Dundee to Vikedal on a Landing Ship Tank (LST). The following year the party flew out.

However in the 1970s a larger and more regular deployment took place when HQ Scotland sponsored an annual patrolling exercise in Southern Norway. Since this took place during the summer holidays and after annual camp, AUOTC of course participated, sending out patrols, one of them formed from the Pipe Band. When not patrolling the 'mini band' help the ambassadorial function by playing at local village fetes. Not that the ambassadorial function needed much bolstering, the British Exercise Bar Stocks and prices ensured the utmost fraternity for decades to come.

Exercise participants assembled at Fort George or Cameron Barracks in Inverness before flying out by RAF from Kinloss to Gardermoen Air Station. Coaches took everyone to the Norwegian Army base at Sessvollmoen,

Patrols were issued with Norwegian kit and duvets for their barrack room bunks. Although mid-summer, the keener young Norwegian national servicemen were always out on their wheeled cross country training skis on the dusty roads night and day. The incentive, beyond Nordic habit, seemed to be that somewhat ironically the best skiers would get to serve at least some of their national service in the Royal Guard in Oslo rather than somewhere beyond the Arctic Circle.

Initial days allowed familiarisation with Norwegian kit, the 'dead man in a tin' field ration, and the constant deluge of dairy products at every mealtime. Competing patrols were then sent out for increasing durations to find their way through the tracks and forests and execute various tasks. Disruptive pattern material (DPM) combat dress of the time included a patrol cap. The traditionalist Major commanding the exercise expressed his disdain for such modern un-Highland items in a direct and four letter word manner. The AUOTC patrol, never slaves to contemporary military fashion, deployed into the woods with individualistic selections from Tam o' Shanters, Pipers' Bonnets and the said patrol caps. The latter, with careful ironing and the accompaniment of round 'John Lennon' spectacles, not uncommon in the Arts Faculty of the day, allowed the wearer to successfully imitate a Japanese infantryman of the Burma War. This could only help freeze the hearts of the Norwegian enemy.

The one Regular Army patrol from 1st Gordons were of course the most professional and elusive in their well tailored Tam O' Shanters. These same Regular Jocks were also so impressed with the Norwegian diet that they were eventually moved to capture the kitchen and produce full fried breakfasts for all.

Patrols were, resupplied at RVs. In the hot dry weather everyone was usually eager to recharge bottles with water. Often however the urns contained not cool clear water but yet more milk.

Radios of the time, even with new batteries, usually allowed only broken conversations at any distance. An AUOTC patrol once contacted HQ to request a resupply of pyrotechnics at the next RV. Bad communications and the 'fog of war' had already led the Exercise Commander to believe, wrongly as it turned out, that one of his patrols (not the Aberdeen one) had successfully captured two innocent Norwegian civilian ramblers. Through the mush of static, he made it clear with a fine selection of expletives that he did not care about pyrotechnics but would prefer that any prisoners should be released immediately.

After a deliberate attack on a Norwegian position, one more long slog brought everyone to a very marshy clearing. Bell Huey helicopters remained in the hover, skids just touching the moss, as everyone got on. Back at base there was more opportunity to sample dairy produce and other aspects of early 1970s Scandinavian culture.

These Norway exercises were tremendous experiences for the officer cadets and a chance to meet a wide spectrum of people. The Norwegian officers were very friendly and hospitable.

One AUOTC patrol included as a reinforcement a very young TA infantryman, a great character, normally employed as a labourer at what he termed the Penicuick 'Skoosh' Factory. Both ends of Scotland's educational spectrum benefited from sharing barrack rooms, ditches and forest bashas. It can be argued that, perhaps counterintuitively, the Services, despite their rank structures and systems of separate messes, have always done more than most contemporary institutions to help bridge social divides.

In the mid 1970s a new HQ for AUOTC was being designed, funded and constructed. On 23 September 1977, the OTC's new building on Don Street , named for its World War II commander Roy Strathdee, was officially opened by Sir Edward Wright, former Vice Chancellor, Principal of the University, UAS commander and strong supporter of the service units. Colonel TJT Nicol, the AUOTC Honorary Colonel, Chaplain to the Queen and former Drum Major, performed the dedication service during the Ceremony. The building's design owed much to architect Colonel Jock Lamb and was aimed at providing flexible accommodation for all the training and social demands of OTC life. It, like the new Elphinstone Hall of the 1930s, included a miniature shooting range.

The move from Bedford Road's huts to the big new single building represented a significant change in the atmosphere of unit life for those involved. Before long of course staff and cadets would know nothing other than unit life and laughs at Don Street. Indeed by the time of the then still distant 2012 Centennial, the unit would have been based in the Roy Strathdee Building for longer than it inhabited the old huts.

The URNU retained their Bedford Road shore base for some time before moving to Gordon Barracks. After the OTC moved out, the University took over the site and eventually the Central Heating Plant with its big chimney occupied one corner. In 2012 many of the old huts still remain in place. The site was used during the construction of the impressive glass cube housing the new University Library which opened in Summer 2011, replacing the neighbouring Queen Mother Library.

In a hectic social period, two days after the official opening of the new building the Pipes and Drums, led by Pipe Major Gordon Campbell, played for the Royal Family at Balmoral. The CO Lt Col David Smith and 2IC Robbie Ewen and their wives attended, as did SUO Graham Bryson, JUO Sheila Gann and WO1 RSM Lawrie who would soon receive his Commission.

Her Majesty celebrated her Silver Jubilee in this year. The next 25 years of her reign would see the Cold War end and some hot wars fought. AUOTC's staff, cadets and alumni would continue to contribute to the protection of national interests.

The old AUOTC Compound on Bedford Road in 2012
Now the site of a Heating Plant and Works Services.
Many huts survive including the arched MT Garage (centre)
and the Cadets Mess and Drill Hall, (hidden on the left by the
Heating Plant). The original entrance was to the right of this
view, on the corner of Bedford Road and Hermitage Avenue.

Chapter 8

THE COLD WAR FROM DON STREET
1977-1991

The Roy Strathdee Building focussed around a large space on the model of the traditional TA drill hall. Down the east side of the Hall ran the miniature range, with the cadets and WO/NCO messes opposite. Toilets and classrooms occupied the ground floor of the two storey section, with the HQ staff having their offices on the first floor. At the south end of the first floor corridor was the Officers Mess. Outside the main building lay stores and garages. To the west of the building, the Seaton Park side, lay the car park come parade ground. Access to the compound was from Don Street by pedestrian and vehicle gates.

The Roy Strathdee Building in 2012
35 years after AUOTC moved in.

While the unit settled into the new space, the annual cycle of recruiting and training of course went on. In 1978, the unit's dancers with those of other OTCs, participated in the Edinburgh Military Tattoo and then crossed the Atlantic to take part in a similar event in Washington DC. Local exercises such as EX LAIRD OF BLACKDOG with the URNU took place on familiar sand dunes in familiar rain and wind. Barry Buddon continued as a frequent weekend destination. One three day exercise was held there with Queens Belfast OTC, the latter again enjoying Scotland's relative peace and security. In contrast to the competition held at Aviemore's hotel complex, Barry Buddon frequently hosted the Northern Lights Inter-Unit Competitions. One of the better spectator events was the driving competition. These involved cadets manoeuvring Landrovers and trailers forwards and backwards through a traffic cone course and changing a wheel, all against the clock. The WRAC included some of the unit's star drivers silencing any chauvinism regarding females at the wheel. The driver training available in the OTC, mostly from driving instructor and occasional Band drummer John Gilbert REME(V), attracted quite a few recruits. Progressing from the basic driving tests, some would soon be qualified to take charge of a 3 Ton Bedford truck. At least one fresher who had been heading for the URNU was swayed by the possibility of gaining a valuable HGV licence with the OTC. Orienteering was another main event of the Northern Lights competitions. The tracksuits of the day were made of material with the absorbent qualities of a sponge. Wet competitions thus required an ability to run with one hand devoted to map and compass, and the other to keeping trousers above knee level.

Less formal competition was based around a popular TV game show of the time. *'It's A Knockout'* was conducted between town teams and involved fancy dress, ingenious obstacles and lots of water being thrown about while contestants attempted silly tasks. A 'school sports day for adults' was one description of the long lasting series.

Aberdeen took its turn hosting a ten day CMT course, accommodating university officer cadets from across Britain in Dunbar Halls of Residence.

Annual Camp 1978 was held once more on Salisbury Plain at Westdown. The initial three days were allocated to sub-unit training. The Engineers worked with 9 Para Sqn RE at Aldershot, and the Signals trained with the HQ Signals Tp of 6 Field Force. The Army conducted a brief and unsuccessful organisational experiment with Field Forces and Task Forces replacing the tried and tested Brigade system. 6 Field Force based on the old 16 Parachute Brigade, provided a competent enemy and excellent communications for the CO's Exercise during the 2nd week. A notable guest at the Camp Cocktail Party was the Inspecting Officer, Air Vice Marshal MacTaggart, a former AUOTC Pipe Major.

Early in 1979, Colonel Jimmy Fraser died. Dubbed the 'Grand Old Man of the AUOTC' he was the last known survivor of World War I's U Company. In the same year Dave Smith handed over command to Robbie Ewen RE(V) an Assistant Secretary of the University. Ewen had not joined the OTC in his time as a student but later was commissioned, led the RE sub-unit and was one of the key mountain leaders for EX COLD COMFORT and other forays into the hills.

The unit celebrated the news that Lt Malcolm Macrae had been presented with the Sandhurst Sword of Honour by the Duke of Edinburgh. During the 1970s, from Bedford Road, and latterly the Roy Strathdee Building, AUOTC helped produce 33 Regular Officers: one to the Royal Marines; one to the RAF; 5 to the WRAC; and one to the WRAF. Of these officers, seven had been at University on Cadetships and one as a Bursar. In the 1970s the TA/TAVR benefited by 59 new officers from AUOTC including 13 WRAC.

With Ewen only just in command and continuing the long tradition of TA COs with University or other Aberdeen education system connections; March 1980 brought the first hints of what some feared would be a major culture shift. The University's Military Education Committee (MEC) received a letter from the MOD's Director of TA and Cadets asking that UOTCs should give early notice of requirements for Regular COs. The MOD stressed that approval of Contingent CO nominations still lay with the MECs and that the Army Board preference was still for OTCs to be commanded by suitable TA officers.

Already looking ahead to when Ewen's appointment would expire in September 1982, HQ Highlands summarised the options for AUOTC:

1. Ewen extends in post.
2. The University requests the provision of a Regular CO.
3. The CO and the MEC nominate another TA officer.

Robbie Ewen preferred the first option but made it clear he intended to break the custom of long command tenures. He pointed out that AUOTC had never had a Regular CO and in his view should never have one if any alternatives existed. He briefed the MEC that a Regular CO, selected by

302

'outsiders', might be of low quality, have a long settling in period, and might never adjust to the OTC environment. Recruiting for the Regulars and Reserves might be perceived as the only OTC role to the detriment of other aspects. Recruiting figures were an obvious performance measure for a CO who might naturally, in the interests of career progression, be influenced more by such things than a local TA man. A Regular, he feared, might also seek to accomplish too much, too quickly. He might seek to be both CO and Training Officer and hence do neither properly. These fears in retrospect proved unfounded. Ewen's concerns, shared by many at the time, looked back to times when the AUOTC could well afford to be insular given the availability of widely experienced TA officers on the University staff and around Aberdeen in general. This marketplace for 'home-grown' officers and COs dwindled rapidly with time.

During session 1979/80 former CO Dave Smith, assisted by the OTC's Capt Loder (who was in fact a member of the University staff) and NCOs Gammack and Wiseman, ran EX FIRST RUNG at Aberdeen as a means of better preparing non-OTC aspiring TA officers for Sandhurst.
In 1981 RMA Sandhurst started training WRAC officers, their own old college, just down the road at Bagshot, being closed.

The unit annual report for 1980 indicated a strength of 169, (49 over establishment). Recruiting was healthy with 63 new cadets. These numbers were just about at the limit with which the new Don Street facilities could cope. The first year of the new decade had produced 12 CMT passes and nine Regular Commissions, including only one for a University Cadetship officer. The wider TA had gained four new officers, and the unit itself two, who would serve with the Contingent until they graduated. 1970s Cadet, Capt Bill Morgan Para (V), resigned due to work pressures, the unit losing a key leader of its mountaineering, skiing and rock climbing activities.

Only eighty had managed to attend Annual Camp at Crowborough. Graduation ceremonies, University field courses and work experience schemes prevented many cadets from attending. Alternatives for people in this category were being actively investigated. One option was for detachment to units and exercises through the summer. Summer 1980 provided an unusually big opportunity in this respect. A massive NATO exercise, CRUSADER, was held in Germany. All of 1(BR) Corps turned out from their barracks including one whole Division required to support and umpire the exercise. RAF(Germany) fielded its Harrier Squadrons and other aircraft in support. Regular and TA reinforcements were activated and moved through the UK, across the English Channel, and up the BAOR lines of communication into West Germany. The exercise is said to have involved the biggest Allied fielding of tanks and other armoured vehicles since D Day. The German and US Army provided two divisions of enemy forces. The Americans combined this exercise role with a test of their own real reinforcement system by flying a whole division in from Texas to their pre-positioned vehicles and equipment. The scale and cost of such exercises demonstrated that the Cold War consisted of far more than rhetoric. Some AUOTC cadets had the chance to witness this huge war game with some reinforcing 2/51 Highland Volunteers, four joining umpire teams and eight WOCdts acting as VIP visitor escorts.

The regular conduct of huge mobilisation exercises;

the equipping and maintenance of a standing Army and Air Force in Germany; the Internal Security operation in Ulster; and numerous small commitments around the world; meant UK defence spending was under constant review by an increasingly squeezed Treasury.

Prime Minister Thatcher's first Secretary of State for Defence, Francis Pym, had resisted cuts on the grounds that they did not reflect the nation's strategic situation. His replacement John Nott however announced large reductions in spending due to the dire financial situation. Any capability for large scale 'out of area' force projection was to be sacrificed in order to maintain a strong NATO anti submarine capability; a strategic deterrent in the shape of the new Trident system replacing Polaris; and a smaller but still quite capable corps in Germany. The effects ranged from decommissioning aircraft carriers at one end of the spectrum to reduced OTC training activity at the other.

Reductions in fuel and cash allocations meant a cancellation of the 1981 Northern Lights Competition. Despite all this the unit recruited over 50 new recruits each year, maintained strength above establishment, and often achieved 100% pass rates in the CMT exams. The unit marked the departure of Elaine Marnoch who in the 1970s had become the Band's first lady member. As Pipe Major, she became the only female one in the Army. Another entry for the record books was her performance as the first female Lone Piper during the Edinburgh Military Tattoo.

Replacing the long tradition of Rothiemurchus exercises, during 1981 an experimental Easter Camp was held at Cameron Barracks, Inverness. Sub-unit training was held in near Arctic conditions. Summer Camp at Strensall, Yorkshire, included a combined final exercise with Glasgow and Tayforth OTCs. AUOTC had taken steps to revitalise its affiliate links with the Gordon Highlanders, particularly the Regular 1st Battalion. The Unit had been assisted throughout the year by the Gordon's Regimental Recruiting Team leader Capt Ewen Chalmers. Both parties were satisfied with the results of closer cooperation. The sapper sub-unit erected a handsome bridge for the Nature Conservancy Council at Derry Lodge. The overall high reputation of AUOTC had attracted an inspection at camp by General Sir Frank Kitson, Deputy Commander United Kingdom Land Forces (UKLF) and Inspector General for the TA.

Robbie Ewen wrote to the University Secretary in March 1982 outlining the procedure for finding his replacement as CO.

1. The MEC had to decide (for the first time ever) whether a Regular or TA candidate was appropriate.

2. If a Regular officer was requested then the MOD would offer its chosen candidate to the MEC for approval.

3. Any TA nominee needed to be suitably qualified and preferably have connections with the University as a member of staff, a graduate, or in some other related professional capacity.

4. The final decision needed the assent of the OTC's Honorary Colonel; the TA Association; Brigadier Commanding 51st Highland Brigade; the officer concerned; and the MEC. By contrast the previous system had merely required a gentlemanly note to the MOD from the University Principal or Secretary.

At the beginning of April 1982 those who woke to listen to the radio news had to get up early in search of an

306

atlas. Somewhere called 'the Falkland Islands' had been invaded. Spurred on by the British plans to scrap aircraft carriers; amphibious shipping; naval dockyards; and the Antarctic Patrol vessel HMS ENDURANCE; the Argentine Government had decided to capture what they called 'Las Malvinas'. Fortunately they moved too early, just allowing the Navy to avoid or postpone the Nott cuts. By the proverbial 'skin of the teeth' OP CORPORATE managed to liberate the Falkland Islanders with the remnants of the Argentine force surrendering on 14 June. The Army helped the Royal Navy and the Royal Marines recapture the islands. Two Parachute Regiment battalions augmented 3 Commando Brigade. 5 Infantry Brigade included Scots Guards, Welsh Guards and Gurkhas. Many men from the other Arms and Services helped insure the success of this hastily improvised exercise in force projection, literally at the range limits of capability.

With the involvement of the Scots Guards, both former and future AUOTC RSMs took part. Capt Arthur Petrie, a 1970s cadet, was a junior staff officer with HQ 5 Infantry Brigade. A Royal Artillery Forward Observation Officer (FOO) with 2nd Battalion The Parachute Regiment, would later command AUOTC. In 2012, the year of AUOTC's Centenary, Op CORPORATE veterans would mark the 30th Anniversary of the many triumphs and tragedies of the Falklands War against a backdrop of increasing regional tension in the South Atlantic.

During their 1982 Camp at Garelochhead, cadets watched the submarine *'Conqueror'* return to base, flying the Jolly Roger to mark her sinking of the Argentinean cruiser *'General Belgrano'*. The final exercise received assistance from the RN Base including the local detachment of the

Special Boat Service (SBS). The Camp suffered very bad weather. The Army Air Corps exercising nearby airlifted in the remains of a dead climber found in Arrochar. The body rested temporarily by the unit's Signals store before being taken to the local mortuary.

WRAC Signallers at work, Garelochhead, 1982

Someone who actively sought extreme conditions was a brief member of the OTC at this time. Benedict Allen was on a post graduate Ecology Course. He went on to become a well known and innovative explorer, author and film maker undertaking arduous expeditions all over the globe. His planning skills, self confidence and determination were probably already pretty well developed by the time he came to Aberdeen. However on a later visit he did tell the local press that 'being part of AUOTC must have helped'.

In Session 1982/83 the unit benefited from a relaxation in training budgets and soon gained approval for improved HQ accommodation with the addition of a kitchen and additional garaging. In December a recruits cadre was held at Ballater, and an Easter Camp at Inverness. The Engineer Sub-unit, with any available reinforcements from the rest of the unit, conducted a series of OP MACC (Military Aid To the Civil Community) tasks throughout the Eighties. In 1982 they built a bridge and culverts for the Nature Conservancy Council in Glen Nevis and in 1983 built two footbridges on Arran.

Bridge Building - Arran, 1983

The concrete and iron remains of Linklater's 'Fortress Orkney' provided OTCs and the TA with challenging demolition tasks for many years. The normal challenges of successfully destroying pill boxes and gun emplacements were often compounded by the need to sweep even the tiniest bits of the resulting debris from nearby fields and golf courses. On Hoy, AUOTC turfed new picnic sites and helped restore land to arable farm use after a 40 year gap.

In 1983 the TA's 75th Birthday was marked by a variety of events including an assault boat race on the River Dee. In the Autumn of that year Lt Col Ronnie Grant MB ChB RAMC(V) took over command from Robbie Ewen. Ewen went off to become the Joint Service Liaison Officer (JSLO) for Grampian and in 1985 became Secretary to Glasgow University. Ronnie Grant had been an officer cadet with the University Air Squadron 1961-1964, before serving as an RAMC officer with Canadian and Barbadian forces. In 1979 he had joined the OTC as a Major.

In January 1984 Grant's unit was officially enlarged by the approval of an establishment increased to 150 cadets. There were no recruitment problems and after selection many joined a waiting list. Despite the official establishment increase a ceiling of 130 cadets was set in light of limitations in allocated Man Training Days (MTDs). To add to programme stress, coinciding with the change of CO was a significant turnover of TA and Regular staff. With MOD talk of 'streamlining' Grant had a long hard look at the unit in the prevailing economic conditions. Although the OTC Charter remained unchanged greater emphasis was to be placed on formal leadership training to the benefit of future Army and civilian careers. Grant hoped to continue a full and varied engagement of OCdts but this would require optimum use of limited resources. Poor results in a military skills competition by an inexperienced team, reinforced the need for careful planning and enough good instructors.

One of Grant's early pieces of staff work involved the unit response to an MOD Paper rather negatively titled 'The Problems of the UOTCs'. Aside from the title, COMEC thought this a 'poor' paper and called for input from all the OTCs so that a strong consolidated reply could be made by the March 1984 deadline.

The paper undoubtedly addressed areas of long debate and recurring controversy. It suggested that the 'problems' stemmed from a lack of priority given to OTCs and the Army's presence in Universities. A planned expansion of the TA would exacerbate an existing shortage of officers. The Government placed strong emphasis on the role of Reserve Forces in time of war. Nineteen UOTC Contingents served 47 universities, and 58 colleges and polytechnics. All of the contingents were well recruited and some, like Aberdeen, had waiting lists. Across the country there were over 3,000 university officer cadets. Having analysed the national statistics for the previous ten years, only around 1 in 17 would gain a TA Commission, and 1 in 35 a Regular Commission. Against this ostensibly poor harvest of officers, the MOD received a steady stream of requests for establishment increases, new detachments and even new contingents. All this challenged the very validity of the 'Officer Training' part of the organisation's title. It had been estimated that on average only one third of any contingent's members were truly potential officer material. If OTC training was only about the few who were eventually commissioned then costs were not justified. If OTC training was only concentrated on those with real officer potential the

MEC's might rightly consider such a move too limiting and elitist. The paper also identified widespread confusion in the Regular Army over the differences between the 'cadets' from the CCF, ACF and UOTCs. All in all the paper suggested, in an echo of the 1948 UTC Structure, that University Officer Cadets, having held that status since the 1950s, might be better designated as University Volunteers (TA).

The lack of a military role led to low priorities for kit against the rest of the TA. Many TA officers perceived the OTCs as insular, lacking sufficient interaction with the rest of the TA, and without a war role. Such feelings were so prevalent that postings to OTCs as COs or Training Majors were perceived by some as 'career fouls'. Clearer military roles might help dispel this feeling. The paper identified that in any case there was a shortage of TA officers, especially within university staffs, the traditional source for UOTC officers. The training and preparation of potential TA officers before attendance at the 2 week TA commissioning course at RMA Sandhurst needed experienced TA officers. None of the Scottish OTCs conducted this formal training, nor did hardly any other contingent.

The existence of special to arm subunits was costly and, the paper claimed, did not make any difference to morale when compared to those contingents who did only leadership and basic military training. There were big differences in the structure of OTCs, some having no sub-units and one consisting of seven. Special to arm weekends at appropriate cap-badge facilities might be an adequate and certainly more economical alternative to established sub-units. As was always the case, travel time to such facilities from Scotland and in particular from the OTC's northernmost outpost, Aberdeen, was not a real consideration. The Army's manning offices had varying success in finding suitable PSIs for sub-units.

Just as other Whitehall papers had done way back in the 1930s, this one identified the mobilisation requirement for district Officer Cadet Training Units (OCTUs) and the role of the Universities and OTCs in supporting them.

The consolidated COMEC response effectively rubbished the paper's conclusions and recommendations. The country's Military Education Committees (MECs) rejected the suggested title change and the allocation of specific military roles. They supported special to arm sub-units stating that doing nothing but infantry training for 3 or 4 years would hit student interest and morale. In any case the TA needed a supply of officers with some training in other arms and services. Thus sub-units should stay where they could be supported. It was accepted that COs should seek better contact with the wider TA. TA officer career planning should explicitly include the possibility of UOTC tours. COMEC pointed out that it was hardly the fault of the OTCs that some parts of the Regular Army could not distinguish between school age and university cadets. In the face of a strong combined rebuttal the paper's authors gave in, rather meekly indicating 'they had merely wanted to assess the situation.' The legitimate issues raised by the paper would not of course disappear, particularly in the future when the Army's size and funding would face even greater strictures.

Meanwhile Engineer tasks included refurbishing the Bailey Bridge at the entrance to the Rothiemurchus track and improving the coastal path at Muchalls south of Aberdeen. A special task for the University, safely moved a valuable book collection from Banff to the King's Library. Demonstrating that the Army was still a global operation, during the

313

summer: 20 cadets went on attachments to Germany; 2 to Hong Kong; 1 to Cyprus; and 1 to the South Atlantic. 25 cadets attended Regular Army courses. Three WOCdts participated in the Berlin Military Tattoo and experienced driving light armoured vehicles, watermanship training and of course memorable sightseeing at this Cold War focal point, including visits through 'the Iron Curtain' to East Berlin.

Session 1984/85 continued the normal routine of training sessions on Thursday evenings and Saturdays with activities for those who could attend on Wednesday afternoons. During the Christmas Vacation the unit went to Barry Buddon and at Easter was back in Ballater. Summer Camp went to Wathgill for the first time. Indicating the unit's heavy reliance on its PSIs, the planned Sapper bridging and MACC camp was cancelled due to their Instructor's illness. In subsequent years of the 1980s the unit would construct: an adventure playground at Crathes Castle; bridges on the isles of Mull and Arran; and bridges and a viewing platform at Pitlochry.

In September 1984 the British tested their contribution to the defence of Europe with EX LIONHEART. This outstripped EX CRUSADER 80, becoming the biggest British Exercise since World War II. Over 135,000 Regulars, TA and Reservists took part. The reinforcement aspect was tested in EX FULL FLOW and the 1(BR)Corps fight in EX SPEARPOINT. New Challenger tanks, tracked Rapier, and the Saxon personnel carrier were deployed. The RAF's Harriers were joined by the new Tornado aircraft. Germans and Americans provided the exercise enemy. The real enemy confirmed their commitment by renewing the Warsaw Pact the following year.

In June 1985 the OTCs received a new Charter in

314

place of the 1972 policy. It was restated that the UOTC was part of Group B of the TA. Contingents could be formed at the request of certain UK universities as agreed by the MOD. Any institution's Military Education Committee (MEC) could recommend disbandment if it was thought that having an OTC was no longer in their interests. A more likely threat would come from the MOD if public money expenditure appeared no longer to be justified. OTCs had four tasks:

1. Forming a practical link between the Army and the Universities. Fostering interest in, and an understanding of, the Army and its role in defence policy.

2. Training for undergraduates in preparation for Regular, TA and Cadet Force commissions.

3. Supervising, administering and training undergraduate university cadetship officers and any Regular Army officers attending University.

4. Informing, advising and assisting undergraduates who are potential candidates for commissions.

MOD policy was to be implemented through HQ United Kingdom Land Forces (UKLF) and the chain of command.

University OTC membership was open to other local colleges and polytechnics. Although students had priority, any young person undergoing professional training outside an institution such as in banking or accountancy, could also apply to join.

OTCs worked within Military Law like the rest of the TA, but would also adhere to relevant University

315

Regulations. The highest priority at all times would be afforded to allowing students to achieve the best possible degree.

Training, under the new MTQ system would develop leadership potential; and provide military experience, knowledge and skills. OTC cadets would be helped to prepare for positions of responsibility in the TA or elsewhere.

The new Charter replaced the Certificate of Military Training (CMT) with the Military Training Qualification (MTQ). Until now the training cycle had involved basic training in the first year, the CMT in the second year, and special to arm training in the third and fourth years. How OTCs did this was largely left to them. The MTQ introduced a more proscribed and rigid syllabus right from the start of a cadet's OTC service.

The MTQ 1, first year syllabus started with a heavy lecture programme in the Autumn Term. Lectures were the one thing students were not lacking and the schedule had a negative effect on the motivation and retention of new recruits. Steps were taken to modularise the training and reduce classroom time in favour of practical training. MTQ 1 consisted of the following elements, all of which had to be successfully completed before the CO could confirm a 'Pass': Workplace Induction; Leadership; Military Knowledge; Skill at Arms including an Annual Personal Weapon Test (APWT); Fieldcraft and Tactics; Communication skills; Map Reading; First Aid/Health and Hygiene; Fitness Training; and Drill.

In a student's second year MTQ2 was conducted and tested. It built on the foundation laid during MTQ1, and focused more on junior officer leadership and management These included: the 'seven questions' estimate (formerly called an Appreciation); the Orders process; more advanced map reading and navigation; Signals skills and public speaking. The overall aim was to promote self-confidence, teamwork and leadership in difficult pressurised situations. Training methods varied between UOTCs but were all based upon a core syllabus issued and overseen by the Royal Military Academy Sandhurst.

MTQ2 Exams ran at UOTCs throughout the UK from late in the Winter term through to Easter. The Exam involved tests of all aspects of the syllabus. Candidates had to prepare and deliver a lecturette on a set subject and perform convincingly on the practical Tactical Exercise Without Troops (TEWT). This involved conducting a formal estimate of a platoon level tactical problem, and then delivering a complete, concise and inspiring set of orders. Successful completion of MTQ1 and MTQ 2 led to higher pay rates and a bigger tax free annual training bounty.

MTQ3 provided special to arm training and qualifications for senior cadets. The whole system, for those who chose, provided a steady progression towards attendance on the Sandhurst TA Commissioning Course.

Changes in Aberdeen's military family were afoot. The closure of the Scottish Infantry Training Depot at Gordon Barracks would require the OTC to pick up extra responsibilities. The OTC set up and administered an Aberdeen based liaison committee to manage increasingly scarce resources and improve training support for the local ACF and CCF. Among other things the OTC staff would take on responsibility for Military Home Defence coordination. Black Dog Range allocations and maintenance would also become an OTC responsibility. It remained officially a Regular Army range with TA, RAF, and NATO allied users

Many OCdts volunteered to assist youth training and charity fund raising activities. The Cadets Mess sponsored the support and education of a Kenyan boy. The social calendar included remarkable costume parties, formal dinners, and a Spring Ball. Regular badminton sessions were held in the Roy Strathdee Building. Teams played volleyball, rugby and hockey and some learned sailing. Ten Cadets walked the 96 miles of the West Highland Way.

The new builds and renovations at Don Street were completed in 1985 including controversial metal railings around the perimeter. This necessary enhancement to the compound's security gradually became accepted as part of Old Aberdeen's architectural ambience. The unit now had a large well equipped kitchen thanks to the generosity of the Highland TAVRA. The facility would it was hoped help attract and train TA cooks, but more importantly would allow greater self-sufficiency in entertaining official guests and holding social events.

In Session 1985/86 the unit strength consisted of:
3 Regular Officers, 3 Regular PSIs, 7 TA Group A Officers, 9 TA Group B Officers (Students), 9 TA Senior and Junior Ranks, 1 Non Regular Permanent Staff (NRPS),
and 145 OCdts (incl 44 WRAC). The main and critical shortage was in the number of cooks.

The usual variety of tasks continued with training and communications assistance to the University and external organisations. The Sappers were involved with planning and surveying road and car park work at Templars' Park Scout Campsite and the transport of a 70 ton cyclotron from Edinburgh to Aberdeen, for use in medical research.

318

The new, from 1985, Military Home Defence role of HQ AUOTC provoked some discussion in the MEC about the mobilisation status of OTC cadets. Only the Group A OTC HQ staff would be mobilised at an early stage to activate the Tactical Area of Responsibility (TAOR) HQ (not located at Roy Strathdee Building) and prepare for Home Defence tasks. Under 1978 TA Regulations, OTCs would not be mobilised as whole units (U Company's experiences were never to be repeated). However cadets were reminded on enlistment and later in Military Law lectures that if matters got to the stage of general mobilisation (the appropriate Queen's Orders having been signed), adjustments to these regulations would be made very quickly, as had happened in 1939. Thus in theory cadets had no greater call-up commitment than their fellow students. However Group B TA, including officer cadets, would in practice represent a valuable contribution to Aberdeen's defence. There would in these circumstances be no shortage of key point security, engineer and communications tasks to cover. It appeared the Cold War would run for some time yet since in 1985 Russia and her East European satellite states renewed the Warsaw Pact.

*WO2 Alan Mearns supervises a WRAC SMG Detail.
In the snow at Black Dog, 1985.*

The demise of the Infantry Training Depot across the Don at Gordon Barracks brought more than additional responsibilities. The OTC got a new Adjt/QM from the closure when Capt(QM) Fraser KOSB replaced Maj (QM) MacDonald RA who set off with a promotion to British Forces Belize, (a deterrent against Guatemalan invasion until 1994. A sizeable jungle training facility survived into the 21st Century).

Of perhaps more historic significance, in 1986 Ronnie Grant handed over command to the Infantry Depot's last CO, Ian Shepherd. Some TA candidates had been considered but distance and other factors precluded them, leaving Shepherd to become the first Regular CO of AUOTC since its birth 74 years earlier. Commissioned into the Royal Highland Fusiliers, Shepherd, a French and Arabic speaker, had to date enjoyed a varied career including loan service with the Sultan of Oman's Armed Forces, Staff College and MOD staff appointments. He had recovered from a very serious injury, caused by a bomb in Northern Ireland, to serve in Moscow as Assistant Military Attaché before taking command at Gordon Barracks. Despite the long held fears and suspicions held by some about Regular COs, AUOTC could only benefit from Shepherd's broad military experience including his time running a major training establishment. His current knowledge of other aspects of Army assets and responsibilities in the Aberdeen Garrison and wider NE Scotland would further help HQ AUOTC with its new role.

The balance between general leadership training and sub-unit training in OTCs was a matter of debate and, as has been described, the subject of regular staff papers from World War II onwards. There is little doubt that the sub-units produced many officers for their own cap badges. This was particularly true in the 1980s in Aberdeen's Signals sub unit. The Scottish OTCs had the time and resources to hold a much greater degree of sub unit training than later became the case. Many factors for this included the post Cold War reduction in the TA's size and distribution. Whatever the reasons, the OTCs produced many more TA officers in the Seventies and Eighties than they would in the early 21st Century.

Although understandably near the bottom of the 'food-chain' for equipment, AUOTC acquired Clansman

Radios before some local TA Infantry much to the latters' displeasure as they continued to hump Larkspur sets around on their backs. AUOTC's signallers enjoyed nothing better than trying to communicate using a Clansman 320 hooked up to a variety of official and home-made antennae. Some, later long serving Royal Signals officers like Domhnall Dods, joined the OTC with infantry aspirations. Like many new Officer Cadets he had served in his school CCF being steeped in the culture and traditions of the local Regiment. On his first summer camp he was injured on the final exercise. He was sent to the Command Post (CP) where he was asked if he could work a radio. After a crash course in radio procedures and watchkeeping from the day shift he found himself on night duty. The signallers seemed to inhabit an alien but cosy world in farm buildings rather than in trenches or under bashas. They had electric lighting and a constant supply of custard creams from Captain Murray. In an age when mobile phones belonged to science fiction, the signals sub unit promised knowledge of what everyone else was up to amid the planned and naturally occurring chaos of an OTC exercise. The unit had a good supply of its own Fitted For Radio (FFR) Landrovers. and fuel. Very few if any students had their own cars, so apart from anything else the Signals meant freedom to roam. Mobility created distance from the hierarchy and once out on the road, an FFR detachment rarely saw their JUO let alone a PSI or officer. In short, a state of unsupervised freedom contrasted well with the up close and constant 'beasting' in the infantry. On occasion there were enough Gaelic speakers in the sub-unit to allow the time consuming use of BATCO to be dispensed with. The use of this 'unauthorised code' was detected once by Royal Signals staff at Catterick who ordered approved methods of encryption to be resumed.

Just as the Engineer sub-unit gained employment on MACC and other tasks, the Signals would deploy in support of a variety of activities. One long lasting and eventually very dull task was however particularly lucrative for the sub-unit members. The MOD was deploying a new Home Defence radio system called MOULD. This worked via hilltop relay sites in much the same way as modern mobile phone systems. The MOULD user handbook required coverage maps. Rather than use some form of computerised analysis, the OTC Signals sub units were tasked to romp around the countryside in their Landrovers doing a radio check every few hundred metres. The task kept everyone busy at the weekend for what seemed like months. It is thought the Signals PSI of the time became unhinged by acknowledging thousands of radio checks since he soon decided everyone should, as in days of old, learn Morse Code. The unit's old practice Morse keys were dusted off and once more 'dahs' and 'dits' echoed through the building. With the OTC's lead role in Military Home Defence (MHD) the unit signallers got to wear civilian clothes while exercising at Grampian Police HQ and elsewhere. These exercises and others were occasionally the target of radio jamming and other tricks courtesy of the Russian 'trawlers' loitering around the UK's coasts. The UK was a target for much Soviet intelligence activity. Apart from what OTCs and other more strategic elements of UK Forces might be up to, the UK was a huge 'unsinkable aircraft carrier' for US Forces. Since 1983, in a reaction to the Warsaw Pact deployment of SS20 missiles, these UK based forces had included nuclear armed Ground Launched Cruise Missiles (GLCMs) at RAF Greenham Common, Berkshire and RAF Molesworth, Cambridgeshire.

The missiles would in the event of war deploy on their specialist vehicles along pre-planned routes to fully surveyed launch sites scattered around the countryside. This controversial aspect of the US presence did not last long but probably helped bring about the Intermediate Range Nuclear Forces Treaty signed by Messrs Reagan and Gorbachev in 1987 as the Cold War neared its end.

In 1986 a local and short-lived controversy ended when AUOTC successfully resisted a Highland Brigade proposal for it to join other units in Aberdeen at combined Remembrance Sunday Parades. The University's long standing and quite special tradition at King's College continued.

The established pattern of four camps also continued. Barry Buddon once again hosted a short Winter Camp in early January involving shooting, and senior cadets planning and conducting battle handling exercises. Easter Camp was spent at Victoria Barracks Ballater focussing on Adventure Training including alpine and Nordic skiing, rock climbing and hill walking. In addition MTQ2 candidates underwent revision. The Contingent went to Crowborough East Sussex for the main Summer Camp. The first week was allocated to specialist training. The Engineers trained with their counterparts from Cambridge UOTC at 3 Training Regiment Royal Engineers. The Lydd-Hythe ranges were used for two days with one night under canvas at Dibgate Camp, Folkestone. The final exercise involved an all arms advance to contact, attacks, defence, and patrolling. The Signallers had to support a skeleton Battalion HQ/Exercise Control (EXCON), a skeleton Company HQ , an A Echelon and F Echelon. The Engineers operated as assault pioneers with the Infantry, protecting their positions with wire obstacles and

324

surface laid Barmines. The gruelling climax was a 23 mile night march along the South Downs Way, with tasks en route, and a final timed 'speed march' leg. After 7 hours rest, cadets were orienteering, and then parading in front of the visiting Chief of Staff, HQ Scotland. The fourth of the annual camps was the Engineer Camp and MACC task.

Reporting at the end of his first full year in command Shepherd had detected a feeling among some that the OTC was nothing more than any other University activity or club, and a very comfortable one at that. He hoped his tour and the promise of a second Regular CO would dispel such notions. The unit had recruited 16 women and 39 men of whom 35 were retained on strength although not all active members. His biggest problem was a lack of instructors with current and required qualifications. He lacked Group A junior TA Officers. Only one Group A officer, the 2IC, was fully qualified to run ranges. All the others were authorised for most range duties but due to lack of time or opportunity, none, including the 2IC, were authorised to run L2 grenade ranges or 66mm Sub Calibre ranges. Shepherd himself had conducted these practices at summer camp. Getting and keeping staff qualified was difficult given their other commitments and getting places on suitable courses. The unavoidable changeover of personnel compounded the problems. The unit asked through the MEC whether or not any young officers could be found from within the University staff as in days of old. The Principal indicated that the University was also under financial pressures and very few new staff were being recruited.

Because a Regular CO was in post the Training Major post was gapped. A bid was submitted to have the post filled particularly in light of the unit's wider responsibilities but the whole Army was experiencing a manning problem at Major level. The clerks post was also gapped and this too hindered Home Defence and Garrison Commander staff work.

A separate case was submitted for a WRAC Lt or Capt to act as Training Adjutant and staff officer for Home Defence matters. The unit was also finding it hard to recruit and retain TA junior ranks. The local job market and the pressures of fulltime jobs took some away and one storeman Private rejoined the Colours. Shepherd also had a pressing need to find high grade senior Lts and junior Capts. He was also simultaneously trying to find placements for two Captains to widen their experience. Budgets and in particular Man Training Day allocations caused some excitement when a training year overspend was predicted. More detailed examination of the issue revealed that the wrong capitation rates were being used and that a considerable under spend would be the actual outcome. Frustratingly the single year budgeting system and the inability to carry funds forward into the next financial year frequently caused panic. Severe cutbacks were almost always immediately followed by urgent calls for expenditure to be made to avoid underspends.

Financial cuts meant that No2 or Service Dress was to be withdrawn from the TA leaving them with Barrack Dress and Combats. Shepherd found this unacceptable particularly for Highland units. His own unit required full No2 Jacket, Kilt, Hair sporran, spats and the rest to properly mark such events as Remembrance Sunday. He believed his cadets also needed No2 dress to allow their full participation during attachments to Regular units, practice attendance at Courts Martial, and other formal events. Removal of No2 Dress, headgear and other accoutrements would disadvantage his cadets.

The gradual slide in the OTC's profile within an expanding University with its own tighter financial constraints, was exemplified by the removal of the Roy Strathdee Building from the University's mail delivery and collection service. Shepherd in his letter of complaint pointed out that having been formed in 1912 the OTC was older than many of the departments that presumably were still on the mail run.

Further improvements to the HQ continued with plans for expanding the Orderly Room to accommodate ever increasing amounts of IT and the additional paper supplies required by every modern 'paperless office'. There was also to be more storage space out in the courtyard. Options for more classroom space were being considered with TAVRA. One option would mean the Band having to practice at Gordon Barracks. The plan, although acoustically attractive for any closet 'Philistines', was rejected.

Shepherd noted that MTQ1 results had been bad and that unit record keeping and progress monitoring needed improvement. MTQ2 results on the other hand had been better but, with other OTCs he was unhappy with the MTQ2 syllabus and had submitted proposals for change through the chain of command. In particular the need for undergraduates to do a written exam was considered superfluous and this aspect was indeed soon discontinued leaving only practical exams.

The AUOTC came 10th out of 24 teams at 51(H) Brigade Military Skills Competition at Barry Buddon. Training for this had been expensive with the Wooden Spoon award going to a young Cadetship officer for rolling and damaging a Landrover and trailer.

The indoor range was put to more use with a monthly small bore competition for what other than the Small Boar Trophy.

The unit sent a team to the Drambuie Marathon along the Caledonian Canal and eight cadets improved their Fieldcraft on an unofficial attachment to a ghillies course on Deeside.

Two cadets demonstrated tenacity and 'maintenance of the aim' when they walked across Scotland on a route originally planned for a team of eight. EX BOAR'S CHALLENGE took them from Aberdeen to Mallaig covering 207 miles and 12 peaks over 3000 ft.

The introduction of new IT systems seldom goes without a hitch and this was the case in April 1987 when the unit received its PAMPAS equipment. This, for the time, ambitious system was rolled out to all units to support pay and general administration. The often heard complaint, even now, that the data entry burden outweighed the perceived benefits, was made. Normal teething and cultural problems were made worse by the software being tailored to TA Group A business rather than that of OTCs. The system as issued did not cope with the unit's training record and standard instruction requirements.

The unit's historic link with the Gordon Highlanders was re-emphasised in Jan 87 with the appointment of a very senior Gordon, Assistant Chief of the General Staff, Maj Gen MacMillan as Honorary Colonel. The following year SUO Marris would represent the unit when Lt Gen MacMillan was installed as Governor of Edinburgh Castle.

Another Gordon Highlander, Maj(QM) Jim Easson, joined the unit from the RMA Sandhurst staff, as Adjutant/Quartermaster. Four years later he would drop a rank and become the first Non Regular Permanent Staff (NRPS) Adjutant. He would complete 12 years service with the OTC in 1999. Perhaps under his influence the Pipes and Drums became the Drums and Pipes in accordance with Gordon Highlander practice. The Drums traditionally bear the Regimental Battle Honours thus taking precedence over the Pipes, in sub-unit title if in nothing else.

The University Royal Navy Unit had a memorable year in 1987 when it replaced HMS THORNHAM with HMS CHASER and at last officially allowed women to join.

AUOTC marked the European Year of the Environment by planting trees around its HQ compound .

MEC discussions at the close of 1987 included the question of war roles for OTCs. In a discussion paper on the topic Cambridge OTC had proposed the notion of OTCs forming TA Group B recce units in the Home Defence role. This was generally rejected given the lack of advanced training and equipment that would be necessary to properly fulfil a particularly skilled and important military role. Shepherd was clear that the existing system should continue. Permanent staff formed the nucleus of a local Home Defence HQ, and the students a reserve of partially trained manpower (and womanpower) for allocation to appropriate tasks as they arose.

The short Winter Camp was held at the Edinburgh Training Centre (ETC) over the weekend 9/10 Jan 88. The ETC provided valuable centralised accommodation and training resources for the TA and cadets. The ETC occupied the old Redford Cavalry Barracks which was of a similar age to AUOTC. With its neighbour, the Infantry Barracks, the Cavalry Barracks had been built before World War One in what was the biggest barracks construction project in Scotland since the building of Fort George in the mid 18th Century.

The Basic Wing carried on with the MTQ1 syllabus while Advanced Wing conducted training with the General Purpose Machine Gun (GPMG) in the Sustained Fire (SF) role. They did more NBC training and attempted to provide timely, appropriate and accurate artillery fire control orders using the Invertron Simulator. This facility provided landscape views on screens where enemy targets could be portrayed and engaged. Communications headsets and sound effects added to the realism. The Invertron replaced the old 'puff ranges' where student fire controllers sat looking over a big terrain model through which a hidden man could project a puff of smoke to indicate fall of shot thus allowing adjustments to be given to the notional guns or mortars being directed. Other training included instruction in the conduct of range practices at Glencorse, and a 12 hour night navigation exercise. A morning was spent with 1RHF, and visits made to the Scottish United Services Museum and the Scottish National Memorial.

Aberdeen hosted Northern Lights the inter OTC competition weekend at Gordon Barracks. During the Saturday competitions were held on the assault course; a march and shoot event was held with the additional burden of an NBC element. Tasks in leadership, first aid and driving skills were set. Sports events included Rugby 7s, Hockey 5s and Basketball. The musical events included individual, quartet and band competitions and the Dancing event was as usual keenly contested. On Saturday evening officers attended a formal Dinner Night in Elphinstone Hall while the cadets held a disco in the Barracks main dining hall.

Hangovers were shaken off on Sunday with a drill competition, tug o' war, and fun games before the prize giving and dispersal of all contingents at noon.

Annual Camp 1988 was held at Beckingham Training Centre, Newark. Special to arm training was held in the first week. Signals work involved VHF PRC 351/349, HF PRC 320, masts, antennae, ancillaries, Voice Procedure, the code BATCO, remoting, and the use of line. Combat Engineering involved preparation of buildings for defence, obstacles, water supply, booby traps, demolitions, and mines. Infantry skills covered battle procedure, patrols, Observation Posts (OPs) including covert ones, house clearing, the Annual Personal Weapons Test (APWT), and throwing the L2 Grenade.

The second week built towards a Final Exercise in the Home Defence Scenario with the set up of a Battalion HQ, Key Point guard forces and a Company level attack. This exercise was seen as a prelude to the later Home Defence Exercise BONNY DUNDEE involving the defence of up to three Key Points.

In June 1988 the OTC took part in an endurance competition with the local TA 15 Para. This involved a 37 kilometre speed march starting at sunrise and including the non trivial obstacles of Cairn Toul, Braeriach, Ben Macdui and Cairngorm. Teams were required to cross the finish line at Linn of Dee within 10 hours.

Through the seventies and eighties Aberdeen, including some parts of its academic community, had undergone rapid expansion and change largely due to the North Sea Oil Industry. This community suffered its biggest tragedy in July 1988 when the Piper Alpha Disaster killed 167 people, 120 miles NE of Aberdeen.

Happier events occurred later in July when AUOTC's MACC camp was established above Dougarie Lodge on Arran's west coast. Despite challenging weather a concrete ford and two Countryside Commission approved 'Galloway' bridges were constructed on the Glen Iorsa track.

The tenure of the unit's first Regular CO came to an end and the sky had not fallen in. The unit had benefited from a fresh 'external' examination and bags of varied experience.

The AUOTC's second Regular CO, was to be Lt Col John Walpole, Royal Engineers. A graduate of the Royal Military College of Science at Shrivenham, Walpole was coming from an appointment within the, Command and Control System, Project WAVELL Team.

As usual an early focus was on the recruiting period after the Summer Break. Sadly but not surprisingly the MEC and the University authorities had not sanctioned a proposal by Shepherd to enliven recruiting. He had hoped the unit would be allowed to conduct a full scale tactical demonstration, with blanks and pyrotechnics, in the grounds of the Hillhead Halls of Residence just up the hill from HQ. At this time not all the accommodation blocks had been built, leaving available enough open ground to put on an impressive show. University concerns over 'appropriateness' and health and safety stymied the idea. There was also concern that only negative and counterproductive PR would be generated by such an event.

As was quite often the case for OTC COs, Walpole had to handle yet another study on the OTCs. The Gibb Review was discussed by the MEC. The report noted that 67% of the Standard Graduate Course and 48% of the TA

Commissioning Course at Sandhurst came from the UOTCs. There was a need to better align UOTCs with current and projected demographics and the expansion of tertiary education. A demographic trough increased the OTC's importance in recruiting. The report called for greater consistency across all contingents, more positive management and the achievement of aims more cost effectively.

Generally content with the report, the MEC did note that the fact of the Scottish 4 year degree system was ignored. The question of mandatory exams in the MTQ system was again discussed in terms of likely effects on recruiting and retention. The Home Defence Roles of permanent staff was noted as was the absence of how additional responsibilities were to be supported particularly in the more militarily isolated locations like Aberdeen. Permanent staff would be required on mobilisation to set up and man the Grampian Tactical Area of Responsibility (TAOR) HQ. Cadets would provide a reservoir of potential officers as required by any developing emergency. The proposal of a recce role for OTCs was again dismissed as being unrealistic. The Report was criticised for including rather outdated language by referring to women officer cadets as the 'girls'. The report's author had detected a swing to the right in University politics. The MEC were unconvinced. Discussions turned to money and former CO John Reid, who served as the Senatus Academicus representative on the MEC for 24 years until 1990, emphasised his belief that bounty payments must be retained as a small reward for committed OTC membership. The MEC told Walpole that despite bids for an increase by his predecessor, the University annual grant to the unit would remain at £250 for the 1988/89 session. However the University retained a high opinion of the unit and its importance and was pleased to report that there had been no complaints over unreasonable demands on any student's time. Indeed they were pleased to note the unit's flexibility as students changed their aspirations and choices.

Unit social life continued with the standard events and in November 1988 a joint 'Beach Boys' Party with the RN and RAF units. The following month the URNU lease at the old Bedford Road site expired. A decade after the OTC had moved out, the University's Naval Unit set up home at Gordon Barracks. Basing the URNU in the Roy Strathdee Building was discussed. The accommodation already being pressed by the AUOTC itself, this option was dismissed.

The usual round of Christmas parties, were held including the permanent staff one which included places for local orphanage children.

The November 1988 organisation was:
HQ; Basic Wing with Buchan and Moray Platoons; Advanced Wing with Engineers, Signals and Angus (Infantry) Platoons; Training Team, Drums and Pipes; QM Platoon.

Adventure training at weekends and on the Easter Camps continued as a major part of unit life but increasingly formal qualifications were being required for instructors and leaders. Efforts were increased to get staff and students placed on popular and oversubscribed Adventure Training Courses. Easter Camp centred on Inverness TC with 35 cadets completing an opening walk through the Lairig Ghru from Linn o' Dee to Coylum Bridge. A total of 70 took part in canoeing, skiing, climbing and abseiling.

Annual Camp 1989 was held at Garelochhead Training Centre. The Drums and Pipes trained with the Tayforth band at Inverness while the rest of contingent went through a first week programme of engineer, signals and infantry skills. The final exercise had a 'Limited War' scenario with platoon and company level operations. On MACC Camp, 28 cadets built footbridges and a viewing platform at Black Spout Wood, Pitlochry for Perth and Kinross Council.

The summer saw the usual Diaspora of cadets on attachments to BAOR, Cyprus, Berlin and the UK. Others took courses in driving, methods of instruction (MOI), First Aid and Basic German. There were 28 attachments to Regular, TA, CCF and ACF camps. Trophies were awarded to the successful and notorious. The Initiative Cup went to the cadet who successfully booby trapped the RE PSI. The Marett Expedition Rose Bowl recognised a successful cross-Scotland expedition. This award had been donated by a recent Training Major who himself had been involved in OP RALEIGH a well known scheme for youth development within challenging worldwide expeditions. The scheme was started by explorer, adventurer and fellow Sapper officer, Colonel John Blashford-Snell as OP DRAKE in 1978. The Wooden Spoon was awarded for the successful targeting of a garage door with a 4 tonne lorry. The Springbok Map Reading Trophy presented by Roy Strathdee at the end of his tenure as Honorary Colonel, was awarded for navigation excellence.

The unit still faced teaching accommodation and storage shortages at its HQ even without the briefly threatened occupation by the Naval Unit. At Black Dog Ranges the Grenade Range was closed permanently, giving the unit sappers a range tower to demolish.

On the broader military education front the University's Department of International Relations revived its participation in the Service Fellowship Scheme which had started 15 years earlier. The University had gained a high profile in International Relations studies particularly with the work of David Capitanchik on international terrorism. Capitanchik served on the Military Education Committee (MEC).

Late 1989 saw minor amendments to the UOTC Charter as a result of the Gibb Study combined with the finding of the wider Military Led Efficiency Scrutiny (MLES). The latter study's title hoped to allay Army fears about exposure to sweeping ill considered cuts by what some termed 'Civvy led bean counters'. The trend for more management information capture and reporting continued, placing ever greater burdens on HQ staffs, without always any obvious compensating improvements in 'efficiency'. The new UOTC Charter identified recruiting as a priority task but was explicitly sensitive to the privileged positions OTCs held within their parent Universities and Colleges. Walpole emphasised to the MEC that he had no intention of turning the OTC into an overt recruiting organisation. He would continue to foster student interest in a future military career by providing sustained, satisfying and enjoyable training for those who wanted it. The new charter indicated that UOTCs would normally be commanded by a Regular Officer but that suitable TA (including WRAC) officers could also be COs. It was hoped to increase the overall national OTC strength to 4059 by October 1990 excluding bursaries, university cadetships and Group B staff. A standardised OTC establishment would have 198 officer cadets organised in three basic wing platoons and three advanced wing platoons or troops. Aberdeen was to be an exception with an establishment of 165 cadets (up from the theoretical 120 and the actual 132) organised in 5 platoons.

It had been found that 50% of the TA's strength was female thus a 35% level was set for women officer cadets.

Two technical arms were allowed per OTC and Aberdeen would continue with Engineers and Signals. An RQMS post was to be established to ease the increasing administrative burden on the Adjutant/QM. The unit would also now be established for an Infantry PSI and a NRPS Chief Clerk.. The Band would later be authorised to have 21 cadets plus SNCOs as Pipe Major and Drum Major.

On mobilisation Regular staff would be appointed to individual posts under the REDRUM scheme. District HQs would take over the remaining rump of the OTCs as command cadres. RMA Sandhurst would conduct a series of 10 week courses producing by the six month point 1,600 young officers trained or under training. In Aberdeen the CO would continue to be the Garrison Commander and one of his TA Group A Major posts would be dedicated to the Home Defence Role.

At a more practical level it had been recognised that most OTC training took place outside of the summer months and that they should be entitled to the issue of waterproofs.

There was no real reason why Aberdeen should be singled out for a smaller establishment. Perhaps the future TA footprint in the area was a factor. It was the 4th most expensive contingent to run out of 19 OTCs and could expect further efficiency scrutiny.

MTQ training continued to be a challenging burden to the unit with decreasing numbers passing at MTQ2 level. It was decided to concentrate MTQ activity at a dedicated camp to avoid everything dragging on throughout the session. The OTC continued to benefit from a throughput of TA officers with varied background and experiences. Architect Edwin Rose had studied in Aberdeen but chose to do his student soldiering initially with 15 Para and then with 2/51 Highlanders. He had not really heard of the OTC when he started his studies but really enjoyed the change of pace and challenges that the local TA provided as a contrast to his academic week. His service had included commanding a Milan anti tank platoon which, with the rest of the battalion, would reinforce 1(BR) Corps in its attempts to stop the Soviet hordes on the North German Plain. Thrown into the challenge of preparing officer cadets for MTQ exams, he found map reading to be the biggest problem (particularly for women he dared to admit). He organised special outings to bring everyone up to speed in navigational skills.

The short 1990 winter camp cramming for MTQ was again held at Edinburgh TC. Early morning PT from 0615 to 0645 took the form of Scottish Country Dancing. Novices learned basic steps, the Eightsome Reel and the Dashing White Sergeant. Intermediate students of the art added the Duke of Perth to their repertoire. The Engineers studied river recce, the Signals set up CPs and Angus Platoon learned more about Soviet minor tactics, patrols and Armoured Fighting Vehicle (AFV) recognition. MTQ Level 3 qualifications were available in Aberdeen's three disciplines of Infantry, Engineers and Signals.

The Easter Camp programme at Ballater had skiing cancelled due to a lack of snow. Other activities including canoeing at Aboyne were enjoyed by all as was evening fitness training in the form of yet more Scottish Dancing lessons.

On the Dee, Easter 1990

The Annual Camp was held at Ripon. Seventy cadets went to Ripon organised as a three platoon company. An internal security/limited war scenario had them building a tented camp and prisoner of war (POW) cages. Road blocks, patrols and rescue operations were conducted. The desired surprise was achieved when the scheduled defence phase suddenly switched to an escape and evasion exercise. Initiative was tested by dumping cadets in Scarborough without money or transport and tasking them to get back to Ripon. Reorganised, the contingent conducted a deliberate company attack to end the exercise.

The Engineer Camp was at Alyth, NE of Blairgowrie, where 30 attendees built a 'wild west' fort and a footbridge. Attachments included three taking on the severe challenge of EX GREEN STUDENT with the Royal Marine Commandos in SW England. Others went off to Cyprus, Belize, BAOR and Canada. Back at Don Street the unit was still facing shortages of space with lots of equipment being stored at Gordon Barracks. Some garage space was converted to storage areas. The Roy Strathdee Building itself got a facelift with a fresh coat of paint.

The big military event of Summer 1990, was the Iraqi invasion of Kuwait. A UN approved coalition response to the invasion included Britain's OP GRANBY the biggest UK deployment and logistic challenge since World War Two. The Army contribution to the First Gulf War centred around 1st Armoured Division with an unusually large slice of artillery, engineer and logistic support. Weapons, doctrine and procedures developed for the Cold War were applied highly successfully to evict the Iraqi Army from Kuwait during DESERT STORM ground and air support operations which commenced on 24 February 1991. By 3 Mar 1991 the Iraqi Government accepted the terms of ceasefire, their invasion force utterly destroyed and the lucky in full retreat. Many Engineers and Infantrymen were involved with POW Cages for real and on a grander scale than the AUOTC efforts at Ripon.

The unit structure for 1990/91 was:

HQ - CO, 2IC, Adjt, SUO, RSM, Orderly Room

A Company - OC, 2IC

      Engr Pl - Pl Comd, JUO, Cadet Sgt, Cadets, RE PSI

      Sigs Pl - Pl Comd, JUO, Cadet Sgt, Cadets, Sigs PSI

      Angus Pl - Pl Comd, JUO, Cdt Sgt, Cadets, Inf PSI

B Company - OC, CSM
       Buchan Pl - Pl Comd, JUO, Cdt Sgt, Cadets, NCO
       Moray Pl - Pl Comd, JUO, Cdt Sgt, Cadets. NCO
Drums and Pipes
Admin Pl - RQMS, MT Sgt, Cadets Mess Sgt, cooks, drivers,
      storemen
Trg Team - Young Officers (cadetships etc), NCO
'Foreign Legion' - Attached non British members attending
      post graduate and other courses.

The training cycle at this time was:

Year 1
       Winter term - enlistment to B Coy, MTQ 1
           Remembrance Day practice and Parade
           Winter camp - MTQ1 trg and exam
       Spring term - MTQ1 infantry trg
              Easter camp adventure trg
       Summer term - move to A Coy, Ex Northern Lights
           Specialist trg
           Annual camp - collective and special to arm
training developing military skills and leadership

Year 2
       Winter term - MTQ 2 and MTQ1 if required,
             Remembrance Day
             Winter camp - MTQ2 and leadership
       Spring Term - Specialist trg and leadership
            Easter camp adventure trg
       Summer term - Northern Lights and Specialist trg
            Annual camp

Years 3 and 4
> Winter term - recruiting, recruit training,
> specialist trg leadership, Remembrance Day
>> Winter camp - recruit trg and leadership
>
> Spring term - recruit trg, spec trg,
>> For those going for commissioning pre District Assessment Board (DAB), and pre RMA Sandhurst training
>>
>> Easter camp - adventure trg
>
> Summer term - Northern Lights, Specialist trg,
>> pre Sandhurst training and Annual camp

The Drums and Pipes followed a separate enlistment and training cycle allowing time for the intensive practice required for Remembrance Parade, Northern Lights, Beating Retreats and other events. Military training and mandatory tests would be completed where possible and being already a close team with strong tribal identity, the Band generally did well.

A long walk through the Lairig Ghru became a regular annual event for the unit normally with a Bar BQ available for the survivors. This exercise took the Gaelic name *Am Fear Liath Mor* in salute to the Big Grey Man of Ben Macdui who haunts the area.

Shooting played a major role in unit life with teams taking part in the Wapinschaw at Black Dog, and the inter-unit Army Skill at Arms Meeting, ASSAM.

Strengthening the affiliation with the Gordon Highlanders was aided by the presence of the 1st Battalion at Fort George.

Some Regular Army corps depots now began to host familiarisation and competition weekends for those UOTC cadets with an interest in their cap badge. The Royal Signals ran EX LIGHTNING STRIKE at Blandford, Dorset and the Royal Engineers held a similar weekend at Minley. The contingent specialist platoons conducted their own series of small exercises throughout the year as time and facilities allowed. Sappering would be done within EX BOARS SNOUT while the Signallers would learn rebroadcast techniques in EX CHAIN CHATTER.

The MEC continued to be involved in discussions regarding the mechanism for the appointment of COs. Some MECs had been upset by a lack of consultation on this matter by the MOD. Aberdeen reiterated, perhaps unrealistically, that its OTC CO should be sensitive to the traditions of the ancient Scottish Universities and if at all possible a graduate of Aberdeen or at least another Scottish University. The MOD in its defence pointed out the challenge it faced in managing the cycle of promotion and appointment boards appointing COs to 19 UOTCs and 130 major units. There simply was no time for extensive staffing of candidate pen pictures to MECs. By the time Universities had stated their preferences most of the suitable candidates would have already been placed.

Aberdeen soon heard that their Sapper CO was to be replaced by a Gunner. Mike Dore RA, an applied science graduate of RMCS Shrivenham, would be joining in Jan 1991, having commanded Rowallen Company at Sandhurst. Rowallen Company was named after Lord Rowallen who had set up the Highland Fieldcraft Training Centre in 1943 to help soldiers who had only just failed to pass War Office Selection Boards (WOSBs) for commissioning. The development of leadership and character on the course helped candidates gain commissions at a time when large numbers of young officers were required for D Day and the subsequent defeat of Germany. Rowallen Company had been established at Sandhurst in 1977 to help the many candidates (70%) who were failing the Regular Commissioning Board (RCB), to mature and develop and successfully achieve commissioning. Rowallen Company was disbanded in 2002.

Lt Col Dore very quickly received the good news that Aberdeen had come third overall at the RE Weekend at Minley. Ice breaking had opened the raft race course sufficiently for Aberdeen to come second in that event.

1990/91 recruiting statistics were studied for lessons to be learned. Aberdeen University had provided 30 male recruits, 6 subsequently discharged. 23 Ladies had joined with 12 being discharged later. Robert Gordon Institute of Technology had provided 8 male and 5 female recruits with 4 males and one female being discharged. Two ladies had joined from the College of Commerce, and two more from the Northern College of Education. From a total recruit intake of 38 males and 32 females, 10 males and 13 females had left mainly due to lack of attendance. Dore concluded that whilst recruiting was reasonably successful retention was not. He wondered if this was partially due to the increasing use of modular exams and assignments throughout the academic session. The days of being able to leave everything to end of session cramming were gone. The MTQ system continued to be a worry. The autumn term still involved a heavy load of MTQ instruction with limited 'fun' outdoor components. A first OTC term of too many lectures meant many did not turn up again in the Spring. He would renew efforts to increase the practical sessions prior to Christmas.

Attendance at the 1991 Summer Camp at Sennybridge had been disappointing. Research indicated that around a quarter of all cadets had, due to financial prudence or necessity, secured full time summer vacation jobs before Camp commenced. Three months of employment would do much to reduce bank overdrafts and this might be the start of a worrying trend under the new student loan system.

At Sennybridge about a third of those who did attend were laid low by a nasty virus which confined many to bed and even sent some to hospital.

The Engineer camp at Jedburgh in contrast was a huge success. In the biggest OTC MACC task to date, a 105 metre suspension bridge, including a 68 metre centre span, was thrown across the River Teviot. Considerable problems had been encountered but overcome. The cadets heard that two Regular Engineer Squadrons had turned down the task due to its complexity. The new crossing allowed ten kilometres of the Dere Street Way to re-open.

In Summer 1991 the CO was faced with a potentially serious challenge of his own. It seemed there might be a serious impediment to his recruiting campaign. Following complaints from the Aberdeen University Lesbian and Gay Society the Students Representative Council (SRC) had informed him that they could not support organisations which practiced discrimination. Thus the OTC and the other service units would not be allowed to advertise in the Fresher magazine or participate in the Recruiting fairs with other clubs and societies. Despite the OTC never having practiced discrimination on grounds of sexual preference, Dore was caught between the opposing forces of student equality activism and the then current Queen's Regulations. He sought MOD guidance on handling the PR and other aspects of this sensitive issue. In 1992 the first challenges against Armed Services policy were made to the House of Commons

Select Committee on the Armed Forces. The Conservative government promised to stop the criminal prosecution of armed service personnel who were 'homosexual'. Nevertheless dismissals and investigations continued while the Ministry of Defence argued that the presence of lesbians and gay men would undermine morale and fighting capability. Not until 12 January 2000 was the ban on homosexuals openly serving in the British Armed Services lifted. Despite the furore, OTC recruiting for 91/92 was successful and no doubt included as it always had done a proportion of 'lesbians and gays' not very dissimilar from the ratios in the whole student body.

The recruiting team under its JUO, persuaded over 100 students to join. Included among the new recruits was Major John Patchett a former Gurkha who would cover the Training Major post while himself being taught to teach. The variety within the new intake was further enhanced by the new Officer Cadet Walker, who had served as a REME Corporal during the Gulf War.

WO1(RSM) Joe Gallagher joined from the Scots Guards and three new PSIs adjusted to OTC life. WO2 Laing of the Gordons became the first Infantry PSI for many years and WO2s Laughlin and Doherty joined the Engineer and Signals wings respectively. The Christmas Term was busy with recruits starting their training with a weekend at Ballater. The Infantry went on exercise at Black Dog eating much of the rabbit population while manning OPs and patrolling. APWTs were conducted at Barry Buddon and the engineers and signallers held their own exercises. The main exercise of the term AUTUMN PRIDE was held on private land at Ballogie with recce patrols having rather too realistic contacts with inadequately briefed gamekeepers who had identified them as poachers. The November 1991 training programme was enhanced by a Gulf War lecture by a team from 1 Royal Scots. They shared their experiences regarding leadership problems at junior command level and other lessons from the front line.

The AURNU had a big year in 1991 taking ownership of the Fast Patrol Boat HMS ARCHER. Their previous and second ship, HMS CHASER, was sold to the Lebanese Navy.

Although it is certain Mike Dore and his AUOTC team would claim no particular credit for it, the Cold War was finally won in 1991. The symbolism of parts of the Berlin Wall being torn down in 1989 was only one event in an increasing rush of change throughout Eastern Europe. In February 1991 the Warsaw Pact members declared the agreement to be at an end. Ten months later the Union of Soviet Socialist Republics (USSR) was dissolved. As at the end of every major conflict, victory would mean great and rapid change to the Regular and Territorial Army as the nation once more adjusted its defence planning and expenditure to a greatly changed situation.

AUOTC had played its role in helping students decide if the Service life was for them whether as regulars or part timers. During the 1980s and the first year of the 90s decade AUOTC helped produce 63 Regular officers including 5 to the RAF/WRAF and 1 to the Royal Navy. In the same period the TA gained 60 officers from AUOTC.

Chapter 9

PEACE DIVIDENDS AND HOT WARS
1992-2012

The growth of Aberdeen's academic institutions in student and staff populations continued and some of the earlier intense local identity began to wane. Particularly among staff, the University and Colleges consisted of many more people with no previous North East connections. At the end of World War II, in 1945, more than half the student population originated within a 30 mile radius of Aberdeen. By 1975 less than a quarter did so. However in the early 1990s, one third of undergraduates still came from the North East and the further Highlands and Islands. The rest of Scotland provided another third. The remaining third came to Aberdeen from the rest of the UK and an increasing number of other countries. Aberdeen continued to grow its postgraduate student populations.

The University property footprint was now heavily centred on Old Aberdeen. By 1990 nearly all engineering and science departments had moved out of Marischal College for new accommodation in Old Aberdeen. Marischal College continued to be used by the University which also maintained its 'New Aberdeen' presence in the shape of the big Students' Union Building across the road on the corner of Upperkirkgate.

Halls of Residence had been increased in number and size making OTC participation at Don Street convenient. Despite needing longer bus rides, getting on for a third of officer cadets were now joining from the Robert Gordon Institute and other colleges and undergraduate schools.

The post Cold War restructuring and reduction of the Armed Forces centred around the Options For Change initiative. Most of this activity would not be perceived by students as they continued the normal round of OTC training and social life. However in the Army, that some of them might join, there were significant changes involving amalgamations, rationalisations and disbandment.

In 1992 a new Adjutant General's Corps was formed from the Royal Army Education Corps, the Royal Army Pay Corps, the Women's Royal Army Corps, the Army Legal Corps, the Royal Military Police, and the Military Provost Staff Corps

The Royal Logistic Corps formed in 1993 from the Royal Corps of Transport, the Royal Army Ordnance Corps, the Royal Pioneer Corps, the Army Catering Corps, and the Postal and Courier Service Royal Engineers.

In 1994 the North East's own Gordon Highlanders amalgamated with the Queen's Own Highlanders(Seaforth and Camerons). The two regiments met on Thomas Telford's old bridge across the Spey at Craigellachie and marched off it as The Highlanders. AUOTC retained the Gordon Tartan and the black buttoned spats adopted by the Regiment in memory of Sir John Moore, the British force commander killed at the Battle of Corunna in 1809.

Perhaps the most obvious change in AUOTC at this time stemmed from the demise of the Women's Royal Army Corps in 1992. Earlier studies had already recommended that Women Officer Cadets should wear the same contingent headdress and cap badges as the men. The women would now indeed wear Glengarries and Tam O' Shanters with the

Boar's Head cap badge. As had happened before in the OTC's history, practical tailoring problems intervened and the ladies would retain WRAC Service Jackets until new uniforms became available in 1994.

On the continent the large military presence established at the close of World War II began to wind down, with barrack and airfield closures and the relocation of units back to the UK. In 1992 the HQ of the British Corps became the nucleus for the multinational HQ of the Allied Command Europe Rapid Reaction Corps (ARRC). In 1994 the British Army of the Rhine (BAOR) and RAF(G) become British Forces Germany (BFG) and the Army presence in Germany reduced to one division.

NATO planning and force structures evolved towards new arrangements for protecting the Alliance's interests from natural and man-made disaster on the margins of the traditional area of interest and even further away in the world. In the mid 1990s the tragic events surrounding the break-up of Yugoslavia led to the huge NATO Operation JOINT ENDEAVOUR authorised by the United Nations to implement a peace agreement. British involvement in the area had started several years earlier in the first OP GRAPPLE deployments under a UN mandate to protect humanitarian aid activities in Bosnia. With years of involvement in Bosnia and later in Kosovo, Army training and doctrine had to accommodate new tactics and acronyms covering a wide spectrum from monitoring, through peace keeping, to peace enforcement. Young officers and their men faced increasing complexity in multinational operations with varying and detailed rules of engagement, all under the ever present surveillance by world media.

For AUOTC, routine carried on against a backdrop of budget squeezes. The unit had lost its winter camp 1991 due to cutbacks and thus had a backlog of MTQ training to complete. Drill nights, which for decades had been on Thursday evenings, moved to Tuesday to facilitate better attendance. Students continued to participate from the University, Robert Gordons Institute of Technology, Foresterhill School of Nursing, the Northern College of Agriculture, the Northern College of Education, and the Schools of Arts and Business Studies. The through-semester pressure on candidates had the Unit Burns Supper competing with exam preparations. Exercise SPRING LEAP pitted Aberdeen against Tayforth OTC in a patrolling skills competition with the assistance of the Ayrshire Yeomanry. Despite fears about the impact of 'Options for Change' recruiting and retention had been successful. Thus cadet strength was encouraging but the unit had only one cook out of an establishment for seven. The supply of Officers to fill Company OC and 2IC appointments remained a concern. Trawls were made to find suitable candidates in the 25 to 37 year age range.

The unit's cross country runners had a busy year with early challenges in February at the Scottish Championships at Penicuik. WOCdt Fulton had particular success and went on to represent Scottish District in the United Kingdom Land Forces (UKLF) Championships.

A UKLF Directive for UOTCs was received and stated that 'the aim of all OTC training is to prepare OCdts for commissioned service in the Regular Army and TA by increasing military knowledge and developing leadership ability'. Although not totally wide of the mark this statement was not in accord with the UOTC Charter and was at least an oversimplification. Yet again a degree of uncertainty and confusion in the chain of command was exposed. Of course encouraging the achievement of Military qualifications and satisfying the broader aims of the OTC were not necessarily mutually exclusive activities, quite the contrary. The CO challenged his PSIs to each produce six MTQ 3 passes in their specialities.

In ! Out ! Drip Camp, 1992

In May 1992 the unit took part in the Wapinschaw and the Band competed at the TA Pipe Band Competition at Alnwickhill. Aberdeen won the Northern Lights Competition for the first time in ten years.

The Summer Ball was held at the Skean Dhu Hotel at Dyce and the Cairngorms once more hosted Exercise *Fear Liath Mor.* Summer Term training weekends were more centralised (combined sub-unit training) than usual to allow for the reduced numbers. The exam schedule at the University and other institutions extended over a long period but finally everyone who could, set off for Annual Camp at Ripon. The main exercise took place in dreadful weather with cadets surviving on what their webbing contained until a joyful reunion with their bigger packs. The MACC Camp went to the north end of Skye and bridged the Kilmaluag River with yet another Galloway Bridge.

The infantry sub-unit joined 1st Gordons in Berlin, for a rare and valuable opportunity to train with Regular soldiers and gain MTQ 3 qualifications. The Gordons CO was himself a former AUOTC cadet and SUO.

A range of other attachments and activities were carried out through the Summer of 1992. Having achieved a number of passes at the Joint Services Mountain Training Centre, a 10 man expedition set off to the Canadian Rockies.

Recruiting preparations took up the final weeks of the vacation, partially funded by an increased annual grant from the University of £500. This allocation supported adverts in the Fresher's Magazine, paid sports entrance fees, and helped meet expedition photography costs.

At the annual get together of all MECs, COMEC, delegates heard about each others efforts in fostering Strategic Studies. The huge changes in Europe provided almost unlimited scope for study, lectures and dissertations. Sir Peter Inge addressed COMEC on the European Security Situation. A former commander of 1(BR) Corps, Commander BAOR and Commander of NATO's Northern Army Group (NORTHAG) he was eminently qualified to do so. In 1994 he would become the last (at the time of writing in 2012) to hold the ultimate rank of Field Marshal.

In Aberdeen, to encourage wider military learning and thought, Mike Dore suggested to the MEC that, like the other Scottish universities, Aberdeen should instigate annual defence lectures. The MEC approved the idea and annual Elphinstone Defence Lectures would be given by authoritative speakers on topical defence subjects. The OTC and other service units would provide most, if not all, of the audiences.

Work at Black Dog Ranges was completed in the summer of 1992 with the 25 metre range rebuilt, the 200 metre range refurbished, firing points relocated and new vedette telephones in place. AUOTC now had full responsibility for Black Dog including its budget, and the range was increasingly busy.

Post Cold War repercussions included a hard look at the TA's property holdings. Aberdeen was considered to have TA accommodation in excess of requirements and official scalings. Options for AUOTC included staying at Don Street in its Roy Strathdee HQ, a TA building built on University owned ground that might be needed for other uses such as more student accommodation. Another possibility was a move to Prince Charles Barracks in Albury Road. The final option was a move to the Bridge of Don Barracks which was eventually chosen as the centralised location for what little would remain of Aberdeen's TA presence. The authorities certainly thought there was no longer a need for two TA Centres (Prince Charles and Bridge of Don). The University reiterated its strong support for the OTC but felt that the question of location was up to GOC Scotland. The MEC's David Capitanchik was firmly against any move from Don Street, given its on-campus location and convenience to halls of residence. Even short increases in commuting distances were indeed a factor in TA recruiting and retention. It is thought by some that many TA infantry volunteers happy to get to the Hardgate for training were not prepared to undergo two bus rides to venture across the Don. Prince Charles Barracks would eventually close and the AUOTC remained where they were on Don Street but using the facilities as required at the bigger barracks across the Don. The University Air Squadron's old premises at Fairfield House was declared surplus to requirements. Aberdeen's squadron combined with others to form an East of Scotland Universities Air Squadron based at RAF Leuchars.

In October 1992, AUOTC entered a team in the Cambrian Patrol Exercise in Wales. Originally set up by nearby TA units, the event grew to become an internationally renowned and gruelling challenge of long distance patrol skills and fitness in the hills and bogs of Wales. Despite a lack of preparation time and appalling weather, the Aberdeen team gained a Bronze Award.

In late 1992 Mike Dore asked the MEC to consider the redesignation of his unit as the 'Aberdeen and Robert Gordon Universities Officers Training Corps'. This would reflect the granting of university 'status' to the Robert Gordon Institute of Technology under the Further and Higher Education Act of 1992. The name change would reflect a broader student base, might help recruiting, and could help stave off attempts to reduce the unit establishment. Both Principals supported the proposal. Wheels turn slowly in such matters and it was not until April 1994 that AUOTC heard via its Honorary Colonel, Lieutenant General Sir John Macmillan, that on 23 March 1994 Her Majesty had graciously approved a change of title. AUOTC now stood for 'Aberdeen Universities Officers' Training Corps'. The formal letter from the Ministry of Defence contained the apostrophe, the existence and placement of which has been a frequent topic of debate. The 2012 view, adopted for this book's cover is to be completely apostrophe free.

Success in unit activities was recognised by the Sword of Honour, the Sash of Honour, the Hewitt Tankard for Best Recruit, the Springbok Map Reading Trophy, the McPhail Massie Shooting Trophy, the Levack Shield, the Marett Expedition Rose Bowl, the Shivas Initiative Trophy, the Taylor CMT Cup (now for MTQ2 excellence), the Buchanan Small bore Rose Bowl, the Shepherd Cup for most improved drummer, a Black Watch Statuette for most improved piper, and a Quaich for Success on a piping course. Everyone remained liable to be recorded for posterity on the Wooden Spoon.

The new special to arm UOTC weekends held at Corps Training Depots and Schools were proving to be a great success. In 1992 Aberdeen sent cadets to weekend concentrations sponsored by the Royal Artillery, Royal Engineers, Royal Signals, and Royal Electrical and Mechanical Engineers.

1992 saw changes at the Royal Military Academy Sandhurst with the previous separate courses for graduates, non-graduates and ladies combined into one course for all British and overseas cadets.

1992 closed with 52 cadets training for MTQ1 and MTQ 2 at a four day Winter camp.

By March 1993 one set of garages had been properly converted to storage space allowing two more classrooms to be allocated. The high numbers of cadets joining and staying put pressure on the available accommodation, budgets and vehicle capacity. However, all in all, problems like these were welcomed. Sixty Eight cadets went to Ballater for Adventure training. Ripon was again the destination for Annual Camp with topical peace keeping tactics being practiced before a week of specialist training.

In July 1993 the long tradition of Scots Guards RSMs came to an end when RSM Rees of the Irish Guards reported for duty. Among his many duties the RSM acted as Bookings Officer for the refurbished and once again popular Black Dog Ranges. The MACC Camp was held at Lagganlia near Aviemore where 20 students completed several tasks including the construction of an adventure play park.

Mike Dore went off to become Defence Attache in Sofia, and in August 1993 the unit once again came under a TA Commanding Officer with the arrival on promotion of Lt Col Gordon McKen MBE TD of the 51st Highland Volunteers. His previous TA post was in Elgin as Battalion 2IC. He had come up through the ranks of the TA 3rd Battalion Gordon Highlanders, later 2/51st Highland Volunteers. He had made a name for himself by establishing or re-establishing TA infantry platoons from scratch in the old Gordon Highlander heartlands. He resurrected vacant and deteriorating drill halls and even church halls, in Keith and Turriff. To fill his new properties on drill nights he conducted active and inspiring recruiting campaigns and training programmes. His knowledge of the TA system, and the best ways of using it or avoiding it, depending on need, would set the OTC in good stead. He was certainly keener on bending rules than some Regular COs might be. An astute and pragmatic businessman in the agricultural industry he listened with wry amusement to some of the inspiring but unrealistic talk from the military hierarchy, about 'doing more with less'. In addition to his passion for training and

358

developing people, McKen loved the challenges of live firing and the real satisfaction and confidence that it had brought to his soldiers. To him military training, properly conducted, could beat just about anything. He believed people joined to 'soldier' above everything else. Such feelings were confirmed when AUOTC shared a camp with another UOTC's cadets. The latter were on an adventure training camp but appeared rather bored and highly envious of Aberdeen's intensive military training programme.

The Summer 1993 vacation saw 16 cadets go to Berlin for a second time, for 2 weeks training with 1st Gordons. Fourteen of them completed MTQ3.

Twelve members of the Drums and Pipes were attached to the Edinburgh Mil Tattoo. This Tattoo was particularly poignant for the Army in Scotland. It would be the last time all of the then existing Regiments would be individually represented in the massed bands before the Options for Change amalgamations were implemented.

AUOTC provided an Umpire team for NATO Exercise ACTION EXPRESS in Denmark during September 1993.

McKen had seen little of the OTC during his previous TA service, the TA/OTC relationship ever a matter of worry and discussion. He tried to encourage more mixing between the two with potential officers from the OTC getting to know the TA and junior TA officers being encouraged to serve in the OTC. McKen, greatly valued the assistance and advice of Honorary Colonels. These senior and experienced men, out of the command chain, could advise COs on delicate matters and occasionally gently influence things among their social peers in the military and university hierarchies. Conversation and persuasion from Lieutenant General MacMillan helped transform a University leadership initially rather suspicious of 'militarism' to one that turned the Remembrance Day Parade into a truly family affair, warmly hosted in the Elphinstone Hall. Even senior academics had to be reminded that soldiers seldom start wars. On a more practical level some of the more 'left wing' observers of the unit were asked which of two options they preferred for the young people in their care. One option involved working long night hours in Aberdeen's bars or some other uninspiring employment. The OTC in contrast provided pay for good training, travel, character broadening experiences and preparation for employment, all conducted in a safe and managed environment.

Unit performance at commissioning boards and on Sandhurst courses had become disappointing. This was identified as being mostly due to a lack of broad all-arms awareness. Instead of staying solely in one sub-unit, everyone started doing a bit of everything throughout their time in the OTC. The unit did its bit for wider TA recruiting by running stands for EXECUTIVE STRETCH. This exercise aimed to give senior businessmen and employers a taste of what the TA involved, in the hope that they would facilitate their employees joining.

With fewer units based in Germany there was increasing bookings pressure on training areas and ranges. UKLF proposed allocating UOTCs to Minor District Training Areas in late June or early July, if any were available. McKen thought most of these minor areas 'quaint' but inadequate for AUOTC ambitions including live firing exercises. To ensure appropriate annual field training the Main Camp would be moved to Easter where they were was a better chance of securing a Major Training Area. Adventure

360

training camp would be held in June.

The change might also allow more cadets to attend the main camp. Differing exam and graduation timetables in the Summer meant that many, especially from Robert Gordons University, could not attend. Some senior cadets, by the time of the June camps, had already graduated and were either in employment or seriously on the job hunt.

McKen's concerns about Summer Camps were to a large extent confirmed by the 1994 Camp at Halton, outside Lancaster. This was a small camp primarily designed for Royal Engineer watermanship training. It had been used many times in the past as an overnight transit stop by AUOTC road parties heading for the deep south of England. The OTC had been bounced out of its original booking at Garelochhead by a higher priority unit. Halton burst at the seams with 106 cadets and 22 staff, and was not suited to infantry based training. This, and signals training, were conducted some distance away at Catterrick, Feldom (near Richmond) and Stang Forest. The COs exercise took the form of a Cambrian Patrol style 48 hour exercise with, depending on map reading, at least 50 miles of walking on the Lakeland Fells with numerous tasks along the way. Despite the considerable physical challenge of the exercise only three cadets were forced to retire due to injury, a tribute to the Contingent's overall fitness and grit. The Signals PSI had his work cut out literally keeping his signallers on the road, given the cadet drivers' penchant for leaving it. Five vehicles required overnight recovery from ditches and other unlikely locations.

Running featured highly in the year's activities with a JUO organising HIGHLAND SLOG, a 24 hour run from Inverness to Aberdeen in aid of Riding for the Disabled.

WOCdt Karen Fulton won the Army UKLF Cross Country Championships at Longmoor a considerable achievement.

Over the summer, 63 officer cadets went away on various attachments in UK, Germany, Cyprus, Hong Kong (British Forces would leave there in 1997) and Canada. The latter involved RSM Rees, Irish Guards, taking 20 cadets to join his Regiment in training. The British Army Training Unit Suffield (BATUS) administered huge training areas leased from Canada in 1971. With the loss of training facilities in Libya in 1969, Canada provided the only space available to the British Army for large scale armoured and mechanised Battle Group training, including live firing. AUOTC would through the years send many parties and individuals on attachments to units exercising in this area. Nearby mountains and rivers also provided terrific opportunities for adventurous training and sightseeing.

In the same Summer, one cadet deployed with OP RALEIGH to Siberia. Even with cadets only being paid for half their time away, attachments were expensive but thought by all to be well worthwhile. McKen placed great emphasis on attachments. Seeing the broader Army gave people a chance to assess 'the real thing' and make up their minds one way or another about future careers. Feedback from host units would also help assess commissioning potential.

The MACC task, with 25 cadets, built a 12 obstacle assault course at Croftinloan School, Pitlochry.

The impact on drill night and weekend attendance of the modular semester system continued to be monitored. Feedback indicated that the impact might not be as great as some thought. Motivated cadets ensured they completed their assignments in good time so as not to limit their OTC participation. In addition to fun, quite good money was on offer.

The 1993/94 daily pay rates were £22-84 for pre MTQ 2 cadets rising to £25-50 for those who had passed MTQ2. With annual camp, at least 15 other training days, and MTQ passes under their belts, cadets were entitled to a tax free bounty payment of £100 in the first year, £130 in the second, and £155 in the third.

Small card handouts gave this information, the names of all those on the staff, and a programme of events for the academic year. To trigger ambition the card also set out the steps to a TA Commission: MTQ1; MTQ2; District Assessment Board; 2 week commissioning course at RMA Sandhurst. Routine training timings were Tuesdays 1915-2130; Wednesdays 1400-1700 optional; Saturdays 0850-1700; Weekends 1900 Friday to 1700 Sunday.

Rightly transparent to cadets, the permanent staff continued to tackle administrative challenges, such as the Defence Costs Study (Front Line First), through what was described as a frustrating and diplomatically awkward time. The assistance of HQ TAVRA staff was valued highly by AUOTC.

The Military Home Defence role began to be wound up, being replaced by an Integrated Contingency Planning (ICP) role. The Joint Service Liaison Officer (JSLO) posts were discontinued. The Aberdeen JSLO post had frequently been occupied by former OTC officers including Robbie Ewen and Mike Hewitt. The CO AUOTC now became the Military Liaison Officer (MLO) for Grampian with responsibility for contingency planning with Grampian Police, and the Chief Executive and Emergency Planning Officer of the Regional Council. The CO would be understudied in this role by his Training officer or other suitable Major on his staff.

The 1994 recruiting effort was slightly scaled back in anticipation of establishment cuts but nevertheless attracted more high quality interest than the unit could cope with.

Aberdeen began to challenge why they had the smallest approved establishment of all the OTCs. With a current actual strength of 193 cadets there appeared no reason for Aberdeen, with five major tertiary education institutions in the City, not to have a standard establishment like Tayforth. The unit was not seeking more equipment, only an increase in permitted personnel and the all important currency of Man Training Days (MTDs). The price of successful recruitment and retention was increased pressure on budgets. In summary there was increasing student demands to expand, versus Army pressures to reduce.

Advertising continued in the press for chefs, drivers and storemen to fill empty staff posts. Without a sufficient number of their own cooks, TA units became increasingly dependent on the allocation of District catering contracts to support their camps. The new Spring scheduled Annual Military Camps began at Warcop in 1995. The facilities there allowed individual, fire team and section level live firing. For watermanship the unit went back to Halton, this time using it in its proper role. Fighting In Built Up Area (FIBUA) training was successful as were long walks in the Lake District. Military training and qualifications included the Basic Fitness Test (BFT), the Combat Fitness Test (CFT) and assault courses. Any remaining energy was expended in sports and socialising.

Ballater hosted the summer camp assigned now to leadership development, adventure training and MACC tasks around Balmoral. Everyone enjoyed a relaxing post exam camp, another argument for the new arrangements.

Under AUOTC management the Black Dog facilities continued to improve. The site of the old grenade range was converted to a Command Post, toilet block and respirator test chamber. Five ISO containers were brought in as target stores and troop shelters. With money being generated by the disposal of training grounds and barracks, AUOTC made a bid for £10,000 on the G4 Common Good Fund. This money had come from the sale of Winston Barracks in Lanark. Aberdeen wanted to use the money for a further series of Black Dog improvements. A range building could be converted to a FIBUA skills house. A new hard target was required to revamp the 94mm Light Anti Tank Weapon Outdoor Trainer (LAW/ODT) range. This system involved firing a 9mm spotting round as a 'moderated noise' cartridge went off simulating the effect of the full weapon. The case was made that better facilities would revolutionise the use of the range. Attempts were still being made to acquire a motor barrow to help move targets around.

Back at Don Street steps were taken to refresh the décor in the changing rooms and kitchen. Hanging railings for service dress uniforms were installed as were power points for the RSM's new computer. Spotlights were installed for the car park area. RQMS Cole's long NRPS service was coming to an end and 30 applications for his job were received. WO1 Thomson RAMC secured the post and would still be there for the Centenary in 2012.

John McConachie, assisted by materials held by the OTC, published his U Company book, *'The Student Soldiers'*, in 1995. This stimulated interest in this aspect of the OTC's origins. The current equivalent of the old Gordon Highlander TF battalions, 2/51 Highland, became 3rd

Battalion Highlanders in February of the same year.

The POTEZ Cup presented by an AURNU Commander back in 1984 continued to be the prize for an annual competition between AUOTC and AURNU at Gordon Barracks. Volleyball, basketball, hockey, rugby, and tug o' war events were keenly contested. The Navy or the OTC took turns to host the ensuing party.

Technical sub-unit success continued with Aberdeen winning EX LIGHTNING STRIKE 95 at Blandford. Two hundred officer cadets from 18 of the UK's 19 OTC contingents participated. The programme included intercepts, jamming, log races, snow shoe races, and dining on pigs heads and dandelion coffee courtesy of survival instructors from 264 SAS Signals Squadron. The AUOTC team led by WJUO Henderson won by the biggest ever margin.

In June, Gordon McKen and his OTC team organised the tri-service marking of the University's Quincentenary with a dinner night in the Academics' Central Refectory complete with a piobaireachd from the Pipe Major. The full Drums and Pipes played a set before everyone moved to the Roy Strathdee Building to 'carry on the motion'. In July a further historic milestone was passed. The arrival of RSM Haughie, Argyll and Sutherland Highlanders, brought to an end the long involvement of the Guards in filling that post. The Scottish Division took on the responsibility.

Aberdeen University maintained a strong interest in Strategic Studies. Research concentrated on the post Cold War shaping of British and NATO forces; the evolution of West European security cooperation and the processes of military economic transformation in Central and Eastern Europe. Degree and diploma courses, and post graduate research opportunities occasionally brought people with service backgrounds from other countries into the OTC. Unpaid, these affiliated members would join in OTC activities as its 'Foreign Legion'. The Department for Strategic Studies also supported short residential courses for British Forces personnel and gave one-off lectures to service establishments as requested. As part of the Quincentenary Celebrations, the Elphinstone Defence Lectures were inaugurated with a talk from Michael Clarke from the Centre for Defence Studies, Kings College, London. The audience consisted of cadets from the three service units, other students and staff, and interested members of the public.

The CO settled into his new secondary role as Military Liaison Officer for the region. No longer a 'Garrison' Commander he became 'Station' Commander for Gordon Barracks. In the Integrated Contingency Planning role HQ OTC would help plan for, and coordinate, any military activity in the area in support of the Civil Authorities (MACA). These could range from responses to Foot and Mouth Disease outbreaks, fire-fighter or fuel tanker driver industrial action, major flooding and of course the response to any major terrorist incident.

During the winter term presentations were given by visiting briefing teams from various parts of the Army. In November 1995 MEC members were invited to join cadets as they listened to talks from the Royal Armoured Corps, the Royal Engineers and Director Special Forces. A second Elphinstone Defence Lecture was given by Chris Donnelly, Special Advisor to NATO, on 'the Future of Russian and European Security'. Himself a long serving TA Intelligence Corps officer, Chris Donnelly was better known to many Sandhurst and Staff College students for his entertaining lectures on matters Soviet.

McKen's tour would end in February 1996. The appointment of his successor, a Regular Officer, James Watson of the Royal Artillery, again caused rather unrealistic bleating from the MEC. Briefed by the MEC, the Principal wrote to HQ Scotland complaining about the lack of consultation and the short notice regarding the appointment. If the University had been consulted, as required by the UOTC Charter, it would have expressed a preference for someone with a strong Scottish University background and an appreciation of the traditions of the Scottish Regiments. It was hoped this principle would be reverted to in future but meanwhile James Watson would be afforded a warm welcome. That was just as well because Watson was bringing a wealth of experience. With a BA Honours Degree and attendance at the Joint Services Defence College Greenwich behind him he was coming from a post in the Policy Division at HQ Allied Forces Europe. Undoubtedly sufficiently 'academic' to satisfy the MEC, he also brought personal experience of war with him. He was the Forward Observation Officer with 2 Para at the bitter Battle for Goose Green in the Falklands, as already mentioned in Chapter 8. Whilst it was regrettable that the University had been given short notice, a trawl in May 1995 had failed to identify a suitable TA officer and the grand aspirations and preferences of the MEC were becoming increasingly daft. The Army struggled against many problems in order to properly manage officers' careers in the turmoil of cutbacks, redundancy schemes and current operations.

Having discussed the CO appointment, the MEC heard that the OTC was 40% overborne at a strength of 207. Brig Jameson commanding the Highland Brigade, informed the meeting that the TA was currently providing 300 of the

13,000 personnel deployed in Bosnia. He also confirmed that the Prince of Wales Barracks was being sold off and that Army assets would consolidate at Gordon Barracks. He admitted that media coverage of post Cold War compulsory redundancies and cutbacks had impacted on Army recruiting generally but that officer recruiting remained satisfactory largely due to the work of UOTCs. The MEC heard that the OTC's sister unit the Air Squadron was experiencing poor recruiting from Aberdeen. David Capitanchik and others put this down to the loss of Fairfield House in 1993. Leuchars in Fife was a long way to go for Aberdeen students in comparison. Travel distances and times would discourage otherwise interested recruits from signing up.

For the 1995/96 Session the University had made a grant of £500. One third of this would be reclaimed from Robert Gordon University as per the 1993 agreement. The 2:1 ratio reflected the cadet population and was also applied to representation on the MEC.

In February McKen handed over command to Watson and with his experience of the TA and the OTC, went off to serve on the TA Commissioning Boards until 2006.

By April 1996 Watson's unit worked to what was termed the Option WHISKY establishment for 140 cadets. There were now across the UK 16 such standard OTCs with, as before, larger ones at Oxford, Cambridge and in London. The Reserve Forces Act of 1996 gave the Army the ability to call-up individual TA Group A officers and soldiers. Students and Group B officers remained free of such liabilities.

One of the privileges of being CO was to reorganise and rename sub-units. McKen's 'wings' were replaced by Watson's 'companies'. Basic Company trained recruits up to

MTQ 1 standards and Advanced Company consisted of the MTQ2 cadre and the three specialist groups of infantry, engineers and signals. The Drums and Pipes maintained their customary independence as a sub-unit in their own right. Some high individual achievements in sport were recorded around this time. WOCdt Guillot set a new Army swimming record for the 100 metre Butterfly and three OCdts secured places in the Army in Scotland Rugby XV

The main military camp was held at Garelochhead with adventure training appetites assuaged on EX TARTAN BOAR based at Ballater. Canoeing, climbing and microlight flying provided the thrills and MACC tasks were completed around Balmoral. The 1990s had seen the unit's old 7.62mm Self Loading Rifles (SLRs) replaced with 5.56mm SA80 weapons. The AUOTC mounted Guard at Victoria Barracks, with four of these and 120 live rounds available if required.

Also in June 1996, a 270 mile walk along the Pennine Way was completed, raising money for charity. Young TA officers wishing for promotion to Captain went off to Edinburgh to complete JOTES 1 training and exams. The unit had now assumed responsibility for Phase 2 TA Potential Officer Training for everyone in the area requiring it, not just University cadets.

At the start of 1997 Brigadier Mel Jameson took over the appointment of Honorary Colonel from Lieutenant General MacMillan. Jameson's role as Director of the Edinburgh Military Tattoo and eventual involvement in overseas Tattoos on the same model, would stand the unit, particularly the Drums and Pipes, in good stead.

In January the MEC noted that the Army was continuing to resist Treasury pressure to make Regular Officer recruitment the primary or even exclusive aim of the

UOTCs. It also noted that the 1996 Reserve Forces Act stipulations regarding individual TA call-up made no change to the mobilisation status of TA Group B university officer cadets.

The main Military Camp was held at Otterburn again giving access to proper ranges and field firing areas. Section level training included a march and shoot with a live fire section attack. A three day company level exercise benefited from helicopter support. Educational visits to regular units and the usual sporting and social events completed the programme enjoyed by 97 officer cadets and 3 TA Group B officers.

In April 97 Cultybraggan was the location for the Northern Lights Inter UOTC competition. The unit returned to Cultybraggan for its Summer adventure training camp and completed MACC tasks on the surrounding Drummond Estate, a large part of which was leased to the Army for training areas. Cultybraggan had also hosted manifestations of the Cold War. From 1960 to 1991 the Royal Observer Corps had maintained one of its nuclear fall-out monitoring stations at Cultybraggan. The Corps was disbanded in 1992 when the threat of nuclear attack was deemed by politicians to have receded sufficiently. In 1990, a modern bunker which would accommodate key regional political and other leaders in the event of nuclear attack was completed at Cultybraggan. Almost immediately it was declared redundant and sold off to the Army. The Army continued to use Cultybraggan Camp until 2004 and in 2007, Comrie Development Trust took over the site known by generations of TA soldiers and cadets of many capbadges.

Getting to know a log - 1997

In Summer 1997 AUOTC conducted a battlefield tour to Northern France and Belgium, tracing the route and key sites of 'U' Company's World War I story. This trip was partially funded from the annual grant from the Universities.

Later in the Summer the Signals PSI and 17 cadets set off for Mont Blanc. Overall 25 cadets went adventure training in Germany, Cyprus, Canada and the UK. Parachuting was included among the usual pursuits. Valuable Unit Expedition Leader (UEL) Certificates were attained on courses. The Drums and Pipes played at the Edinburgh Military Tattoo, pitting their livers against the nocturnal lifestyle that this involved. Robin Barr, a 1970s AUOTC cadet and piper, retired from the 2IC post, after 21 years service as a TA Royal Engineers officer.

In September 1997, reports indicated that against the establishment for 140 cadets, AUOTC had 240 on the books. This consisted of 148 males and 92 females, with 80% belonging to the University of Aberdeen and most of the remainder coming from Robert Gordon University. With excellent recruiting and retention, shrinking resources continued to be a management concern especially in allocated Man Training Days (MTDs). MTDs were reduced in 1997 and HQ Scotland was searching for further savings. All four UOTCs in Scotland were 100% over establishment. COs were reminded that they were only funded for 140 cadets and that this might soon drop to 120. HQ Scotland perceived that the four OTCs ran unique programmes with different emphasis. Part of this resulted from the mismatch between UKLF directives and available resources. Much was left to the interpretation and initiative of COs. With resource levels only likely to deteriorate further, GOC Scotland launched a study with questionnaires going out to all COs. Each unit's approach to recruitment, selection, training, and commissioning was recorded. For example Tayforth included a high number of Group B TA officers. Aberdeen had a high conversion rate from Group B to Group A commissions. Aberdeen's retention of cadets was good with over 71% of cadets being eligible for bounty payments as against 50% in the other contingents. Comparing like with like in such studies was always difficult. Scottish Universities and hence OTCs attracted a high proportion of the Army's cadetship and bursary entrants. There was always the question of just how many students would join the Regular and Reserve services even without the opportunity to join an OTC. Many went up to University having already enjoyed CCF or ACF membership while at school. It seemed likely however than many would lose interest in military careers without the option of joining a UOTC. University Contingents if nothing else would allow people to really make up their minds about future options. The OTC process acted as a filter for those who were not really sure or who were not really suited to commissioned service.

The training syllabus was also examined. MTQ2 actually exceeded the RMA Sandhurst entry requirement but was only achieved with real difficulty in the training time allocated to it. The question of special to arm sub-units was once again put under the microscope. Each OTC differed in its structure depending on what sub-units they contained, and the size of the local 'black economy' for suitably qualified trainers of the right quality. Geography in relation to the distribution of the TA across Scotland was also a factor. At the time Glasgow was over strength in TA Majors while Aberdeen had only one, plus one temporary Regular Major. Aberdeen though did have a surfeit of TA Captains.

Accepting that UOTCs would continue to be near the lowest priority for equipment, these scalings would also be reviewed. Aberdeen had: 124 SA80s, 18 LSWs, 12 pistols; and four 51mm Mortars. For communications Aberdeen owned: 16 PRC 349s; 10 PRC 351/2s; 6 PRC 320s; and 6 MOULD sets for the Integrated Contingency Planning (ICP) role. The vehicle fleet consisted of: one staff car; two short wheelbase Landrover Defenders; one long wheelbase Landrover Defender; three 4 ton trucks; and 2 Minibuses.

HQ LAND undertook to reverse short sighted amendments to Materiel Regulations. It was recognised that current, good quality uniforms and personal equipment were required to attract and retain recruits.

The GOC Scotland study produced valuable recommendations for change but any implementation had to be put on hold pending the outcome of Secretary of State for Defence, George Robertson's Strategic Defence Review (SDR). The SDR, having assessed the likely future world situation, set out just what number, duration and level of operations, Britain's Forces would be expected to sustain. Numbers, organisation and equipment would be designed to fit the requirement. The TA was to be reduced in size but modernised to make it more readily deployable and more fully integrated with the Regular Army.

Lt Col RGJ Carrow of the Royal Green Jackets took over from Watson in July 1998. Quickly thrown into the build up to recruiting he noted with regret the exclusion of the university service units from the main hall at the Freshers' Fayre. The OTC however continued to 'help cadets mature in a protected environment'. A small team went to explore the World War II Normandy landing beaches. Exercise TARTAN INCA got 3 staff and 8 cadets to the top of Mount Chimborazo in Ecuador. Unit heritage was saluted by dancing a Dashing White Sergeant at the summit. At a height above sea level of 6268 metres, and lying on the Earth's equatorial bulge, AUOTC had reached the point on the planet, furthest from its centre.

Also added to the unit's calendar was entry in the Nijmegan Marches. The world's largest walking event, it started in 1909 and had been based in Nijmegan since 1916. Once largely a military event, it now involves thousands of civilians, but retains a large and challenging military category, with different distance and load carrying requirements.

The unit's other major 'walking' event, the Cambrian Marches, suffered awful weather. AUOTC, first out on the route, were eventually forced to retire after a third of the teams behind them gave up. Eventually 18 of the 25 teams withdrew. However a good lesson in leadership and prudence had been learned by not choosing to press on regardless and avoiding inevitable casualties. Unit participation in the Wapinschaw Shooting Competition continued with Martha Ingleby securing her place as top lady shot. The team sent to the REME UOTC weekend bemused other OTCs, with REME sub-units, by coming first.

The Royal Marines from Arbroath were assisted in their conduct of a sponsored abseiling event in aid of Childline. On the admin front bids were made for more computers and internet links for cadets. Project CAPITAL brought more resource accounting and budgetary fun to the permanent staff.

Housekeeping and adjustments continued at HQ with redecoration in the main hall and the acquisition of a separate portacabin for the Band. The indoor range which ran down one side of the main hall was decommissioned, providing more space for classrooms. Support to the wider community included fund raising initiatives and logistic support to Rotary activities. Communications were provided for a Christian Aid event, and radio and logistic support was given to Cornerstone Community Care. Local disadvantaged children were once more hosted at a Christmas Party.

MACC tasks went on as a key part of training and unit pride with SUO Laura Ferrand and the RE sub-unit building four bridges on the Speyside Way. A grateful distillery provided the celebratory barbeque.

In December 1999 the OTC's last formal report to the MEC of the 20th Century looked back on another successful year. Emphasis had been placed on properly training the recruiting team and conducting a formal selection weekend for those new students hoping to join. The SDR ramifications had no direct impact on the OTC but led to Group A TA officers and NCOs transferring to the OTC. Despite this Carrow still lacked a Training Major, an Admin Major and four chefs.

Mrs Cruickshank a civilian member of staff left in November 1999. Her 29 years of service was recognised when Brigadier Grant presented her with the Imperial Service Medal during his own last visit to AUOTC as a serving officer. 1999 had also seen the long serving Adjutant, Jim Easson hand over the reins to Dave Chapman. Easson assisted by Ian Murray and others, had made a great effort to collect and record information pertinent to unit history.

Five staff and 24 officer cadets went to Gibraltar in August. A MACC task had them freshening up the famous Mediterranean Steps. Military training included FIBUA in the Rock's tunnel system. A day trip to Morocco confirmed that they should bid for an Annual Camp at Gibraltar in 2001.

Pipe Major and Rock of Gibraltar

Battlefield tours had included a trip to Berlin. Although no Cambrian Patrols had been held that year due to heavy operational commitments, the urge to get blistered feet was satisfied by participation in the Nijmegan Marches. The unit had produced six candidates for the Regular Commissioning Board and six for the TA Board. A successful Army Open Day had been instigated at Gordon Barracks with local TA recruiting responding favourably. Former AUOTC CO John Walpole was providing help and guidance in his role as the local Army Careers Advisor.

Not mentioned in the MEC report but certainly of some concern to the OTCs ICP involvement was the contingency planning for the horrible events that might occur late on Hogmanay 1999, due to the Millennium Bug. The representation of dates in some older software caused global concern that microprocessors would fail spectacularly as the Year 2000 was entered. Everything from domestic microwave ovens and washing machines to advanced share trading, air traffic control and defence systems might fail. In the UK, one of the unpleasant scenarios thought most likely was the sudden default opening of sewage overflow gates. In the event nothing terrible happened and AUOTC safely entered the 21st Century.

Early in the new millennium, AUOTC's Drums and Pipes, reigning TA Champions, went off to Shetland to perform and promote piping and drumming. The Contingent continued to operate well above establishment as these March 2000 figures show:

	Group A	Group B
Estb	10 offrs + 18	140
Actual	11 + 18	5 offrs + 221cadets

The year 2000 was an unusual year with a record number of sporting achievements and competition results. Retention had been poor however, as had success at MTQ1 level. At the other end of the pipeline RCB and TCB statistics were good.

Among the staff, the post SDR influx of new instructors continued to find their feet. A drive towards more diversity in unit activities was being made while still maintaining high standards in traditional training. New women cadets were dropping out more than men, and the male:female ratio had dropped from 50:50 to 70:30. This was partially attributed to the dispiriting conditions on early field exercises.

The climax of military training had been at Camp at Stanford, Norfolk. Deliberate attacks were practiced against training villages. Chinook helicopters arrived unannounced one breakfast time to take the cadets to their final assault on Sculthorpe Airfield. One Chinook immediately suffered mechanical problems, this being blamed on the RSM's existing 'Jonah' relationship with Chinooks.

Adventure training was again held at Ballater with a summer mountain proficiency course and MACC tasks. Battlefield tours covered three wars with visits to Waterloo, Arras, Cambrai and Arnhem. Climbers visited the Pyrenees and Aberdeen was the only UOTC entrant in the Nijmegan March. The Band replaced the Edinburgh Military Tattoo gig with one at the Royal Military Tattoo held in London on Horse Guards Parade as part of the Queen Mother's Centenary Celebrations. The band moved on to Brittany for the Festival Interceltique. Six cadets joined the Lowland Volunteers on Exercise ORIENT EXPRESS in Belgium, while another five went with Tayforth OTC on the Berne Marches.

AUOTC's keen skiers back in the 1950s, 60s and 70s had to be content with Abergeldie, Glenshee and Aviemore as winter sport destinations. The 21st Century's winter warriors increasingly went to the Alps to follow the tradition. Aberdeen won the Scottish Division team downhill event and Shona Robertson secured many medals in multiple events. The British Ladies Army Ski Team (BLAST) included two Aberdeen WOCdts.

The unit won both the Engineer and Signals UOTC competitions, the first time a Scottish OTC had won both, and the first double win by any OTC for eight years. The Band excelled itself at the Bagpipe Committee Pipes and Drums

Competition at Inverness, winning solo drumming, quartets and March, Strathspey and Reel. The Northern Lights Contests were adjusted to accommodate English OTCs now included in the post SDR Divisional area. GOC 2 Div had nine OTCs in his area.

In 2001 Carrow handed a big and active unit to new CO, Lt Col Robin Wardall, Royal Artillery. His tour was tragically cut short by his sudden death in June. A Memorial Service was held at King's Chapel in October with a Reception in Roy Strathdee Building. A MACC task bridge, at Loch Muick on the Balmoral Estate, was dedicated to Robin Wardall after its official opening, with members of his family present. The summer of 2001 was also marred by the death of former CO John Mann and his wife in a road accident.

The year's training and other activities of course went ahead with things being held together by Adjutant Dave Chapman and his team. A successful deployment by C130 Hercules aircraft to Gibraltar was assessed as probably being more economical than most UK based camps. A Foot and Mouth outbreak curtailed many activities later in the year and some staff deployed on MACA tasks to help control it. Among other things the Wapinschaw was postponed to October. The OTC did not shoot but helped logistically.

Internally there was some tension regarding the allocation of Man Training Days. Those responsible for getting cadets through MTQ thought far too much resource was going to adventure training 'jollies' particularly to a few good skiers and other 'usual suspects'.

Lt Col Andrew Preston REME had been keeping a watching brief on the unit since his surprise appointment in tragic circumstances. He took up his post properly in

November 2001. He had served in Germany, Hong Kong and the UK. He brought with him recent operational experience in Bosnia and Kosovo. His staff appointments had mainly concerned equipment procurement and he had specialised in field artillery developments. Preston appreciated the hard work that had gone into keeping things moving. Chapman later received an MBE for his conduct through this difficult period.

The whole world had entered a long lasting and difficult period with the 11 September terrorist attacks on the USA at the World Trade Center in New York and the Pentagon, just across the Potomac from Washington DC.

The CO's other role as Station Commander recorded another successful Open Day at Gordon Barracks. The training year closed in traditional fashion with the Officers, Warrant Officers, and SNCOs serving Christmas Dinner to the cadets at Barry Buddon. Food and alcohol revived everyone from the physical and mental fatigue associated with giving and receiving combat estimates and orders in Barry Butlin's bitingly cold winds.

Perhaps appropriately during a command tenure by a REME officer, the cost and quality of maintenance associated with the unit's 'green fleet' of military vehicles and trailers, and other equipment raised real concern. The decision was made to get rid of the 'green fleet' and make use of the cheaper 'white fleet' system. Distinct technical sub-units for the Royal Engineers and Royal Signals had been effectively discontinued already, but this settled matters for good

However, Engineer and Signals training for all cadets at all stages of their training, would continue under the two PSIs. Signals and Engineer JUOs would continue to be appointed and specialist training would focus on preparation

382

for the Corps UOTC Weekends and MACC tasks.

In Spring 2002, the diminishing Army presence in Scotland was illustrated by the redesignation of 51st (Highland) Brigade to 51st(Scottish) Brigade. The AUOTC lost two majors to civilian employment commitments and the CO noted that, like all mortals, his TA staff continued to age. Replacing them from the ever dwindling local military community would become increasingly difficult. Even more distant trawls for staff transfers had limited success. Investigations through various Regimental Associations were hampered by geographical realities and the Data Protection Act.

By contrast the British Army presence in Afghanistan was growing under OP HERRICK. Over the next ten years (at least at the time of writing) many ex-cadets and OTC staff would find themselves in areas once described by old soldier and King's College Sacrist, Dan Dankester, before the First World War. In Afghanistan and Iraq, young officers would be involved in dangerous high intensity operations very early in their careers. Training staff joining the unit would bring with them their experience of many tours in hot places under most challenging circumstances.

Easter Camp 2002 was held at Wathgill, once again with helicopter supported exercises including an attack on the Whinny Hill FIBUA village. Leadership Camp went once more to Ballater, with two bridges being built on the MacRobert Estate. Lady MacRobert established a trust to commemorate her three aviator sons. One was killed in a civil flying accident and the other two during operational RAF sorties in 1941. She funded the construction of a Stirling Bomber, 'MacRobert's Reply'. She later bequeathed the estate to the Trust, and Douneside and another of the big houses retain service connections.

Twenty officer cadets went to Chamonix for ice climbing, mountaineering and canoeing. The unit skiers and snowboarders enjoyed Exercise SPARTAN HIKE and SNOW LION. The Winter term 2002 kicked off with new recruits learning how to 'live in the field' on EX ROOKIE BOAR at Black Dog. November was busy with the Remembrance Day Parade, a Bronze Medal performance at the Cambrian Patrols, and 'advance to contact' exercises for Advanced Company on Finzean Estate.

During late 2002 and early 2003, the CO was distracted by his ICP role and the planning and conduct of OP FRESCO, the military response to a series of fire-fighter strikes. Later Elgin's worst floods for many years would cause another flurry of activity. As Station Commander he also had responsibility for the Aberdeen Military Show and the Union Street Parade.

In January 2003, Brigadier Charles Grant became Honorary Colonel. He knew the unit well having been its boss in the chain of command, and having led the GOC's study into the workings of all the Scottish OTCs. His experience and counsel would be highly valued by future COs, and he took a frequent and active role in unit activities. One of his other interests, the history of the 51st Highland Division, provided valuable input and assistance for Battlefield Tours.

Through February and March a series of exercises developed skills and self confidence. Basic Company conducted ROAMING BOAR at Black Dog and BOARS HUNT at Barry Buddon. BOARS BAPTISM practiced ambush and recce techniques on Durris Estate. Advanced Company conducted UN style Protection Force tactics at

Barry Buddon on SPRING LEAP.

Aberdeen hosted an MTQ exam session for its own cadets and some from Birmingham and Tayforth, out on Scotstown Moor, near the unit's World War II 'killing areas'.

Out in the wider world the Second Gulf War, OP TELIC for the British, started in March 2003. The British Army would be involved in combat operations in Iraq until May 2009 and would complete its involvement in 2011, eight years after the start. Iraq and the long involvement in Afghanistan were not quite what had been envisaged in the Strategic Defence Review and other rationalisation exercises. Britain's armed forces would be put under great strain, involving repeated operational tours, each with protracted pre-deployment phases. The steadily mounting statistics for the killed and injured brought intense media scrutiny and coverage. Almost unprecedented levels of radio and TV discussions were held on detailed manning, tactical, logistic and equipment procurement issues. Soon the lower end of the media were dubbing soldiers either 'heroes' or potential 'war criminals' with apparently nothing much in between.

Despite all this media attention, a true understanding of the realities of soldiering and military life, was increasingly lacking. This was evident in the Universities and their Military Education Committees. GOC 2 Division hosted a lunch for all his MECs. They came from the four Scottish UOTC catchments, Liverpool, Manchester and Salford, Northumbria and Sheffield. Central to discussion was the fact that MEC members were tending towards the 'elderly'. Fewer had any personal military experience or military contacts. No serious 'anti-military' feelings had been detected but there was a serious lack of knowledge on which to base MEC decision making and responses to MOD papers and studies. One University had actually abolished its MEC after a review of committees, unaware of the statutory requirement to have one wherever a university service unit continued to exist. Many university service units, including those associated with Aberdeen, were being charged full commercial rates for stands at Fresher Fayres. Relations with Student Unions waxed and waned as they always had done depending on world events, the Army's deployments, individuals and historic relationships. Perhaps providing other university clubs with qualified instructors and other support would help bring the units back into the fold with other clubs and societies.

OP TELIC in Iraq and no impact on OTC recruiting and retention improved. Of significance to the TA was the fact that of the 9,500 reservists mobilised only 420 came from the Regular Reservist pool. The remainder came from the TA, indicating they would be an essential part of any future large scale expeditionary deployment. As ever the TA would need a constant supply of young officers.

The Elphinstone Defence Lectures continued to involve high grade presenters. Professor Freedman of King's College London gave a timely talk entitled 'The War on Terror - a Preliminary Assessment'. Freedman had been the official historian for the Falklands War. He also provided Prime Minister Blair with guidance on how to test the rights and wrongs of liberal military interventions. He later was a member of the Chilcot Iraq War Inquiry.

For cadets a full programme of military and other activities kept them occupied. Aberdeen hosted and won Northern Lights 2003, and the unit's, particularly the RSM's involvement with the Wapinschaw grew. Longmoor hosted the Camp and the Leadership and Adventure Training camp at Cameron Barracks, Inverness helped select the next year's hierarchy of Junior and Senior Under Officers. The summer's MACC task was special in the construction of a new Chimpanzee area at Edinburgh Zoo. Sixteen officer cadets went adventure training in Norway.

The 2004 Easter Camp went to Sennybridge and Kinlochleven was the base for Adventure Training. In the Summer Preston handed over command to a TA Officer. This one was truly home-grown, being a former AUOTC cadet and SUO. Kevin Wilkinson had served with the Royal Engineers TA and had been 2IC of Edinburgh UOTC. Familiar with the OTC world he read himself in to the broader tasks of his appointment, his new unit being the main Army presence in the North East of Scotland.

Back in 2000, Graham Shanks, Maggie Barr and others had tracked down enough OTC people of the 1970s era to hold a very successful and well attended reunion weekend. Informal gatherings at the OTC, bowling alleys, pubs and other rendezvous led to a formal dinner at Crombie Halls in Old Aberdeen. Few, including this author, realised they were dining on top of the Contingent's old World War II training ground. The Roy Strathdee Building sustained late night gossip and reminiscence. Hangovers were nurtured during a Sunday morning visit to the Gordon Highlanders Museum.

The success of this event, a contact database partially populated, and the support of Kevin Wilkinson led to the formation of the AUOTC Accociation. The unofficial title, 'The Old Boars', came from the 'Old Boars Dining Club' instigated by Andrew Jeffrey in the 1980s with a primarily 1970s Infantry membership.

A committee was formed and a series of reunions were held over the following years. Initially events, for practical reasons, centred on decade cohorts of former members and staff of the 1970s and 1980s. This gave way to all-comer events as the committee and unit strove to expand

The 1980s Menu Card Graphic of the Old Boars Dining Club. The name passed to the AUOTC Association. Reproduced with the kind permission of Andrew Jeffrey and of Loon Cartoons, Muir of Ord. (www.looncartoons.co.uk)

interest among 'younger' Boars thus ensuring the Association's longevity. Graham Shanks set about creating a photo archive on the association website.

Wilkinson exercised the CO's right to tweak the organisational chart and rename things. U Company's first OC Duncan, and later Sniper Sergeant Forbes, gave their names to sub-units as did interwar CO, and later Honorary Colonel, Harry Butchart.

Technology marched on with the recently received

PAY 2000 software package failing to support OTC requirements particularly the cadet pay rises following MTQ2 success. A temporary manual workaround kept cadet 'pooches' filled.

One positive result of the heavy Army commitment in Iraq and Afghanistan was the increased availability of adventure training courses and expedition destinations. Twenty one cadets went to Alberta for high altitude climbing on glaciers, white water canoeing, parachuting, horse trekking and biking.

The concept of a virtual 'leadership academy' was being increasingly explored. Through MTQ and later, the future leaders of industry, business and perhaps even the armed forces could benefit from increased exposure to military and non-military leadership and managerial challenges. The unit encouraged individuals to set their own personal development programmes which would include self administered leads on sport, adventure training and social events. Assistance in improving a student's employability was given a new focus and plans were set to increase the awareness among local employers about just what a product of the OTC had to offer.

U Company Dinners were now a firm part of the social calendar and the 2004 Dinner was graced by the presence of the author of *'The Student Soldiers'* Dr John McConachie and his wife Margaret. The dinners gave cadets an opportunity to develop their public speaking by delivering verbal snapshots of the U Company story between the meal's courses. Often actual diary entries made by their forebears in Bedford, France and Belgium were quoted.

A less formal, much less dignified, and politically incorrect mess event was the Gallon Run, a three-legged pub crawl competition.

The CO, Training Major, Adjutant and RSM shared a requirement for maintaining a 24 hour/7 days per week contact. ICP work, such as flood response, required satisfying a 30 minute Notice to Move (NTM) to an operational location. As the main military presence in the area, HQ AUOTC was also responsible for the sad duty of casualty notification and supporting the families involved. With operations in Iraq and Afghanistan such work was an increasingly likely occurrence but would also involve tragic training accidents in the local Cadet Forces.

Brig Grant gave the Elphinstone Lecture on the topic 'War - Does It Have Future'. He continued his active support of the unit and involvement in its activities. He firmly believed that more than half the value of the UOTCs was developing those cadets who would not join the services. Meanwhile RMA Sandhurst noted that 83% of its entrants were now graduates. World events, seldom declared formally as 'wars' these days, indicated that they would indeed continue to have busy 'futures'.

Wilkinson reversed a ten year trend by holding his main military camp in the summer. At Strensall, cadets became familiar with sniper rifles and various weights of machine guns. The longest ever field exercise was held and cadets were further challenged by being dropped in York without money or mobile phones. They were tasked among other things with getting themselves on local radio and eating boar while dressed as one.

Initiative and determination developed on the streets of York were put to the test on summer expeditions. Some went to the Czech Republic for hill walking, trekking and rafting. Others joined Tayforth on their trip to Uganda, working on community projects and navigating the Nile on kayaks and rafts.

A large detachment went to join their US equivalents on the Leadership Development Assessment Course at Fort Lewis, Washington State. This course is a key stage in the US officer cadet progression through their college units towards US Army commissions. Aberdeen's cadets enjoyed the opportunities to fire and control 155mm artillery. They got to fly in the American's famous Black Hawk helicopters. The AUOTC detachment moved on to British Columbia and the thrills of the Fraser River Canyon, its Hell's Gate, and the sights of Vancouver.

A JUO led Battlefield Tour to Belgium allowed respects to be paid at the graves of U Company members and AUOTC pipers played at the Menin Gate Memorial to the Missing in Ypres.

The annual Royal Engineers competition at Minley included a 6 bay Medium Girder Bridge (MGB) build. Training for this event took place in the Roy Strathdee Building car park while the unit had temporary possession of a palletised MGB bridge set. Inflatable and Mark 5 Assault boat handling, demolitions, assault course and command tasks completed the weekend. Summer engineer tasks included the construction of an information centre at the Kingussie Wildlife Park.

The once again 'Easter' Adventure Training Camp included rafting on the Findhorn, gliding, and mountain navigation inside ice clouds. The unit's snowboarders won the TA Competition in France and rugby players went to Cyprus.

A good and well recruited Band played in Brittany, and in the Brabanthallen at Hertogenbosch in the Netherlands, the Edinburgh Military Tattoo and the Braemar Gathering. One of the unit chefs deployed to Iraq.

Military Liaison Officer duties included preparations for the G8 Summit at Gleneagles. MACC tasks included further landscape gardening in Edinburgh Zoo.

In July 2005 the OTC helped Archaeolink at Oyne to simulate the construction of a Roman Marching Camp, watched by the TV cameras of the Time Team.

Despite the ending of distinct technical sub-units, Engineer and Signals knowledge remained an important part of everyone's training. From the Signals PSI, MTQ1 cadets received an insight into the capabilities of the Royal Signals and were taught the basics of communications. For MTQ2 they worked with PRC349 and PRC 351 radios, and learned the code BATCO, and Voice Procedure. They were introduced to the platoon to company PRC352 radio with its 28km range. They were required to be competent military map markers for up to company level operations. They were introduced to High Frequency (HF) communications and the PRC320 company to battalion radio with its 35km range. At MTQ3 level cadets became competent in setting up and running a Command Post up to company level using PRC352 and PRC 320.

In Winter 2005, the unit produced the first edition of its high quality magazine, ' *Student Soldier*', which would run until its Summer 2007 edition when costs became prohibitive. One edition included a contribution from 1950s WRAC cadet Anne Murchie who had co-edited a much less lavishly produced Unit Magazine in 1959, price 3 (Old) Pence. Her magazine had included an invitation to the Unit

Ball at the Marcliffe Hotel, Double Ticket 25 Shillings.

In 2006 Aberdeen was now in the top three of Britain's UOTCs for recruiting. There were high pass rates in the MTQ exams and growing interest in TA Commissions. Leadership and management skills were honed by participation in the city-wide Malawi Project. Easter adventure training was held at Capel Curig in the heart of Snowdonia with the usual activities supplemented with land yachting, and power boating through the Menai Straits tidal bore. Military activity concentrated at Otterburn. The main management challenge during the escape and evasion exercise was convincing the hunted that the exercise had really finished. Watermanship training made use of Kielder Water. The Band marked the Queen's Birthday at a joint engagement with Glasgow's Band at Stirling Castle.

An active Officers Mess social programme included a foray out to Delgatie Castle, near Turriff, for a formal dinner night in grand surroundings.

JUOs, with a little help from their seniors, led an expedition to Kenya. Phase 1 took the team to the summit of Mount Kenya at an altitude of 5199 metres. This was the Adjutant's second visit to the top. Phase 2 was a landrover safari through the Tsavo East National Park. Refreshing dips in the sea followed on Phase 3 on a sub-aqua diving course at Mombassa. Elsewhere in Africa other cadets joined Tayforth UOTC in Uganda. Trips to Washington State and Canada were again on the menu and the year's battlefield tour focussed on Normandy. The Drums and Pipes performed in the Halifax Nova Scotia and Edinburgh Tattoos.

Two of the unit's chefs deployed to Iraq, as did Rhys Jones who was taking a sports studies course at the School of Medical Sciences. He deployed with his parent TA unit, 4

Para.

The unit strove to widen its contacts with Old Boars offering expedition support to anyone who made it to South Africa or Chile. The OTC fostered stronger links with its Royal Navy and Royal Air Force equivalents and was pleased to inform the MEC that it was the envy of many other OTCs in the support it got from its parent universities. Attempts were made to increase recruitment from RGU. This was helped by the removal of Fresher Fayre fees at the RGU event. Fees for the University of Aberdeen event remained but were reduced.

The local mountains, as ever, provided unlimited scope for enjoyment and challenge. One weekend In November 2006 the unit was out training but on returning to Aberdeen heard that one of their new recruits, Richard Hardy, a fit young man with his eye on a Royal Marines career, had died near Cairngorm's Northern Corries. Not far from safety, he and his climbing partner had been overwhelmed by extreme storm conditions while returning from Coire an t-Sneachda. At the time he had not been under OTC training, but the incident was a reminder to all staff and cadets that if underestimated, or if just a little too much bad luck occurred, the mountains could still kill.

In 2006, amid much controversy, the six remaining Scottish Regiments were brought together as the Royal Regiment of Scotland (SCOTS). Numbered Regular and TA Battalions retained some of their original distinctive characteristics. Amalgamations and disbandment were not new to the British Army and very quickly young officers and soldiers would know nothing else. The merits of 'super regiments' or even an Infantry Corps, versus old, now mostly single battalion Regiments, had long been debated. There were significant personnel management advantages to the new system. A SCOTS, formerly Royal Scots, officer was about to take command of AUOTC.

Lt Col Charlie Wallace arrived in January 2007 having finished a tour as the Chief Planner for the Multi National Division (South East) in Iraq. He was glad to have Wilkinson's long OTC experience available to help him adjust from operations in Iraq to operations in Aberdeen.

Wallace was struck by the unit's strong identity and sense of history. As usual for OTC COs he had arrived on the back of a fairly detailed review of UOTCs which had not drawn any particular conclusions. The review however had caused some consternation amongst some MECs around the country. The unit's connections with the two universities in Aberdeen seemed fine but Wallace was struck by how little the wider Army understood UOTCs and the potential that they had. For some, these organisations were nothing more than a recruiting mechanism for RMA Sandhurst. For others, they were a luxury that could be done without, especially when the focus of the Army was on two significant operations in Iraq and Afghanistan. Much had changed in society since the OTCs had been set up in 1908. No longer was the military at the forefront of peoples' minds despite 24 hour media coverage of operations. No longer could the majority claim to know someone who was serving or who had served. It was clear that the true value of what the military, particularly the OTC, could offer was not understood. Wallace detected this starkly when engaging with the University of Aberdeen and indeed the wider Army.

Accepting that only a small minority of cadets would go on to the Regular Army and TA, it was important that the

OTC continued to give something to students that would be valuable to them in later life. In return, cadets would hopefully be extremely grateful that the Army had given them a skills-set putting them ahead of their competitors for jobs and promotion. They would thus think and speak highly of the organisation and recognise its value. These aspects were after all part of the UOTC's Charter. Detailed discussions were held with the Chambers of Commerce and the Confederation of British Industry as well as the oil industry in Aberdeen. The single most frustrating factor they all saw in new graduates seemed to be the lack of understanding of responsibility and team-work. There was also a real sense coming from the employers that universities in general were not properly preparing graduates for the workplace. Here was a niche that AUOTC could explicitly offer to fill, building on the work by Wilkinson and earlier COs.

The universities were approached to see if an OTC supported leadership module could be inserted in their degree courses. Perhaps the more vocationally focussed, Robert Gordon University staff were very keen. The University of Aberdeen, more keen to preserve academia for its own sake, was less so. After considerable effort a, degree points earning, leadership module was agreed with The Robert Gordon University. It was based on the Management and Leadership Development Programme (MLDP) which was replacing the MTQ system.

Wallace welcomed Brigadier Charles Grant's continuing support as Honorary Colonel, including during a notable crisis of corporate morale near the end of a very tough Warcop final exercise. It was clear there were not many enthusiastic senior ex-military men around to consider as replacements. This allowed a change of tack completely

396

and after some discussion, it was decided to invite the Principal of Robert Gordon University, Mike Pittilo to be the next Honorary Colonel. Pittilo's appointment did indeed further strengthen the linkages between the academic world and the UOTC until his untimely death in February 2010.

Together with all the activity to match the COs aspirations for the unit, much of the traditional routine continued. Some things were cancelled or postponed. These included the Northern Lights Inter-OTC Competition and a planned combined climbing trip and battlefield tour to the Italian Dolomites.

Fifteen cadets however went once more to Fort Lewis and four joined 4 SCOTS for 32 days living out of armoured vehicles. Local attachments were made to the Police and an oil firm. The success of the Wapinschaw as a community event, continued with police, TA and local civilian participation as of old.

The Band which had previously fallen away a bit due to people moving on, supported a regimental Burns Night over in Paderborn, Germany. Having recruited 8 new pipers and 4 drummers, a band of 19 pipers and 8 drummers proved the Cold War was well and truly over by performing in Lithuania and Moscow.

An impressive 49 students maintained the unit's links with snow by attending ski championships in France. In earlier years these trips had occasionally even attracted pay. Harder times led to an increasing personal contribution from participants. Even on field attachments cadets would sometimes only be paid for half their days away. These were 'penalties' readily accepted.

A team completed the tough 'three peaks (Ben Nevis, Scafell and Snowdon) in 24 hours' challenge.

Leadership was developed in 'civvies' at Kinlochleven in March 2008, and in uniform at Catterick in the summer. Low level weekend exercises continued in the surrounding hills and woods. The unit finally got to the Dolomites on the postponed Exercise ITALIAN BOAR, hanging off the *via ferrata* above impressive drops while investigating World War One tunnels and trenches. Northern Lights, funded this year, was won by Aberdeen.

The Unit and its Association, celebrated the TA's 100th Anniversary in grand style. An impressive massed band of current and former pipers and drummers entertained everyone on Friday evening and again on Saturday morning. Former band members included a Pipe Major and Drum Major from the 1950s. Old Boar teams risked injury on the sports fields in keenly contested games against current unit members. The Beach Ballroom housed the Ball. It had been increasingly used by the OTC for its own Annual Balls. These were followed by continued merriment back at the Roy Strathdee Building with a Survivors' Breakfast at dawn for those with sufficient stamina and/or self-control.

One minor event that occurred during Wallace's tenure is nevertheless of historical interest. Cadets of all descriptions wearing uniform while on the way to or from drill nights had always been subject to the attentions of Aberdeen's street 'comedians'. A more sinister atmosphere surrounded the attentions of a group of young men towards an Officer Cadet passing the Spital Mosque in uniform. Given British involvement in Iraq and Afghanistan this was a period of real tensions between some parts of the Moslem community and the British 'establishment'. Talks between Wallace and the Mosque leadership, pointed out that the OTC included Muslims in its ranks. It was agreed that the incident was unacceptable and should not be repeated.

Wallace handed over to Matthew Wardner of the Mercian Regiment in June 2009. Another new regiment, his one had been formed from the Cheshire, Worcester and Sherwood Forester and Staffordshire Regiments.

As the British economy ran into serious trouble Wardner would experience probably the tightest resource challenges suffered by any AUOTC CO since World War Two. All elements of defence were under 'value for money' scrutiny, with the highest priority obviously going to current operations, primarily in Afghanistan. For the UOTCs the squeeze manifested itself in three way: budget reductions including Man Training Days; less training ammunition; and gapping of established posts. In 2009 the AUOTC budget took two successive cuts of 10% before, in October, being effectively reduced by 90% and stopping Officer Cadet pay. With a big reduction in training activity the unit hardly noticed a massive reduction in ammunition allocations. The third area of concern was the most damaging. The TA and Regular staff were operating at only 50% of establishment with a PSI, the Training Major, the 2IC and the Chief Clerk posts all being gapped. By April 2010 things began to ease and it was hoped to fill the gapped posts by September. The response of the Officer Cadets was extremely positive and even with a six month period without pay, a nucleus of 75 regular attendees had completed worthwhile training. Easter Camp was once again the opportunity for military training and at Garelochhead students caught up on the Management and Leadership Development Programme (MLDP) at levels 1 and 2. The first week of Summer Camp 2010 had one group on a Battlefield Tour studying the events leading to the surrender of the 51st Highland Division at St Valery in 1940. This group joined the others for the second week.. Aberdeen took the lead for an OTC exercise to Georgia, USA and deployed around 40 cadets out of a total of 110 participants. Financial issues unsurprisingly cancelled the 2009 Ski Trip to the Alps but it resumed in 2010. Munro-bagging for charity formed the basis of other summer activity with ascents of many Scottish peaks above 3000 feet.

Remembrance Sunday Parade 2010 had an additional phase when SUO Aine Scott was presented with a Certificate of Commendation from GOC 2 Division for highly meritorious service. While en route to the Battlefield Tour the previous summer, she had taken charge of a serious road accident on the M6, prioritising and treating casualties in difficult circumstances.

SUO Aine Scott and her Mother. Remembrance Parade 2010.
Since the WRAC's demise, women cadets had been wearing
the same headgear as the men. Some became SUO.

The unit visited Catterick and Inverness for its main camps in 2011. All staff and cadets on the Summer Camp, young and old, climbed to the top of Ben Macdui to mark the unit's 99th year. Two Old Boars of 1970s vintage, Bill Morgan and Jim Duffus, had gone up earlier and were searching in the cloud for the old Sapper Bothy ruins near the top. Nineteenth Century Sappers of the Ordnance Survey built this hut while establishing that Ben Macdui did come second to Ben Nevis. The Association representatives were guided back to the summit rendezvous deep in the drizzly clouds by the sound of the pipes. The OTC had arrived.

Am Fear Leath Mor, The Big Grey Man, kept out of the way as lunch was taken and the new RSM took his WOs and NCOs off into the gloom for his first Mess meeting. The minutes record that members were keen that future meetings be held in more accessible and comfortable surroundings. A group photo was taken before the column began the long descent. Once out of the clouds another, somewhat clearer, photograph was taken, with the old OTC stamping grounds around Rothiemurchus as the background.

Other 2011 exercises had included VIKING BOAR to Shetland; Special to Arm weekends including COMMANDO STUDENT and AIRBORNE STUDENT; and the customary exposure on Barry Buddon's ranges.

The unit's long association with Aberdeen's Wapinschaw ended as Regular and Reserve Forces no longer supported it, or took part, for financial and other reasons. In the Army, 'gravel belly' competition shooting for a long time had been a declining activity, no longer greatly encouraged, and deemed largely irrelevant to the realities of combat shooting.

In September, the Old Boars held their AGM and a very pleasant dinner in the Royal Scots Club, Edinburgh. This was an attempt to facilitate attendance from the many 'Not So Old Boars' living in the Central Belt. A respectable number of the Central Belt wing of the Old Boars had braved bad winter roads for their own get together some months previously. Three AUOTC COs attended the AGM: Kevin Wilkinson, now the Association's Committee Chairman; Matthew Wardner; and the newly appointed Lt Col Matt Thorp MBE Royal Regiment of Fusiliers.

Thorp would, in addition to his normal unit and Station Commander activities, have a Centenary to organise in competition with Her Majesty Queen Elizabeth II's Diamond Jubilee. At the end of 2011 his unit's actual strength sat healthily at 151 against an establishment for 134. All his Majors posts were filled but there remained gaps among Captains and other Group A instructor posts. The Band was particularly healthy after recruiting, with a strength of 25, not including the Pipe Major and Drum Major. The Band played at the unveiling; by HRH Prince Charles, Duke of Rothesay; of the Gordon Highlanders Memorial Sculpture at the Castlegate.

Cadet strength was increasingly diverse with students from many parts of the Commonwealth alongside British nationals of many family backgrounds.

For the HQ staff, AUOTC's role as the main Army presence in NE Scotland increasingly involves coordinating assistance to all serving and former members of the Army, and in practice the other services. Under the Armed Forces,

402

'Firm Base' system, the CO is tasked with ensuring the nation's cradle to grave 'covenant' with servicemen and servicewomen is enacted in practice at the local level.

Long serving Adjutant Dave Chapman moved on to a post at Inverness with the Highland Reserve Forces and Cadets Association. For several years he had confused observers by alternating between the uniform of an RE Captain and that of a full Colonel in the Army Cadet Force.

Early 2012 activities included an Easter Camp at Garelochhead and the special to arm Corps UOTC weekends. The Aberdeen team were delighted to receive, from Commandant RMA Sandhurst, the prize for best overall team at the RE weekend at Minley. The short weekend had included Corps capability displays; a fancy dress party; setting and blowing 'confidence' demolition charges; the Medium Girder Bridge competition; watermanship training, the military swim test; a cross country run; jungle survival and the climactic boat race on Hawley Lake conducted, not for the first time, in a thick snowstorm. Aberdeen's success was recognised by a well supported Motion of Congratulations in the Scottish Parliament.

Overall Lt Col Thorp remained content that nothing he planned to do had been stopped for resource reasons. A recent annual AUOTC output had produced 5 new officers for the Regular Army, notably none for the TA. Many cadets have trained with Regular and Reserve units all over Scotland, in Cyprus and in Kenya. Cadets continue to support the local police in contingency training exercises.

The Government have ambitious plans for the TA, bringing it up to full strength and gearing it to a full role in the nation's defence. But real practical problems stand in the way. Parliamentary debate includes expressions of deep concern regarding TA officer recruitment. Will conditions of service be sufficiently attractive? Not only the size of the TA matters. Its distribution across the country seems key. There needs to be a reasonably local TA for people to join. The clue lies in the 'T' of the abbreviation. There is even some chance, not for this book to quantify, that those keen to soldier will someday be able to choose between British and Scottish units.

Aberdeen's military geography is a weak echo of the strong TA presence established in the 1900s and carried through well into the Cold War. Troops now exist where once squadrons were; platoons, where once companies and even battalions drilled.

The City's urban geography has of course transformed beyond recognition through one hundred years. Marischal College with its magnificent granite façade is now home to the City Council. The archway through which generations of OTC squads and Torcher Charity Processions marched is now glassed over. The Union across the road is gone. Robert Gordon University is set to pull its remaining presence in Schoolhill in to its modern campus at Garthdee. The City's student population in addition to being of much greater diversity, is at least tenfold larger than it was at the close of World War Two.

Further away, Cultybraggan Camp is in the control of Comrie Development Trust and the RE bridging camp at Drip, outside Stirling, is a garden centre. Many old OTC destinations do however remain. Black Dog provides a handy tactical training area but with the ranges primarily being used by school cadets. For range work, the OTC's students continue to frequent Barry Buddon, a destination since U Company days. Garelochhead, Fort George, and of course

Scotland's hills, lochs and forests remain available for interesting challenges and fun.

The current government's Strategic Defence and Security Review undertook to *'maintain the important role of the tri-Service cadet and university units.'* The Army recognises the important role played by UOTCs in preparing potential officers for Sandhurst. A high proportion of its best output comes from an OTC background. The quality and experience of those coming in from UOTCs allows staff to concentrate on the initially weaker entrants. Commandant Sandhurst is now firmly in the chain of command above OTCs. A scheme is under trial whereby UOTCs might be grouped into Officer Training Regiments (OTRs). In some ways this would be not too far from the days when Aberdeen shared its Adjutant with Glasgow and was commanded by a Major. It is envisaged that individual OTCs will retain their own capbadges and traditions. There is much to retain.

As this book heads for the 'presses' the unit and the Association's Committee are working hard in preparation for the Centenary Celebrations in June. Old Boars from far and wide are likely to attend, including serving brigadiers. Thoughts will be with the eight former members serving in Afghanistan.

The Friday 'at Home' event at Roy Strathdee Building will include the first performance of *'Non Confundar'*, Malcolm Coombe's winning tune in the Centenary 6/8 March Composition Competition. The unit's Drums and Pipes, boosted by former pipers and drummers, will lead a parade down Union Street before a Civic Reception in the Beach Ballroom. This venue will be reorganised in time for the Centenary Ball, while gladiators young and old take to the playing fields. The very next day the unit's Camp will commence at Kinloss, a base recently vacated by the RAF and soon to be home to an Engineer Regiment.

This last development may bring new opportunities for the unit's Engineer training. The Signals PSI hopes to receive the Bowman system before too long. The acquisition of secure-voice radios may finally remove the need to learn codes such as BATCO. Gaelic may however still occasionally grace the unit's radio nets. Later in the Summer, the Band will deploy to the Basel Tattoo, and a small team are preparing to mark the Centenary with an ambitious overseas expedition.

To end the story so far, this author can do no better than use the words Roy Strathdee chose 66 years ago to close his history:

'Some one may, in the years to come, continue this story. .... Whatever the future has in store, the Training Corps, and this Contingent in particular, has every reason to be proud of its past'.

Non Confundar !

CAMPS

The destinations listed are generally for the main military camps. Through time these moved from Summer to Easter.

Camps sometimes included a mix of military and adventure training. Winter warfare, CMT/MTQ training, Adventure Training and Engineer (MACC) Task Camps were also held. Rothiemurchus, Barry Buddon, Edinburgh Training Centre, Cameron Barracks Inverness, and Victoria Barracks Ballater were other very frequent camp destinations.

(Medical Contingent)
1913 Aldershot, 1914 Salisbury Plain, 1915 Rumbling Bridge, 1916 Peebles, 1917 Gailes, 1918 Barry, 1919 -21 No Camps, 1922 Fleetwood, 1923 Ramsay

(Medical and Infantry Contingents)
1924 Fleetwood, 1925 Kinnel Park, 1926 No Camp, 1927 Blair Atholl, 1928 Scarborough, 1929 Peebles, 1930 Nairn, 1931 Dunbar, 1932 No Camp Training at King's College, 1933 Blair Atholl, 1934 Peebles, 1935 Dunbar, 1936 Catterick, 1937 Peebles, 1938 Peebles, 1939 Aboyne, 1940 No Camp, 1941 Ballater/Lonach, 1942 Lonach/Glenbuchat

(Medical, Infantry and Signals)
1943 Glenbuchat, 1944 Colquhonnie, 1945 Fochabers, 1946 Dunbar

(Medical, Infantry, Signals, RE, REME, and Int Corps)
1947 Dunbar, 1948 Berwick on Tweed, 1949 No Camp, 1950 Comrie, 1951 Spey Bay, 1952 Comrie, 1953 Garelochhead, 1954 Barnard Castle, 1955 ABTU and Attachments, 1956 ABTU and Attachments, Pipe Band to Stobbs with 5/6 Gordons

(Whole Contingent with women cadets)
1957 Glencorse, 1958 Barry Buddon, 1959 Magilligan,
1960 Cultybraggan, 1961 Garelochhead, 1962 Monmouth,
1963 Benbecula, 1964 Bedford Road (Typhoid Epidemic),
1965 Leek, 1966 Cultybraggan, 1967 Benbecula, 1968 Benbecula,
1969 Longmoor, 1970 Folkestone, 1971 Rollestone, 1972 Ripon,
1973 Crowborough, 1974 Westdown, 1975 Folkestone,
1976 Nesscliffe, 1977 Strensall, 1978 Westdown, 1979 Nescliffe,
1980 Crowborough, 1981 Strensall, 1982 Garelochhead,
1983 Folkestone, 1984 Nescliffe, 1985 Wathgill,
1986 Strensall, 1987 Crowborough, 1988 Beckingham,
1989 Garelochhead, 1990 Ripon, 1991 Sennybridge, 1992 Ripon,
1993 Ripon, 1994 Halton, 1995 Warcop, 1996 Garelochhead,
1997 Otterburn, 1998 Warcop, 1999 Wathgill, 2000 Stafford,
2001 Gibraltar, 2002 Wathgill, 2003 Longmoor, 2004 Sennybridge,
2005 Strensall, 2006 Otterburn, 2007 Warcop, 2008 Wathgill,
2009 Benbecula, 2010 Warcop, 2011 Inverness, 2012 Kinloss

APPOINTMENT HOLDERS

HONORARY COLONEL

1951-53 Col HJ Butchart DSO OBE TD
1953-57 Col The Lord Strathcona
1957-64 Lt Col RB Strathdee OBE TD
1964-73 Col Sir TB Smith QC DCL LLD FBG
1973-82 Col TJT Nicol MVO MBE MC
1982-87 Brig DW Anderson CBE
1987-97 Maj Gen (later Lt Gen) JRA MacMillan CBE
1997-2003 Brig MS Jameson CBE
2003-09 Brig CS Grant OBE
2009-10 Professor RM Pittilo MBE
2011-   AEH Bradford Esq

COMMANDING OFFICER

1912-15 Maj GA Williamson RAMC(TF)
1915-19 Capt JP Kinloch RAMC(TF)
1919-25 Maj GA Williamson RAMC(TF)
1925-33 Lt Col HG Butchart DSO TD
1933-35 Maj A Fowler TD RAMC(TA)
1935-40 Maj A Crichton TD Gen List (TA)
1940-48 Lt Col RB Strathdee OBE TD Gen List (TA)
1948-50 Lt Col W McNeill MBE Gen List (TA)
1950-55 Lt Col TB Smith GORDONS(TA)
1955-56 Lt Col FG Burnett GORDONS(TA)
1956-65 Lt Col J Reid TD Int Corps(TA)
1965-68 Lt Col PEG Mitchell TD RAMC(V)
1968-74 Lt Col CJH Mann OBE TD RAMC(V)
1974-79 Lt Col DF Smith MBE TD PARA(V)
1979-83 Lt Col R Ewen OBE TD RE(V)
1983-86 Lt Col RW Grant TD RAMC(V)
1986-88 Lt Col I Shepherd RHF

1988-91 Lt Col JAF Walpole RE
1991-93 Lt Col MIV Dore RA
1993-96 Lt Col G McKen MBE TD 51 HIGHLAND
1996-98 Lt Col JNE Watson RA
1998-2001 Lt Col RJ Carrow RGJ
2001 Lt Col RC Wardall RA
2001-04 Lt Col AD Preston REME
2004-07 Lt Col K Wilkinson TD RE(V)
2007-09 Lt Col CP Wallace SCOTS
2009-11 Lt Col MR Wardner MERCIAN
2011-   Lt Col MCR Thorp MBE RRF

SECOND IN COMMAND

1962-64 Maj DW Girvan GORDONS
1964-65 Maj PEG Mitchell TD RAMC
1966-69 Maj AJC Wood SEAFORTHS
1969-74 Maj AE Urquhart TD RE(V)
1974   Maj DF Smith MBE TD PARA(V)
1974-78 Maj MR Hewitt TD 51 HIGHLAND(V)
1978-79 Maj R Ewen TD RE(V)
1979-81 No appointment
1981-83 Maj RW Grant TD RAMC(V)
1983-84 No appointment
1984-89 Maj WA Johnston TD RE(V)
1989-95 Maj SV Duggan TD 51 HIGHLAND(V)
1995-97 Maj RD Barr TD RE(V)
1997-98 No appointment
1998-2001 Maj JF Geddes TD R SIGNALS(V)
2002   Maj DS Harris TD RE(V)
2004-07 Maj MA Strachan TD R SIGNALS(V)
2007-10 Maj AMG Phillips R Wx YEOMANRY
2011-   Maj SJ Lambirth RAMC(V)

TRAINING OFFICER

Infantry
1942-45 Maj T Murray Kemsley CAMERONIANS
Signals
1943   2Lt WF Hossack R SIGNALS
1944-45 Lt BG Whitmore R SIGNALS
1945   Lt NI McClary R SIGNALS
1945-46 Lt CWG Hodge-Brooks R SIGNALS
Contingent
1947   Capt AP MacDonald R SIGNALS
1947-49
1949-52 Capt JD Hendry MC TD HLI
1952-53 Maj RG Pollock McCall BW
1954   Maj RW Petrie GORDONS
1954-56 Maj JGH Patterson GORDONS
1956-60 Maj TF Oxley CAMERONS
1960-64 Maj AJC Wood SEAFORTH
1964-66 Maj I McK Robertson GORDONS
1966-68 Maj JMG Somerville A&SH
1968-70 Maj JR Buchanan KINGS
1970-72 Maj CJK Campbell BW
1972-75 Maj JAR Taylor RHF
1975-77 Maj AJ Bartholomew WFR
1977-79 Maj JAR Taylor RHF
1979-81 Maj DH White GORDONS
1981-83 Maj MP Taitt GORDONS
1983-85 Maj SJM Barnetson QGM RS
1985-87 Maj PJ Marett RE
1987-93 no appointments Regular CO in post
1993-95 Maj MRM Gibson MBE GORDONS
                    (HLDRS wef Sep 94)
1997-99 Maj PJ Wotton TD CHESHIRE(V)
1999-2001 Capt R Craig RA(V)
2001-04 Maj MA Strachan TD R SIGNALS(V)

411

2004-07 Maj NP Canning RLC
2007-10 Maj PA Rorie TD SCOTS
2010-11 Maj M Braithwaite-Exley SCOTS
2011-   Maj MJ Vicca TD SCOTS(V)

ADJUTANT/QUARTERMASTER

Adjutant shared with Glasgow UOTC (resident at Glasgow)
1923-27 Capt RA Grant Taylor OBE MC RSF
1927-31 Maj JR Peploe HLI
1931-35 Capt FRH Morgan Border Regt
1935-37 Capt KID Stewart BW
1937-38 Capt JFM Macdonald KOSB
Adjutant shared with St Andrews (resident in Aberdeen)
1938-40 Capt RC Cottrell-Hill MC Border Regt
Adjutant
1941   Lt PELA Myers GORDONS
1941-42 Lt T Murray-Kemsley CAMERONIANS
1943-44 Lt P Thomson GORDONS
1944-48 Capt JE Macarthur HLI
1948-49 Capt AG Close GORDONS
1949   Capt RC Gascoyne SEAFORTH
1949-50 Maj AG Close GORDONS
1950-51 Capt GP Wood MC A&SH
1951-52 Capt RH Webber A&SH
1953-54 Capt J Neish GORDONS
Adjutant/Quartermaster
1954-57 Capt KM Howitt GORDONS
1958-62 Maj(QM) WJ Robertson BW
1962-76 Maj SJ McGrath GORDONS (formerly REME)
1976-77 Maj(QM) EF Cameron QOH
1977-79 Capt(QM) E Elcock QOH
1979-81 Capt(QM) W Waddell RTR
1981-83 Maj(QM) H Bell R SIGNALS
1983-86 Maj(QM) W MacDonald RA

1986-87 Capt(QM) R Fraser KOSB
1987-91 Maj(QM) JC Easson GORDONS
Adjutant Non Regular Permanent Staff (NRPS)
1991-99 Capt(QM) JC Easson Gen List (V)
1999-2012 Capt D Chapman MBE RE(V)

REGIMENTAL SERGEANT MAJOR

1913-14 WO1 J Todd RAMC
1916-18 WO1 JM Humphreys RAMC
1937-42 WO1 H Atkinson SG
1942-49 WO1 W McCready SG
1949-54 WO1 KM Howitt SG
1955-56 WO1 A Young SG
1956-57 WO1 F Adams SG
1957-59 WO2 J Leslie SG
1959-61 WO2 JI Grant SG
1961-63 WO1 GA Whyte SG
1963-65 WO1 G Adams SG
1965-69 WO1 J Leslie SG
1969-71 WO1 A Armitage SG
1971-72 WO1 F Lawrie SG
1972-75 WO1 D McMillan SG
1976-77 WO1 E Lawrie SG
1977-79 WO1 D Murphy SG
1979-81 WO1 R Milne SG
1981-83 WO1 LM Ingram SG
1983-86 WO1 AB Grant SG
1986-87 WO1 IA Kaye SG
1987-90 WO1 BB Sulley SG
1990-91 WO1 IR Shand SG
1991-93 WO1 JP Gallagher SG
(22nd and last Scots Guards RSM)
1993-95 WO1 JC Rees IG (the last Guards RSM)
1995-97 WO1 JJ Haughie A&SH

413

1997-2000 WO1 JR Culling KOSB
2000-01 WO1 GW Eaton HLDRS
2001-04 WO1 IJ Peel HLDRS
2004-06 WO1 MJ Whyte HLDRS
2006-08 WO1 GR Hogg SCOTS
2008-09 WO1 AD Steele SCOTS
2009-11 WO1 AR Campbell SCOTS
2011-   WO1 JR Mathieson SCOTS

REGIMENTAL QUARTERMASTER SERGEANT (RQMS)

1980-95 WO2 FB Cole
1995-   WO2 LJ Thomson

PIPE MAJOR

1936-37 P Mitchell ('Ark Force'; MC in Italy 1944)
1944-46 DK MacTaggart
1946-48 WK MacTaggart
1948-51 I Forsyth
1951-53 PL Cromar
1953-56 KT Melvin
1956-59 GW Anderson
1959-61 KT Melvin
1961-63 G Whyte
1963-64 A Hunter
1964-65 WR Fraser
1965-66 A Hunter
1966-71 WR Fraser
1971-72 W Donaldson
1972-75 JL Taylor
1975-76 A MacInnes
1976-78 G Campbell
1978-80 E Marnoch
1980-82 R Bisset

1982-83 A Esson
1983-84 E Marnoch
1984-86 K Sprott
1986-87 C Junor
1987-88 A Sprott
1988　　D Steele
1988-89　C Kennedy
1989-90　M Forbes
1990-2004　BJ Elrick
2004-　　MA Laing

DRUM MAJOR

1930s　　Tom Nicol　(MC, Hon Col)
1950s/60s　Olly Urquhart
　　　　　(World Champion, OTC RE Offr, MEC Member)
1960s　　Sandy Jessop
1990s　　Gordon Elrick
2005-　　Neil Jamieson

ROYAL ENGINEERS

1952-53 WO2 H Spencer
1953-57 WO2 G Le Warne
1963-66 WO2 S Turner
1966-71 WO2 G Smith
1972-74 WO2 P Scanlon
1974-76 WO2 P Lance
1976-78 WO2　J Highlands
1979-80 WO2 J Simmers
1980-83 WO2 N Thompson
1983-86 SSgt JS Grant
1986-88 WO2 PG Davidson
1988-90 WO2 JT Barker
1990-91 WO2 P Gibson

1991-95 WO2 MJ Laughlin
1995-96 WO2 SJ Fletcher
1996-99 WO2 GA White
1999-2003 WO2 BM Stuart
2003-2005 WO2 DS McAdam
2005-07 WO2 A Simpson
2007-2010 WO2 J Donnelly
2010 -   SSgt J Hazell

ROYAL SIGNALS

1942   Sgt R Phillpot
1942-43 LCpl G Patterson
1943-45 WO2 AD Glanvill
1945   LCpl Bazodis
1945-46 Sig JB Whyte
1948-49 WO2 FW Davies
1949   WO2 E Peacock
1949-50 WO2 FG Ferguson
1951-52 WO2 WA Richardson
1952-53 WO2 CK Taylor
1952-53 Sig C Cowan
1953-54 Sig GW Blyth
1953-55 WO2 L Parry
1954-55 Sig AD Walker
1954-56 WO2 S Percival
1972-75 WO2 W Dick
1975-77 WO2 Upton
1979-81 WO2 Foster
1981-83 WO2 J Wooley
1983-86 WO2 J King
1986-89 WO2 M McDermott
1989-92 WO2 DAM Bennett
1992-93 WO2 MV Doherty
1993-96 WO2 KJ Bywater MBE

1996-98 WO2 DL Palmer
1998-99 WO2 VR Miller
1999-2002 WO2 KJ O'Neill
2002   WO2 B Gillies
2002-04 SSgt HD Berry
2004-06 WO2 R Ayling
2006-07 WO2 M Eastman
2007-09 WO2 M Preece
2009-11 WO2 A Bedward
2011-   WO2 B Harvey

INFANTRY

1924-29 Sgt R Smillie Argyll &Sutherland Highlanders
1929-30 Sgt TA Baird Scots Guards
1930-31 Sgt A McDonnell Scots Guards
1931-35 Sgt J Edgar Scots Guards
1935-36 Sgt J Hull Gordon Highlanders
1936-37 Sgt J Smith Gordon Highlanders
1940-45 Sgt JS Duncan Gordon Highanders
1941-42 Sgt C Adam Gordon Highlanders
1941-43 Sgt HH Duncan Gordon Highlanders
1942-43 Sgt R Runacres Cameron Highlanders
1943   Sgt J Smithson Gordon Highlanders
1944-45 Sgt T Kay Black Watch
1944-46 Sgt DM Gallacher Gordon Highlanders
1945-46 Sgt JN MacDonald Gordon Highlanders
1946-49 Sgt E Humphrey Suffolk
1946-47 LCpl E Croom Worcestershire
1947   Cpl AF Niven Scots Guards
1947-48 Pte G Paton Seaforth Highlanders
1948-50 LCpl JM Mills Gordon Highlanders
1949   WO2 W Wilbur Scots Guards
1949-51 Sgt E Ives Scots Guards
1949-52 WO2 A Ward Cameron Highlanders

1949-54 WO2 Kynoch Gordon Highlanders
1950   Pte Swindley Black Watch
1951   Pte Gavin Seaforth Highlanders
1952-55 Cpl W Gray Gordon Highlanders
1955-56 WO2 A Young Scots Guards
1955-57 Cpl SJ Livingstone Gordon Highlanders
1956   WO2 J MacGregor Seaforth Highlanders
1956-58 WO2 J Bell Argyll & Sutherland Hldrs
1957-58 Cpl W Richardson Gordon Highlanders
1957   Pte GP Gerrard Gordon Highlanders
1960-67 WO2 J Banno Black Watch
1967-69 WO2 W Joss Gordon Highlanders
1991-93 WO2 GG Laing BEM Gordon Highlanders
1993-95 WO2 AT Hastie Gordons

                                    (Highlanders after Sep 94)
1994-96 WO2 K Masson Gordons
                                    (Highlanders after Sep 94)
1996-98 WO2 K Drelincourt Highlanders
1998-99 WO2 D Lundie Black Watch
1999-2002 WO2 KW Adams Highlanders
2002-03 CSgt E Cowan Argyll & Sutherland Hldrs
2003-05 WO2 MJ Door Light Infantry
2005-07 CSgt PC O'Neill Argyll & Sutherland Hldrs
2007-09 CSgt D Florence SCOTS
2009-11 CSgt D Campbell SCOTS
2011-   Sgt J Campbell SCOTS

ROYAL ARMY MEDICAL CORPS

1921-22 Sgt WH Nelson
1922-24 Sgt JJ Murray
1924-26 SSgt H Quelch
1926-28 Sgt Wilby
1928   Sgt AT Leggat
1928-30 Sgt T Hipkiss

1930-34 SSgt TH Hearnshaw
1934-39 SSgt TF Jouning
1939   Sgt SG Watson
1941-42 QMS HM Roberts
1942   Sgt C Bownes
1942-43 Sgt WJ Birdwhistle
1942-44 QMS EE Bishop
1944-45 QMS JP Chadwick
1945-47 QMS J Mackay
1947-50 QMS CG Anderson
1952-53 WO2 WL Lewis
1953-55 WO2 GA Mellalieu
1955-58 WO2 FL Pritchard
1958-59 WO2 GT Bevan
1959-61 WO2 G Cooper
1961-63 WO2 GW Marsh
1963   WO2 AW Francy
1967-69 WO2 C Cross

ROYAL ARTILLERY

1952-54 WO2 RC Bryant
1955   LBdr RE King
1955-57 Gnr A Davidson

ROYAL ELECTRICAL AND MECHANICAL ENGINEERS

1946   Cfn A Chalmers
1946   Cfn J Lightbrown
1949-52 WO1(ASM) MF Kinshott
1952-54 WO2 P Fitzhugh
1953-55 Cfn G Bishop
1953-55 Cfn T Walker
1955-57 A Bevan

ARMY PHYSICAL TRAINING CORPS

1942-43 Sgt RM Smith
1943-44 Sgt W Matthews
1944-55 Sgt MR McIntyre
1945   WO2 C Gadd
1945   Sgt D Miller

SENIOR UNDER OFFICER

Annual appointments by decade, with subunit where known

1963   M Plowman, GJ Knowles, HG Cameron,
DM Rothwell, PJ Shearer, unknown, RJM Macdonald

1970   R Bishop (Med), J Dalrymple-Hamilton (Inf),
AJM Durcan (Inf), D Macniven (Eng), J Taylor (Pipe Band),
WA Watt (Inf), JB Duffus (Pipe Band), GKD Corsar (Inf),
G Bryson (Sig), A Clarke (Pipe Band), I Miles (Inf),
DH Nattrass (Inf), S Ahmed (Sig)

1980   K Wilkinson (Eng), GML Coutts (Eng), S Scoones,
HD Maclean (Eng), AH Fulton (Inf), BS Matheson (Inf),
AI Gray (Inf), RG Marris (Inf), LM Barron (Eng),
MW Hogarth (Eng)

1990   AJG McCulloch (Eng), TA Johnston (Inf), EP Garden
(Sig), GB Ingram (Inf),A Walker, MS Kemp, MA Cadman,
L Cameron, LT Fernard, GR Greenhowe

2000   GJ McGhie, D Hirst, N Cargill, SC Porterfield,
G Fisher, FCS Robertson, T Bird, WG Guy, CH McRobbie,
LJ Elliott

2010   A Scott, D Wilman

SASH OF HONOUR

Presented Annually to a Woman Officer Cadet.
Award Initiated and Sash Presented by Lt Col TB Smith on handing
over as CO in 1955.   Listed by decade.

1955   Sgt BJ Hunt, LCpl EP Farrel, Sgt MA Moir,
Cpl AA Lyall, Sgt MT McCallion

1960   LCpl AB Yackiminie, Sgt A Murchie, JUO H Nicol,
JUO L Greig, JUO MF Geddes, JUO ECJ Cardno,
JUO HM Lindsay, JUO N MacPherson, JUO EM Hay,
OCdt LD Willets

1970   JUO LD Willets, OCdt K Howie, JUO E Craig,
JUO A Smith, JUO K Hunter, JUO VB Duthie,
JUO P Watkins, JUO E Storey, JUO S Gann, JUO F McGrath

1980   JUO C Hoskins, JUO H Buchan, WOCdt R Lodge,
JUO L Kirk, JUO E Marnoch, JUO SL Prosser,
JUO SL Prosser, JUO SM Mann, JUO LM Barron,
JUO FJ Harvey

1990   JUO DJ Simpson, JUO S Watson,
WOCdt FB Walker, JUO LA Chapman, JUO SL Milton,
JUO KJM Henderson, JUO KA Fulton, JUO KA Fulton,
JUO JA Lamb, SUO LT Fernand

2000   JUO EL Bosher, JUO RJ Ricketts, JUO C Eustace,
JUO IV Kahane, SUO SC Porterfield, JUO S Houston,
SUO F Robertson, DSUO C Shaw, WOCdt F Pringle

Not awarded after 2008, male and female cadets being eligible for
the Sword of Honour.

THE DRUMS AND PIPES, THE PIPES AND DRUMS, - 'THE BAND'

Photographic and documentary evidence, the latter including records of expenditure on 'instruments', indicates the AUOTC Medical Contingent had pipers supported by a few drummers right from the start in 1912. The contingent formed at a time when just about every organisation had its own band. The University catchment area in the North East, the Highlands, and Islands ensured many Freshers arrived already practiced to one extent or another in the dark arts. Some even came from Dundee, Fife, Perthshire and even further away !

The Pipes and Drums were properly established in 1925 after the Infantry Unit joined the Medics and became the Drums and Pipes in the late 1980s in accordance with Gordon Highlander tradition and the wishes of a Gordon Highlander Adjutant . The posts of Pipe Major and Drum Major were established within the Permanent Staff in the 1990s. Before then student cadets, and occasionally returning TA officers with the necessary skills, would fill the roles. In the 1980s RSM Dixie Ingram Scots Guards, already a big name on the competition circuit, took a special interest in the Band which won the World Pipe Band Championships in Grade 3 in 1983.

Generally 'the powers that be' have accepted that to maintain standards (in music if in nothing else), the band must operate its own programme away from everyone else. However when involved in the more martial aspects of Contingent life, the band's special camaraderie and team spirit generally delivers a good result, often besting the other sub-units. Many individual band members have gone on to military careers joining the Regular and Reserve Forces. Band alumni include some Colonels, Brigadiers and even an Air Vice Marshal. Within the unit some have been appointed Senior Under Officer thereby forcing them to perform outside the Band's ranks at Remembrance Sunday Parades. This was particularly the case in the 1970s when three out of ten SUOs came from the Band.

The Band has often included extremely good pipers who have gone on to gain great recognition in the piping world.

Again (apologies to other vintages) taking the 1970s as an example, one young Gus Clarke was finally attracted to the OTC while sitting in his room at Hillhead listening to the piping programme on the radio. The programme featured recordings from the recent competitions at the prestigious Northern Meeting solo piping competition, ending with the winner of that year's Gold Medal for Piobaireachd. The listeners were informed that the year's winner was, Jack Taylor, medical student from Aberdeen and Pipe Major at the OTC. The Pipe Sergeant, another medic, was Bill Wotherspoon, who himself would become a Gold Medallist. Doctors Taylor and Wotherspoon, as at 2012, are respectively President and Honorary Secretary of the Piobaireachd Society.

Taylor and Wotherspoon had played under the previous Pipe Major, William Donaldson, another Doctor but not of the medical variety. Donaldson's PhD Thesis was on Jacobite song. This started him off on a long and widely praised career in the study of traditional Scottish performing arts. He coordinated the publishing of classic pipe music manuscript collections on the Ceol Sean internet site. Knowledge of the historic repertoire was reflected in some of the little known older tunes and settings included in his light music collection, the first to be wholly produced on CD-ROM. The collection included his own tribute to AUOTC's early origins with a Retreat Air, entitled *'U Company'*. His books are recognised to have increased the scope of piping literature immensely, if in places controversially.

Another band member of the time, himself not afraid of generating research and intuition based controversy, was Allan MacDonald a highly respected piper, gold medallist and clasp winner (twice over). He is renowned for his work on the relationship between Gaelic song and piobaireachd and for his innovative approach to light music. He is today a well known composer, musical director, piper, singer, workshop leader, and

424

lecturer. Discussing the finer points of piping, its origins and its future, MacDonald shared many a drink with another OTC piper Peter Forbes, a mature student and former National Service piper with the Highland Light Infantry.

Ian Duncan would go on to great success in the Pipe Band world. He became Pipe Major of Tayforth UOTC. He is perhaps best known however for taking bands such as Vale of Atholl, from local non-competitive status, up to the highest realms of Grade One. Another innovator, he tested the Band Competition 'Establishment' with novel approaches to repertoire and style.

With a team like this and other strong pipers like Jim Menzies and John Lovie, new pipers joining the OTC could only improve. The Band at this time routinely won Northern Lights and once entered and won the TA Championship.

Gus Clarke, who admits his early performances at Edinburgh Castle and on the foredeck of URNU's HMS THORNHAM were not his best, went on to become Tayforth UOTC's Pipe Major. By the mid 2000s he was one of many contemporary TA Pipe Majors with AUOTC Roots. Gordon Campbell was PM of the TA 71 Engineer Regiment's Band, Brian Elrick was PM 51st Highland, and Mike Laing PM of the AUOTC itself. Getting on for 50% of Scotland's viable TA Pipe Bands were under 'formerly of AUOTC' management. Brian Elrick also took Stonehaven's Band through the hard journey from Grade 4 to Grade 1.

One AUOTC Pipe Major deserves special mention. The Band's first female player, Elaine Marnoch became the Army's first lady Pipe Major and the first lady Lone Piper at the Edinburgh Military Tattoo.

Many members of the Band, Dr Bill Fraser and Gordon Campbell to name but two, have gained distinction as teachers and judges. Excelling in quantity as well as quality, 1970s players held an official Guinness Record for Marathon Quartet Playing, achieved in the Officers Mess, Bedford Road, much to the pleasure of the neighbours.

The Band of the 1950s even included a World Champion Drum Major, Olly Urquhart, who maintained a long link with the OTC as a TA Royal Engineer officer and long serving member on the Military Education Committee. He got the mace out again at the OTC's TA 100th Celebrations leading the Association's 'Old Boar' Band. His contemporary Pipe Major Walter Anderson played at that event in the ranks with many former Pipe Majors, pipers and drummers. Robert Gordon College and Aberdeen Grammar School provided a steady supply of OTC cadets for many years, including many pipers and drummers. These were supplemented by others from more distant CCF bands across the country and from those who had learned their music elsewhere.

In the late 60s and early 70s, Aberdeen Grammar School produced several embryonic drummers thanks to Russell Gray, himself an OTC drummer who returned to the Grammar as Geography Teacher, CCF Officer and Drumming Instructor. Waiting for fresh students was Drum Sergeant Ken Boddie, a Gordonian. A former member of the Bucksburn and District Band, at that time the North East's only Grade 1 Band, he strived long and hard to get his corps playing anywhere near his level.

The band has represented the unit far and wide, in too many places and situations to mention. The broader and younger band community across Scotland has benefited when the AUOTC has 'blown through' on the 'Pipers' Trail'. Mini bands deployed to Norway as long distance patrols in the 1970s; and places as disparate as Stonehenge, Red Square, and the Rock of Gibraltar have echoed to the music of the AUOTC Band. Although going since the start in 1912, the Band's own 'official' Centenary will come in 2025. Before then someone may write a fuller account of its achievements and its many musically charged parties.

SOURCES

Books

Aberdeen Newspapers Ltd. 1928
A Record of Events in Aberdeen and The North 1801-1927.

Barnett, Correlli. *Britain and Her Army 1509-1970, A Military, Political and Social Survey.* Pelican Books 1974.
ISBN 0 14 02.1751 7.

Carter, Jennifer J and McLaren, Colin A.
Crown and Gown 1495-1995, An Illustrated History of the University of Aberdeen. Aberdeen University Press 1994.
ISBN 1 85752 240 0 (pbk).
(<u>NB</u> It wrongly states that there was no AUOTC before and during World War One.)

Fraser, W Hamish and Lee, Clive H. Editors.
Aberdeen 1800-2000 A New History. Tuckwell Press Ltd, 2000
ISBN 1 86232 175 2

Hickman, Tom. *Called Up, Sent Down. The Bevin Boys' War.*
The History Press, 2010. ISBN 978 0 7524 5749 9

Jones, RV. *Most Secret War, British Scientific Intelligence 1939-1945.* Hamish Hamilton Ltd 1978. ISBN 0 241 89746 7.

Lake, Deborah. *Tartan Air Force. Scotland and a Century of Military Aviation.* Birlinn Ltd. 2009. ISBN13: 978 1 84158 806 3

McConachie, John. *The Student Soldiers.*
Moravian Press Ltd, 1995. ISBN 1 870151 05 4
(NB Suggests nobody transferred from U Company to AUOTC in 1912 and later when in fact several did, some forming the experienced core of the new unit.)

Osborne, Brian D. *The People's Army, Home Guard in Scotland 1940-1944.* Birlinn Ltd 2009. ISBN 978 1 84341 043 0.

Pirt, Asher. *GHQ Liaison Regiment (Phantom): A Nominal Roll with Short Biographies.* Walmer, Lulu 2011.
ISBN 978-1-4452-9099-7

Rule, Alexander. *Students Under Arms.*
Aberdeen University Press. 1934.

Salmond, JB. *The History of the 51st Highland Division.*
The Pentland Press Ltd. 1994. ISBN 1-85821-245-6.

Sinclair, Donald. *The History of the Aberdeen Volunteers.*
Aberdeen Daily Journal Office 1907.

Strathdee, Roy B. *Aberdeen University Contingent, STC.*
W&W Lindsay, Aberdeen, 1947

Taylor, William and Diack, Peter. *Student and Sniper-Sergeant, A Memoir of JK Forbes MA.* Hodder and Stoughton, London, 1916.

University of Aberdeen Special Libraries and Archives

University Memorial Rolls and Rolls of Service
University Annual Review Vols XXXIV toXLI (1951-1966)
University Magazine Alma Mater Vols 31 to 51 (1911-1934)
Military Education Committee Minutes and Correspondence.
- MSU 895 Minutes, 1912-1952. (3 Volumes).

- Accession 465. Unsorted and incomplete MEC papers late 20th Century

Papers of WM McNeill, 1947-50 Update to Strathdee's 1947 book. MS3830

University Oral History Collection. Transcriptions of Interviews. MS 3620

MS 3620/1/43 Interview with EM Wright
  (UAS, WW2 Intelligence, Chair of Maths, Principal)
MS 3620/1/82 Interview with RV Jones
  (WW2 Intelligence, Chair of Nat Phil)
MS 3620/1/33/1 Interview with Dr Harold Watt
  (OTC, STC, UAS)
MS 3620/1/136 Interview with Dr Harold Bowie
  (LDV, Home Guard)
MS 3620/1/179 Interview with Alexander Adam
  (OTC, STC, Home Guard)

AUOTC Roy Strathdee Building - Records and Files

Unpublished supplements to Strathdee's History covering their periods of Command by Lt Col TB Smith (1950-55) and Lt Col J Reid (1956-65)

Miscellaneous unit records, photographs, artefacts, historical summaries and Annual Unit Reports.

Miscellaneous Publications

Territorial Army Officer, Skills for Business, Leadership for Life. Ministry of Defence, Army Recruiting Group. RG/BRO/141 August 2009.

Royal Navy's Museum of Radar and Communications, HMS Collingwood, Fareham, Hampshire
Research and access to the online virtual museum, courtesy of Bill Legg and Jeff Dykes, on the details of the World War One Naval Wireless Station at Stoneywood guarded by Gordon Highlanders.

Personal Interviews or Written Contributions

Aitken, Stuart - 1950s Cadet, Natn'l Svce and TA Officer
Barr, Robin - 1970s Cadet, Piper, Officer, 2IC AUOTC
Barr (nee Shanlin) , Maggie - 1970s Cadet
Cameron, Ranald - 1970s cadet, drummer
Cantlay, Les - 1960s/70s cadet
Chapman, Dave - Adjutant 2012
Clarke, Angus - 1970s Cadet, Piper, TA Pipe Major
Copland, Bill - 1940s Cadet
Dodds, Domhnall - 1980s Cadet, TA Officer
Duffus, Mary - 1970s Cadet, TA QARANC Officer
Harvey, B - WO2, Signals PSI 2012
Hazell, J - SSgt, Engineers PSI 2012
Hewitt, Mike - late 50s/60s Cadet, TA Officer
Jeffrey, Andrew - 1970s Cadet, TA officer
Laing, Mike - Cadet, Piper, Pipe Major 2012
Mathieson, JR - WO1, RSM 2012
McKen, Gordon - CO AUOTC
Milne, Alan - Cadet, TA officer, AUOTC Medical Officer
Morgan, Bill - cadet and officer 1970s
Morgan (nee Petrie), Carol - Cadet 1970s
Philips (nee Storey), Eleanor - 1970s Cadet, TA Officer
Rose, Edwin - TA Officer 1980s/90s
Shanks, Graham - 1970s Cadet, TA Officer
Thomson, Les - RQMS 2012
Thorp, Matt - CO AUOTC
Urquhart, Olly - 1950s Cadet, Drum Major, TA, MEC
Wallace, Charlie - CO AUOTC

Wilkinson, Kevin - 1970s Cadet, TA Officer, CO AUOTC
Willis, Andrew - 1970s, TA Officer
Youl, Rob - 1970s, Royal Australian Engineers

ACKNOWLEDGEMENTS

Graham Shanks has been a friend since CCF days. He and Ros Shanks, have devoted a great deal of time to gathering the pictorial record of AUOTC. Their efforts with pictures inspired me to gather some words.

Many folk gave time to interviews or written recollections. Pipe Major Mike Laing conducted an admirable archaeological effort on Band appointments. Commanding Officers Matthew Wardner and Matt Thorp, their permanent staff and officer cadets, have all willingly helped my delving in the Roy Strathdee Building.

I thank Deputy Archivist Andrew Macgregor and the Reading Room staff for their help and guidance particularly as they were in the midst of preparing for their own historic move to the new University Library now towering above Bedford Road near the old OTC Compound. Thanks are also due to them for permission to reproduce extracts from the Roll of Honour and the use of photographs of Marischal College, Principal Smith and George Williamson.

For proof reading I am particularly indebted to Mike Hewitt. Of course any howlers in coherence, consistency, fact, style, grammar, or spelling remain all my own work.

Seeing me across the leap from computer files to books were Neil Harrison, .Alison Allan and their colleagues at Robert Gordon University's Gatehouse.

Jim Duffus, Huntly, 2012

AUTHOR

Colonel (Retired) JB Duffus MSc BSc
late Royal Engineers

Jim Duffus was born and raised in Aberdeen. He joined the Aberdeen Grammar School CCF, the descendent of the Junior Division OTC, hanging on long enough to become Drum Sgt and Cadet CSM. At the end of his fifth year, Highers out of the way, he helped to fill the depleted drummer ranks of AUOTC's Pipe Band in time for the 1971 Summer Camp on Salisbury Plain. This experience helped him choose which University to enter in 1972. Happy years were spent with the OTC, and occasionally the Geology Department, and he hung around long enough to become Drum Sgt and SUO before graduating in 1976. He spent the next 26 years in the Regular Army and, as advertised, 'saw the World'.

In 2002 he and his family settled in Huntly. Visits to the 'Toon' have included participation in the formation and fun of the AUOTC Association, 'The Old Boars', even on occasion including some drumming.

His sister, Mary, joined AUOTC too. She was later commissioned in Queen Alexandra's Royal Army Nursing Corps, QARANC(V).

He was exposed to 51st Highland Division history from an early age, his father having served with the Division in North Africa, Sicily, France, Holland and Germany.

Further back in the period covered by this book his paternal Grandfather emigrated to the USA in February 1912, six weeks ahead of the *Titanic*. In 1915 he paid his fare back to Scotland to serve with 2nd Battalion Gordon Highlanders on the Western Front and in Italy. He won a Military Medal at the Crossing of the River Piave in 1918. Jim's mother lost four potential paternal uncles in World War One. One was killed serving in 1st Battalion Gordon Highlanders, two while with the Australian Infantry and one at sea with the Royal Navy. Tragic but not uncommon statistics.

435

AUOTC AT BEDFORD ROAD
- CIRCA 1960s/70s

Not to scale and very approximate being compiled from an amalgam of several recollections.

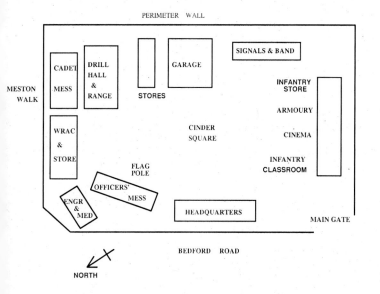

Non Confundar (The AUOTC Centenary)

March

Malcolm M Combe

Design

large format printing

calendars

book printing and binding

professional binding

pull-up banners

creativity

photo copying

convenience

business cards

colour printing

YOU

added value

the future

postcards

photography

digital printing

year books

4

THE GATEHOUSE

DESIGN & PRINT CONSULTANCY AT RGU

USE OUR IMAGINATION

Garthdee Road,
Aberdeen AB10 7AQ
T: 01224 262945
E: orderform@rgu.ac.uk

www.rgu.ac.uk/gandp
www.rgu.ac.uk/photolibrar

wedding stationery